THE K STREET GANG

THE
K STREET
GANG

THE RISE AND FALL OF THE
REPUBLICAN MACHINE

MATTHEW CONTINETTI

DOUBLEDAY

New York   London   Toronto   Sydney   Auckland

PUBLISHED BY DOUBLEDAY

Copyright © 2006 by Matthew Continetti

All Rights Reserved

Published in the United States by Doubleday, an imprint of The Doubleday
Broadway Publishing Group, a division of Random House, Inc., New York.
www.doubleday.com

DOUBLEDAY and the portrayal of an anchor with a dolphin are
registered trademarks of Random House, Inc.

Portions of this work were originally published, in different form,
in *The Weekly Standard*.

Book design by Tina Henderson

Cataloging-in-Publication Data is on file with the Library of Congress.

ISBN-13: 978-0-385-51672-X
ISBN-10: 0-385-51672-X

PRINTED IN THE UNITED STATES OF AMERICA

1 3 5 7 9 10 8 6 4 2

First Edition

To my mother and father

What the Republicans need is fifty Jack Abramoffs.
Then this becomes a different town.
—GROVER NORQUIST

CONTENTS

THE K STREET GANG

THE DECEMBER REVOLUTION

TOM DELAY AND THE RISE OF THE K STREET CONSERVATIVES

THIS IS A crime story.

It begins in October 1993, more than a year before Republicans took over Capitol Hill, when Illinois Republican Bob Michel, the House minority leader, announced that he would retire at the end of his term. Michel was eighty years old. He was first elected to Congress in 1956. His face was streaked with wrinkles, he wore thick glasses with lenses the size of car windshields, and he had little hair. He looked like a relic.

In a way, he *was* a relic. Michel's career almost perfectly traced the decline of the Republican congressional majority. By the time Michel retired from Congress, the last year Republicans had controlled the House of Representatives was in 1954. That was two years before he had been first elected to represent Illinois's 18th District. Michel had come to Congress just when his party was on the way down.

Yet, as the party declined, Michel rose through the ranks. He became minority whip in 1975, and minority leader in 1981. In both jobs he shepherded Republican legislation through the House as best he could. He was often referred to as an "institutionalist"—someone who exploited the rules and regulations of the House for tactical gain. But more often than not conservatives referred to him as an "accommodationist"—someone with no sense of overall strategy who was all too eager to make deals with the House Democratic leadership.

Michel was soft, conservatives grumbled. He was afraid to take a stand against the Democrats, who, after decades in power, had grown decadent and corrupt. And Michel knew, too, that the younger a Republican House member was, the more he was itching for a fight with the opposition. As Republican representation in the House had shrunk, it had also become more conservative—far more conservative than Michel. At the press conference announcing his retirement Michel admitted he was "much more comfortable" in the Washington that existed "when I first came to Congress."[1]

One of Michel's harshest critics—and the frontrunner to replace him—was Newt Gingrich, who had represented Georgia's 11th District since 1979, and who had been elected minority whip in 1989, after Dick Cheney left that post to serve as President George H.W. Bush's secretary of defense. Gingrich was Michel's opposite in almost every way. He was fiercely ideological, tirelessly combative, and endlessly inventive. Before he entered electoral politics, Gingrich had been a history professor, and so his mind, he said, was attuned to the faint vibrations that signaled the rise, decline, and renascence of civilizations.

Also, unlike Michel, whose midwestern Republicanism had its roots in 1950s budget-cutting and isolationism, Gingrich was a true Reaganite. He was a supply-sider who thought that lower marginal tax rates would spur economic growth and increase tax revenues. He believed in American power, a strong national defense, and standing up to the tyrannical Soviet Union. And though his conservatism was not religious, he was nonetheless a cultural warrior, and thought that a libertine Boomer elite, reared in the student revolts of the 1960s, governed the country from the coasts in an increasingly out-of-touch manner.

Gingrich was also famous. His political celebrity had been growing for some time. He had first gained prominence in the early 1980s, when he used after-hours "special orders" speeches, broadcast live on the C-SPAN television network, to harangue the House Democratic leadership. He led ethics crusades against Democratic Speakers Tom Foley and Jim Wright. He argued that the Democratic Congress was plagued by scandal—scandals at the House bank, scandals at the House post office, scandals at the highest reaches of congressional power—and that only a thoroughgoing purge would set things right. He tried to combine the wisdom of a public intellectual with the guile of a public official. A simple conversation with Gingrich would be inevitably laced with references to Napoleon, science fiction, Churchill, the futurist authors Alvin and Heidi Toffler, Franklin Roosevelt, and Peter Drucker. He preached a transformative politics that would break the old systems of the past and help move America forward into the Information Age. Gingrich was the first example of the paradoxical species that would eventually proliferate throughout Washington: the progressive conservative.

He was an ideologue. But Gingrich could also be incredibly charming, at least to Washington conservatives, who swooned whenever the minority whip gave a speech about rescuing American civilization from liberal elites, unleashing the dynamism of the American economy through tax cuts and deregulation, and changing the culture of Washington so that power rested with the American people, not special interests. And all of Gingrich's speeches and articles, delivered at conservative think tanks and retreats and reprinted in the pages of the small conservative magazines, had one thing in common: They would usually end with assurances that one day, perhaps sooner than people thought, there would be a congressional Republican majority.

But this would not happen, Gingrich argued, as long as someone like Bob Michel ran the House Republican caucus. It came as no surprise, then, that within hours of Michel's announcement on October 4, 1993, Gingrich had, in turn, announced his candidacy for minority leader. It was no contest. As minority whip, Gingrich had already rallied a majority of the conference to vote for him—more than a year before the Republicans would hold leadership elections in December 1994. Michel allies were left in the dark. A new power was rising in the Republican party, one that was uncompromising, loud, and visionary.

The problem was, the *actual* rising power wasn't Gingrich. In fact, Gingrich's rise was so stunning, his personality so polarizing, his visage so ubiquitous, that his quick elevation to minority-leader-in-waiting obscured another fissure in the House Republican leadership. That fissure was opened by the race to replace Gingrich as minority whip. And the man who won that race, which began the same day Gingrich locked up the post of minority leader, was ultimately to have more power on Capitol Hill than Newt Gingrich ever dreamed of having.

It is in the nature of revolutions that they consume their most passionate advocates. The vanguard's ideals are replaced by the faction's brass knuckles. The chain of events that Robespierre set in motion led to his death by guillotine in 1794. Trotsky fled from Stalin and met his fate with an ice pick to the head in Mexico in 1940. The dynamics of political revolutions in a constitutional republic such as the United States are nonviolent, but the parallels between political insurgencies remain. One group comes to power pledging reform; the reformers' newfound power attracts a troop of opportunists and hangers-on; the opportunists eat away at the reformist impulse from within. Newt Gingrich's Republican Revolution would turn out to be no different.

Three candidates ran to replace Gingrich as minority whip, yet only two really mattered. (Florida representative Bill McCollum always trailed the others.) In one corner was Gingrich's longtime ally Robert Walker, the fifty-one-year-old congressman from Pennsylvania's 16th District. Walker had been Gingrich's chief deputy whip—responsible for "whipping up" support on key votes—since

1989. He had the requisite experience, and he was committed to Gingrich's ideals and programs. His association with Gingrich began long before he joined the whip team. With Gingrich and Minnesota Republican Vin Weber, Walker had cofounded the Conservative Opportunity Society in the early 1980s, a sort of in-house think tank that sought to tilt the Republican caucus to the right.

With Gingrich, too, Walker had pioneered the use of after-hours speeches on C-SPAN. In Walker's case, however, this sometimes proved to be embarrassing: Once, as he delivered a televised special orders speech, House Speaker Tip O'Neill ordered the C-SPAN cameras to pull back—revealing that Walker was speaking to an empty chamber. But such embarrassment did little to hurt his relationship with Gingrich, who had often said that Walker was his "closest personal friend in the House."[2] Loyalty mattered, after all.

In the other corner was Tom DeLay, the forty-seven-year-old representative from Texas's 22nd Congressional District. DeLay was an experienced politician and a hard-core conservative. It was his fury at Texas's environmental regulations that led him to run for the state legislature in 1978. It was his distress at the burdens the Federal government placed on business—more regulation, heavy payroll taxes, an intrusive Internal Revenue Service—that sparked his run for Congress in 1984. Caught in the Reagan whirlwind, DeLay came to Washington at a time when free enterprise, not government, was sexy. Clearly DeLay would sympathize with business interests. He was one himself.

In December 1992, DeLay had been elected secretary of the Republican Conference. In a House filled with scalawags, layabouts, and diehards, DeLay was unusual in that he combined the convictions of an ideological conservative with the street smarts of a machine politician. When DeLay first arrived in Washington, he had quickly aligned himself with Bob Michel. The move made sense at the time—above all, DeLay wanted to be close to power—but within a few years it became clear that it was damaging his career.

This was because DeLay had made allies with the old guard. He had sided with pols who were on their way out. At no time was DeLay's miscalculation clearer than in 1989, when Gingrich first ran for the position of minority whip. At the urging of Bob Michel, who loathed Gingrich, DeLay had backed Edward Madigan, from Illinois—not only *backed* him: DeLay was his campaign manager. Which turned out to be a bad move. Gingrich won the post by two votes, 87-85. And once elected, he, like all politicians, immediately started rewarding his friends and punishing his enemies. DeLay was at the top of that enemies list.

Bob Walker, on the other hand, was at the top of Gingrich's list of friends. Walker had run Gingrich's campaign for minority whip, and afterward became Gingrich's chief deputy. DeLay was left with zilch. "You could consider that moment my downfall," DeLay later told Fox News reporter Major Garrett. "But I think I helped myself right after. That same day Newt had to whip a vote. And on that very day I went into his office and I had to swallow my pride. I had to start from scratch. That's when I set my sights on a new path."[3]

In truth, the new path looked a lot like the old. DeLay's standing had been hurt by Gingrich's elevation to minority whip in 1989, but not by much. After all, DeLay's candidate, Madigan, had lost by a narrow margin. He still had support. And DeLay was a prodigious fund-raiser; he had been nicknamed "The Hammer" for his ability to nail down contributions. Yet a leadership position still eluded him.

DeLay's strategy was, on the one hand, to ally himself with Gingrich and the confrontational House members as best he could—he led the charge against the first President Bush's 1990 budget deal, which raised taxes—while building support within the caucus through spreading around his fund-raising largesse. It was this strategy that led to his victory in the contest for Republican Conference secretary, which had put him in the position to run for whip.

DeLay also understood that in order to ascend further in the ranks of House Republicans, he would have to build a constituency within the caucus—one untapped by Gingrich and his favored replacement, Walker. In this, timing worked to DeLay's advantage. It was no accident that Michel announced his retirement as minority leader a little under a year before the 1994 midterm elections. Michel felt that the 104th Congress, which would take office in January 1995, should have new leadership. Throwing his hat into the ring, DeLay saw his opportunity: Republicans had been gaining momentum in the past few elections—forty-seven Republican freshmen were elected in 1992—and there would likely be additional Republican freshmen in 1995. If he could not develop a sizable constituency in the 103rd Congress, why not try for the 104th?

DeLay set to work. He hired political consultant Mildred Webber. Then he chose Dennis Hastert, a backbencher from Illinois, to whip support.[4] The election wasn't until December 1994, but DeLay couldn't afford to waste time. He founded his political action committee, Americans for a Republican Majority—known for short as ARMPAC—to raise money for Republican challengers across the country. His consultant Webber also doubled as an in-house adviser to Republican challengers in the midterm elections. DeLay set up a phone line that candidates could call to ask for advice. He organized a training school where candidates could learn the intricacies of road signs and meet-and-greets. He traveled to twenty-five states to raise money and appear at events with various candidates. "I wanted them to think of me as their brother," he later told reporter Elizabeth Drew.[5]

DeLay's ARMPAC was soon awash with money. He told reporters that he stopped counting after he reached $2 million, which he apportioned to about eighty Republican candidates. Most of those were challengers. But money wasn't everything. One challenger, Ohio Republican Bob Ney, later told the *New Republic:* "He made sure we understood he was just a phone call away. There were times we called at 1 A.M. in the morning just to ask a question. Sure, his money was crucial. But when you're out there alone, the encouragement is a big help."[6]

As Washington trudged slowly toward the midterm elections, DeLay kept one eye on securing additional Republican House seats and another on winning Gingrich's old post as minority whip.

And then, suddenly, as DeLay worked toward his goal, something remarkable happened. After years of defeat and decades spent in the political wilderness, Congressional Republicans had a major success: They defeated President Clinton's chief domestic initiative, health care reform. The president's support began to erode, and Republicans felt energized. They began to see a possible congressional majority in their grasp. The internal politics of the House Republican caucus would have to wait. National politics took precedence.

This was also about the time, as we learn from the histories of Republican triumph published over the last decade, that Gingrich made the decision, in consultation with his pollster Frank Luntz, outside advisers Ed Gillespie and Vin Weber, and top congressional allies like Robert Walker, to nationalize the 1994 elections—which is to say, run a unified campaign across the country that would serve as a referendum on the first two years of Bill Clinton's presidency. In a canny electoral gambit, the Republicans would attempt to win over the voters who had supported Ross Perot in the 1992 election—almost 20 percent of the national electorate that year— by rallying behind a reform program that centered on term limits, accountability, balanced budgets, and a strong defense.

On September 27, 1994, more than 300 Republicans—both elected officials and candidates—appeared on the Capitol steps, where they unveiled the centerpiece of the Perot-influenced reform program. This was the Contract with America, which "aimed at restoring the faith and trust of the American people in their government" through "major reforms" including a balanced budget amendment, welfare reform, an expanded death penalty, tax cuts, tax credits, tort reform, and term limits. The Contract promised "a Congress that is doing what the American people want and doing it in a way that instills trust." And it concluded: "If we break this contract, throw us out. We mean it."

Gingrich was on the Capitol steps that day, as were Bob Walker and Tom DeLay. One of the Contract's architects, the voluble Richard Armey of Texas, took the stage and proclaimed, "We enter a new era in American government."

"We are united here today," Armey went on, "over 150 current members of the House and over 200 candidates, united in the belief that the people's House must be wrested from the grips of special interests and handed back to you, the American people."

It was a stirring moment, reflecting the political atmosphere of the time. Change was in the air, brought about by disillusion with Clinton's program and disgust at the Democratic mismanagement of the Congress. Congressional Republicans had a bold program of reform, a set of ideals and policies they were ready to enact. All they needed was power. Yet what was lost in the excitement of the moment was a recognition that, once again, the engine of revolution had begun to purr, and the great wheels of historical irony that crush grandiose principle and replace it with petty graft were starting to turn.

The first sign that November 8 was going to be a good night came not long after the polls had closed. In Indiana's Fourth District, Representative Jill Long, a Democrat, was defeated by Republican Mark Souder, a former congressional aide running in his first election. From Indiana all eyes turned to Kentucky's First District, where Representative Thomas Barlow, a Democrat, lost to Republican Ed Whitfield. From Kentucky to South Carolina's First District, where another neophyte candidate, Republican Mark Sanford, trounced Democratic state legislator Bob Barber. From South Carolina, to Louisiana. From Louisiana to Texas. From Texas to California.

One after another, all the liberal lions—local, state, and national—fell. In New York, Mario Cuomo lost to George Pataki. In Texas, Ann Richards lost to George W. Bush. Also in Texas, Jack Brooks, the chairman of the House Judiciary Committee, lost to Republican Steve Stockman. In Illinois, Dan Rostenkowski, the legendary chairman of the House Ways and Means Committee—who was under a twelve-count indictment at the time of the election—lost to Republican Michael Patrick Flanagan. In Maine, Sen. George Mitchell retired and was replaced by Republican Olympia Snowe. In Washington State, House Speaker Tom Foley fell to Republican George Nethercutt—the first time a sitting speaker had been defeated since 1862.

On the morning of Election Day, the Democrats held 256 seats in the House. The Republicans held only 178. By November 10, the Republicans would hold 230 seats in the 104th Congress to the Democrats' 204 (not counting the Independent from Vermont, Bernie Sanders, who typically votes with the Democrats).

On Election Day, the Democrats held 57 seats in the Senate. The Republicans held only 43. By November 9, the Republicans would hold 52 Senate seats in the 104th Congress to the Democrats' 48. Then, after Alabama Democrat Sen. Richard Shelby switched parties shortly after Election Day, the number would be 53 to 47. And in March 1995, when Colorado Democrat Sen. Ben Nighthorse Campbell also switched parties, the numbers would be 54 to 46.

President Clinton, who had spent the week before the election stumping for Democratic candidates nationwide, received the largest off-year rebuke to a president and that president's party in American history. Not only did the Democrats lose the Senate, they lost the House; they lost a majority of governorships; they came close to losing a majority of statehouses. Most stunning of all: Not a single Republican incumbent, anywhere, failed to win reelection. A new majority party had risen, more or less overnight.

The newly elected Republican representative from California's Forty-fourth District, former pop star Sonny Bono, best captured the mood. "The last thing in the world I thought I would be is a U.S. congressman," he told the *Washington Post*, "given all the bobcat vests and Eskimo boots I used to wear." In this, he spoke for us all. So did a man at Dan Rostenkowski's headquarters on election night, who shook his head at the election results and muttered to no one in particular: "Unbelievable." And so did the midlevel Clinton administration policy analyst working on the State Department's 1996 budget who walked into his office after the election, looked at the "detailed paperwork outlining foreign aid allocations" sitting on his desk, and thought: "Should I toss this in the trash? Should I go forward as if nothing changed? Is there going to be any foreign aid? My God, what do I do now?"

Newt Gingrich spent election night at a party in his hometown,

Marietta, Georgia. There was a large television screen at the far end of the room where election results were announced to raucous cheers. As the night progressed, it became clear that Gingrich would no longer be minority leader in the 104th Congress. He'd be the Speaker of the House—the first Republican speaker in forty years.

The lavish event was emceed by a local conservative radio talk show host named Sean Hannity. Gingrich's staff handed out blue and white bumper stickers that read "Speaker Gingrich." People danced and laughed and guzzled champagne. It seemed as though Gingrich was headed in every direction, simultaneously: greeting friends, thanking supporters, rallying the troops, giving interviews. He took the stage and told the adoring crowd, assembled at his feet, that now that the Republicans were in power, the stakes were high—"every day we fail to act, children are at risk . . . Every day we fail to change things, people literally die." He told the crowd that the election results "sent a signal for less government and lower taxes and a change in direction." And he added that now "every bill or committee report filed in Washington will be available instantly on computer."

It was a funny tic of Gingrich's personality—Republicans take over Washington for the first time in decades, and his first thought was about computers—but such a statement was also reflective, in its own way, of the victorious Republicans' boundless idealism. In Washington, D.C., on election night, Kansas senator Robert Dole, who was set to become the first Republican Senate majority leader since 1986—and who was not known for his sunny disposition— was almost giddy in his remarks to supporters. "We're winning governorships all across America," he said. "We're going to change America. We're going to give America back to the people!"

Shortly after the election, Gingrich's pollster Frank Luntz wrote a *Washington Post* op-ed in which he argued that "Election Day was a public scream to change the entire way Washington does business." Another Republican pollster, Ed Goeas, said: "We have to take the power given us and use it to dismantle Washington." First things first, Ohio Republican congressman John Boehner said: "If we're going to change Washington, it's going to be very difficult unless we change Congress. It's Congress that's created this monster. It's Congress that sustained it. It's Congress we must change so we can get at this monster." Republican congressman Jim Nussle told one paper that the change in power on Capitol Hill was "not only a transition. It's a transformation." Nussle told another paper that Republican rule heralded "a new order."

Flush with success, Gingrich returned to Washington on November 10 and spoke to a business roundtable assembled at the Willard Hotel. He upped the stakes; upped the idealism. "I am not prepared to compromise," he said. "I think Medicaid needs to be looked at. I think the Job Corps needs to be looked at. I think that Head Start needs to be looked at, I think that everything from the ground up has to be looked at." He paused. "That doesn't mean it has to be abolished."

By "it," of course, Gingrich meant "everything." "Everything" needn't be abolished. But a lot would be, if he had his way—and why not? The central Republican conservative idea is that government should be small and responsible. The Republicans had promised the American public an era of systemic reform.

The conservative think tanks and talking heads and op-ed pages and policy staffs had been waiting for this moment for a long time. They were hemorrhaging plans. Plans to eliminate at least three cabinet-level departments—Education, Commerce, and Energy— and perhaps even the Department of Agriculture. Plans to trash thousands and thousands of federal regulations. Plans to eliminate patronage positions on Capitol Hill and restructure Congress. Plans to eliminate the National Endowment for the Arts, the National Endowment for the Humanities, and the Corporation for Public Broadcasting. Plans to reform welfare and abolish Aid to Families with Dependent Children. Plans to slash taxes further than Reagan did, maybe even replace the progressive income tax with a one-size-fits-all national sales tax or flat tax. Plans to partially privatize Social Security, ban partial-birth abortion, and reform Medicare and Medicaid.

And there were plenty of young foot soldiers ready to put these plans into practice. The conservative movement, and Gingrich's triumph, had inspired thousands of young men and women who shared conservative ideals and thought conservative thoughts. They had read conservative books and magazines and had listened to conservative speakers, and they wanted to see their government behave under the conservative precepts of prudence and austerity, modesty and restraint. They wanted a government without an upturned, priggish nose, one that refused to tell its subjects what to eat, what (not) to smoke, which "lifestyles" were appropriate, and which were not. Such young people went to work at papers and legislative offices, on campaigns and in activist groups; thousands came to Washington every year, and continue to come, thinking that conservatism is about starving government, not fattening it up and then living off its excretions.

I know this was—and continues to be—the case. I know it because I'm one of them.

I came to Washington a few years ago, almost a decade after the Republican Revolution, to work for a conservative political magazine. It was quite an opportunity. I'd spent the previous four years at a school in New York City not known as a hotbed of conservatism, to say the least, and like a lot of conservatives I enjoyed the contrarian spirit that comes with being an intellectual minority. What I found in Washington was different. I found a city where Republicans controlled all three branches of government, had their own radio and television networks, and dominated public debate and policy in a way similar to that of the massive liberal majorities that governed the New Deal and Great Society. I found a city that had grown rich and fat and happy, filled with expensive gourmet restaurants, chic bars, and a social life reminiscent of, if not comparable to, New York City's. But I also found that the ideological fervor of the Gingrich revolution was fading; that too many conservatives had made too many compromises with their own principles; that clouding all the fun was a widespread sense of peril, of living on the edge. And I found a city dominated by K Street Conservatives,

named after the street in downtown Washington where most lobbyists have offices, people who mouth conservative principles while
getting rich off conservative power. The city of the K Street Conservatives was a city on the brink of major scandal.

All of this can be directly traced to the leadership election the
newly victorious congressional Republicans held in December 1994.

In all, seventy-three freshmen Republicans were elected to the
House of Representatives in 1994. This meant that more than a
third of the Republican caucus had won office in the last two election cycles. It was an overwhelmingly young, vibrant, and conservative crowd—indeed, probably the most conservative House caucus
in decades. And the person the surge of new blood into the House
benefited most of all was Tom DeLay, who had campaigned tirelessly on behalf of challengers across the country. DeLay had been
the second-biggest congressional fund-raiser in the 1994 election
cycle; only Newt Gingrich's GOPAC had raised more cash. And
while GOPAC spread its resources thin, donating to the widest
number of candidates possible, DeLay understood that to maximize support, you have to *provide* maximum support. He gave all
of his eighty candidates the maximum allowed contribution. In
contrast, Robert Walker raised only $1,000 for one Republican
challenger in 1994 who went on to become a member of the fresh-
man class.[7]

DeLay seized his opportunity. He asked his consultant Mildred
Webber to manage his campaign for minority whip in the month
before the leadership elections on December 5, 1994. Dennis Hastert
assembled a twenty-member vote-gathering team to whip support
among the Republican Conference.[8] They weren't afraid to play
dirty. The *Washington Times* reported that DeLay's allies were
accused of telling "several freshmen" that "a Walker reception for
them had been canceled." They were also blamed for spreading
rumors, the *Washington Times* continued, that Walker "was about
to withdraw from the race."[9] (Delay denied this.) DeLay's team was

fierce, and it was fast—an harbinger of things to come. Before the first vote was cast, DeLay had the guaranteed support of fifty-three of the seventy-three GOP freshmen.[10]

Walker—and Gingrich—were left grasping at straws. By mid-November 1994, conventional wisdom on Capitol Hill was that DeLay had the race locked up. In a last-ditch effort to prevent DeLay from winning, Gingrich—by far the most popular member of the House Republican caucus—began to tell members that he supported Walker. But Gingrich's private campaign had little effect. (DeLay would later tell reporters that Gingrich never publicly campaigned for Walker because "he knew that I make a terrible enemy.")[11] On November 27, 1994, a week before the leadership elections, DeLay was already predicting victory. "I've got it on the second ballot," he told the *Dallas Morning News*. "I think Walker will come in second."

On December 5, the House Republicans met in a large room inside the Cannon Office Building on Capitol Hill to select their new leadership. By all accounts, the room was filled with energy, and Gingrich was nominated Speaker of the House with unanimous consent. People shouted his name: "Newt! Newt! Newt!" Next, Texan Dick Armey quickly won approval as the new majority leader. No doubt the legislators' eyes were wide at the prospect of retaking power, enacting serious and irrevocable reforms, busting the Washington bureaucracy, and returning power to the states and to the people.

Sometime during the meeting, Newt took the floor and addressed all of the House Republicans—his shock troops in the coming Revolution.

"When you see a large government bureaucracy," Gingrich asked, "is it an inevitable relic of the past that can't be changed, or is it an opportunity for an extraordinary transformation to provide better services and better opportunities at lower cost—exactly what every major corporation is going through?"

The Republicans listened closely.

"I think you're going to see over time a more decent and a more open and a more idealistic and a more romantic vision of what self-government's all about," Gingrich said.

The speech was vintage Gingrich—grandiose, optimistic, propulsive, and overwhelmingly confident in the idea that you could run the federal government like a large corporation. But it also was evidence of a divide among Republicans. On one side was Gingrich, who used business metaphors to describe his vision of government because he thought that markets responded better to change than tired bureaucracies, and that government could learn from them. Bob Walker felt similarly. But on the other side were Tom DeLay and his allies, who viewed government *as* a business—one that maximized the advantages of business so that business would then donate to their political war chests. The whip election was between those who viewed power as a means to the end of limiting government and those who viewed power as an end in itself. And this election would go a long way to determine which side of this Republican divide emerged victorious.

There, in the Cannon Building, the House Republicans voted for their next majority whip. The vote was by secret ballot. DeLay's prediction from a few weeks earlier turned out to be wrong—he won 119 votes in the first round, four more than was necessary to avoid a run-off. Walker got eighty votes. It's clear now that he never had a chance.

Everyone was looking one way at the election results from November 1994—the Republican Revolution, as it was quickly named. And everyone was looking at Newt Gingrich as he dazzled supporters and infuriated critics with his arrogance, charm, quirky erudition, and boldness. But the actual revolution in American politics occurred with the elevation of Tom DeLay. His election to the whip position was the first step in the creation of a new Republican machine—one that would keep Republicans in power by tightening the grip the business lobby had on the conservative caucus.

It was a grand design, but it was also fraught with risk. There had always been a danger that business's hold on Republican lawmakers would become dictatorial. A danger that Republicans would start to see business interests as the public interest. A danger that, while Republicans would hold office, corporate lobbyists and special-interest groups would hold all the actual power—writing bills, shaping public discourse, and using the apparatus of big government to their own advantage.

These dangers were soon realized. The November revolution turned into the December revolution—in which power was decisively transferred not from Washington to the American people but from Capitol Hill to K Street. This second revolution, it should be said, had ideological cover: Conservative Republicans are generally pro-business, which is to say pro-free market. They prefer competition to monopoly.

Similarly, conservatives have an ideological distaste for regulation. They argue that regulations end up hurting more than they help. They believe government should get out of the way whenever possible, leaving individuals and businesses to fend for themselves in the free market. Tom DeLay is such a conservative. Ever since DeLay had arrived in the Texas state legislature in 1978, he had been known as "Dr. DeReg."

But as the Republicans took over Capitol Hill, the free-market conservatives forgot, it seemed, that open markets and competition are not in the interest of most businesses. If you are a smart businessman, you'll know that less competition increases your market advantage. Therefore, you'll turn to the government to maximize profit. Which means you'll not only lobby for subsidies, antitrust protections, and tax loopholes; you'll also seek to end government regulations limiting your profits, regardless of whether or not those regulations serve the public interest. Businessmen don't do this out of malice. They don't do it entirely out of greed. They do it because they truly believe that everyone will be better off if they make more money.

Certainly, Republicans would be better off. The more profit a corporation makes as a result of GOP-backed legislation, the more donations a corporation's political action committee can make to

Republican lawmakers. There's a certain Zen circularity to this logic. But that's how things ran, more or less, in the forty years that Democrats ran Congress.

It was only a matter of time, then, before the Republicans handed the business lobby the keys to Capitol Hill.

The moment came sooner than anyone expected. On December 14, 1994—about a month *before* Republicans took power—whip-elect DeLay held a press conference. Standing next to him was Bruce Gates, a friend and the vice president for public affairs at the National American Wholesale Grocers Association. Gates's job was to lobby for legislation that would help grocery corporations make more money. But now he had a new job: He was going to head a broad-based, "grassroots" campaign to deregulate industry. He wanted to "change the process by which the government regulates." As he put it later to the *New York Times:* "What this is all about, is changing the fundamental process from a system where people are serving regulations, to one where the regulations are serving people."

Surrounded on both sides by tall, tall piles of federal regulations, Gates and DeLay answered questions and unveiled their "100 Day Agenda," along with a toll-free number—1-800-XS-REGS—that Americans could call to voice their complaints about how government do-gooders were harming consumers and strangling business. (If you call the number today, there's no answer.) And they gave their project a name: Project Relief. Because deregulation was a matter of life and death, apparently. At the press conference, DeLay said government regulators were "Gestapo-like."

Project Relief was a consortium of more than 350 corporations, trade associations, lobbying firms, and special-interest groups, including representatives from the drug industry, the construction industry, BellSouth, FedEx, the Beer Institute, Boeing, the National Restaurant Association, the Cato Institute, Americans for Tax Reform, the Heritage Foundation, the Christian Coalition, the U.S. Chamber of Commerce, Ross Perot's United We Stand America, the FMI, the

National Grocers Association, the Grocery Manufacturers of America, the Adolph Coors Co., the Associated General Contractors, the Chemical Manufacturers Association, the Conservative Caucus, Chevron, General Electric, the lobbying firm Hill & Knowlton, the National Association of Realtors, the Unocal Corporation, and Wal-Mart.

Members of Project Relief's "Steering Committee" were asked to make a "voluntary contribution" of $1,000, but most gave much more than that. Project Relief's communications budget alone was $500,000. One estimate put the total amount of money spent by members of Project Relief in the first six months of 1995 at $30 million.

Project Relief members met once a week. The meetings mostly were about how to pass the Job Creation and Wage Enhancement Act of 1995, a massive deregulation bill that would have imposed a thirteen-month moratorium on federal regulations. The bill had been written by Gordon Gooch, who was not a congressman or a member of any congressman's staff. He was a lobbyist—a high-paid representative for the oil and gas industries. And he had no illusions about whom he ultimately was working for: "I'm not claiming to be a Boy Scout," he later told the *Washington Post*. "No question I thought what I was doing was in the best interest of my clients."

Gooch's first draft of the Job Creation and Wage Enhancement Act initially limited the moratorium on federal regulations to 100 days. But soon other lobbyists came in and extended the ban to thirteen months. Then the lobbyists stuffed the bill with special giveaways to companies like Union Carbide and Boeing. It was a field day. "We're no longer on the defensive," one lobbyist said.

The modus operandi of the K Street Conservatives was apparent even before Newt Gingrich was sworn in as Speaker of the House. And it would be replicated over and over again: First, assemble lobbyists from throughout corporate America and ask them what they want. Then create a "grassroots coalition"—in this case, Project Relief—that can conduct a media campaign to gin up support. Next, publish op-eds that push all the right free-market buttons, such as the one Bruce Gates published in the *Washington Post* in early 1995: "What proponents of regulatory reform (as outlined in the Job Creation and Wage Enhancement Act) are really interested in," Gates wrote, "is a more flexible, realistic approach to government intervention that injects common-sense analysis into the regulatory process." Next step: Never identify the author of these op-eds as a corporate lobbyist—Gates, for example, was simply identified as "the chairman of Project Relief." These intermediary steps should provide enough cover to pass whatever you want.

On January 3, 1995, on the eve of "Opening Day"—when Gingrich would officially open the 104th Congress—DeLay opened the doors to his lavish leadership suite inside the Capitol Building to members of Project Relief. DeLay's staff wasn't finished unpacking his things, so the office was a mess—a collection of busybodies, copy machines, reams of white paper, and ringing telephones. The lobbyists went through draft after draft of the deregulation bill. They were the new legislators.

When Newt Gingrich took the dais the next morning, he spoke of none of this. Instead, he repeated what he had said in the previous months. In one interview that day, Gingrich told reporters: "What I can do between now and Easter is break up the Washington logjam, shift power back to the fifty states, break up all the liberal national organizations—and make them scramble to state capitals in Texas, Georgia, and Missouri." In another interview Gingrich said that "the whole language of politics is in the midst of transformation."

It was quite a contrast—Gingrich talking of transformation while DeLay handed over the legislative power to paid interests. One wonders whether Gingrich even knew what was going on—and indeed, in a televised debate with Democratic Senate minority leader Tom Daschle in 1996, Gingrich said he did not recall Project Relief lobbyists ever working out of the leadership offices. He could have been lying, of course. But he also just could have been aloof.

DeLay didn't have that problem. The Job Creation and Wage Enhancement Act passed the House Committee on Regulation, where DeLay ally Mildred Webber now played a prominent role. On February 1, 1995, DeLay held a meeting with about fifty Project Relief lobbyists. He told them he wanted the deregulation bill to be veto-proof, which would require bipartisan support. Project lobbyists came up with a list of seventy-two potential Democratic votes—Democrats who had voted in January for the balanced budget amendment. A Project Relief lobbyist was assigned to each of the seventy-two targets.

On February 24, 1995, the House passed DeLay's bill, 276-146. More than fifty Democrats voted for the moratorium. The next week DeLay attended a reception in the Caucus Room of the Cannon House Office Building—the same room where he had been elected whip about three months earlier—to celebrate. His staff had built a five-foot Statue of Liberty and wrapped it in red tape. It sat in the middle of the room. Someone handed DeLay a pair of scissors, and he started cutting, cutting away, a toothy grin on his face. Bruce Gates, who had recently left the National American Wholesale Grocers Association for a more lucrative job at the lobbying firm Oldaker, Ryan & Leonard, joined in the fun. People laughed and sipped cold drinks.

"You've got to understand, we are ideologues," DeLay once told journalist Elizabeth Drew. "We have an agenda. We have a philosophy. I want to repeal the Clean Air Act. No one came to me and said, 'Please repeal the Clean Air Act.' We say to the lobbyists, 'Help us.' We know what we want to do and we find the people to help us do that. We go to the lobbyists and say, 'Help us get this in the appropriations bill.'"

It was a stunning admission, unnoticed at the time: Lawmakers, DeLay was basically saying, relied on paid lobbyists to get bills passed, not the other way around. The federal government was so complex, the challenges of leadership so difficult, that lobbyists were more likely to get things done than the people's representatives. And DeLay, because of his "ideology," was happy to play along. The age of K Street had arrived. The Republicans were just along for the ride.

CHAPTER ONE

THE GANG

HOW THE COLLEGE REPUBLICANS
LAUNCHED THE CAREER OF A CON ARTIST

I think the revolution is happening. It's going to stick.
I don't see what could happen to move it back. The trouble is,
there will be a lot of whores trying to jump on the bandwagon.
Like young professionals who decide to go to Washington
and be a Republican.
—GROVER NORQUIST

ON MONDAY MORNING, August 20, 1984—the first day of the
Republican National Convention in Dallas, Texas—the twenty-
six-year-old president of the College Republicans, Jack Abramoff,
approached the podium, gazed out into the half-filled convention
center, and addressed the crowd. "Fellow Republicans," he began,
"I come before you representing American students." His voice was
nasal but assured. He had great confidence. "Today," he went on,
"our party readies itself to mount the wave of the future. Will we
ride that wave to glory, or will it send us crashing ashore?" And
then he began to rhyme. "If we're the party of tax cuts," he said,
"and not the party of 'ifs' and 'buts,' then we're riding our wave."

Applause.

"If we're liberating students from Grenada, and not bowing
down to a Cuban dictator, we're riding our wave."

More applause.

"But if we equivocate, capitulate, accommodate, and negotiate, we'll crash ashore."

Yet more applause.

"If we try to outspend big fat Tip O'Neill, or rush to Geneva to cut a deal, we'll crash ashore."

It was a quirky speech—at times sophomoric, at other times too clever for its own good—but it also served an important purpose. Abramoff was the spokesman for a new generation of conservative activists, young men and women who had come of age just as their party was coming into power. This was a generation of conservatives who possessed ideological zeal coupled with an oppositional demeanor. A generation that—unlike its elders in the conservative movement—had been attracted to politics in the wake of the Reagan election. It was also a generation, it would turn out, that was corrupted by power before they knew what power was. They took their cues from an unlikely source: the student activists on the left who had immediately preceded them on campus, who thought that ideological fervor, coupled with bold action, was the avenue to, and predicate of, political power. They shared a susceptibility to extremist tactics on the one hand, and underhanded behavior on the other. This was an unhealthy combination. It made these young conservatives unpredictable, reckless—out of control, even. No one knew where they were headed. No one cared to know.

Consider the career path of the young man standing on the dais that day in 1984, urging Ronald Reagan's reelection.

In retrospect it might seem a perfect symmetry that the man who would become known in Washington, D.C., as "Casino Jack" Abramoff was born in Atlantic City on February 28, 1958. Notwithstanding where he was born, his childhood was placid, normal, even dull. Abramoff's father, Frank, was a businessman. Abramoff's mother took care of the kids. When Jack was born, his dad worked at Arnold Palmer Enterprises in New Jersey. When Jack was ten, the family settled in Beverly Hills, where his father had taken a job at the Diner's Club.

Needless to say, it was a privileged youth. Abramoff went to Beverly Hills High School, where he was a jock. On the weight-lifting team he squatted 540 pounds. He played football and he was popular with the girls. He was a member of the student government. He was patriotic, an establishmentarian, in a manner similar to that of other affluent children who are interested in politics—interested in protecting the sort of lifestyle to which they are accustomed. His family was Jewish but not particularly religious. At twelve he saw *Fiddler on the Roof* and had a religious awakening. "I made the decision that I would become religious in order to preserve the faith in our family," he has said. After watching the movie, he spent all the money he had saved on Judaica. He studied the Torah. Eventually, he would become Orthodox.

Abramoff's family did not follow him into Orthodoxy. Later, when they visited him in Washington, they would stay at a hotel rather than observe the strictures of his Orthodox household. Though they had religious differences, Abramoff's politics tracked closely with his father's. Frank Abramoff was a Republican with ties to Ronald Reagan. Like his father, Jack Abramoff was a Reaganite—if Reagan was for it, so was he. Abramoff was a fusionist. He believed that a virtuous society required unfettered markets. Beyond that, his politics were vague. He was a party man. What could he do for his party? And, more important, what could his party do for him?

In 1977, Abramoff graduated from high school. He went straight to Boston, to Brandeis. He graduated in 1981, but he did not move on—at least not right away—because over time his love of politics had turned professional. Central to this transition was a young man who shared his convictions, his passion, and his ambition: Grover Norquist. Together, they would remake the College Republicans in their own, hard-core image. And their friendship would outlast their activism. It would continue for decades, as the two traded favors, used each other's connections, and promoted each other's careers, not to mention each other's clients. Norquist would become famous, Abramoff remaining in the shadows. Eventually, that would change. Abramoff's dizzying lobbying career would make him famous, too—before it made him infamous.

The two friends had met in Boston, volunteering for Ronald Reagan in the 1980 presidential election. In that election, of course, Reagan went on to sweep forty-four states, including Massachusetts—for which feat Abramoff and Norquist would often claim partial credit. Norquist was older than Abramoff; he was a student at Harvard Business School when they first met. He was less charismatic. He was more intellectual.

Norquist had been born on October 19, 1956, and had grown up in Weston, Massachusetts, a suburb of Boston. Norquist's father, Warren, was a Polaroid executive. Norquist's mother stayed at home. Both his parents, we learn from his biographer, Nina Easton, were Rockefeller Republicans. Today, the Rockefeller Republicans are for the most part gone, victims of the Republican Party's southern, conservative realignment. Those who are left are confined to rotten boroughs in the Northeast, politicians like New York governor George Pataki and Republican senator Lincoln Chafee. Like their guru Nelson Rockefeller, once governor and senator from New York, these Republicans embodied a patrician ethic that coupled pro-business economics with a live-and-let-live (or let die, as the case may be) attitude toward social issues. "Ideology" wasn't for them. Neither was a confrontational foreign policy.

This did not suit the young Norquist. For him, accommodation was what should be absent from politics, not ideology. In this he resembled his grandmother, a Nixon supporter and longtime subscriber to *Human Events,* a conservative newsletter. His grandmother would give Norquist copies of that paper when she had finished with them. It was she who, Nina Easton tells us, provided Norquist with an introduction to "the concept of 'totalitarian liberals,' the 'leftist bias in academia,' threats posed by Big Labor, and American weakness in the face of encroaching 'Red Tyranny.'"[1]

Norquist's conservatism was the result of reading—reading that provoked sentiments about power, the state, and the United States. A precocious teenager, he read J. Edgar Hoover's *Masters of*

Deceit, Whittaker Chambers's *Witness*, and Herbert Arthur Philbrick's *I Led Three Lives*, among other titles. These books introduced him to a world where cells of foreign agents were attempting to penetrate and undermine American institutions and American strength, a world in which two all-encompassing and diametrically opposed ideologies competed for global dominance. In these books, there is no such thing as an innocent bystander. One is forced to choose sides. Norquist's choice typified those of a generation of young conservatives. He chose democracy over tyranny. He chose capitalism over controlled economies. He chose the Constitutional Convention over the Third International, Whittaker Chambers over Alger Hiss. What was curious about Norquist's political awakening, however, was that, while he committed his life to ending communism and promoting freedom, over time he began to imitate the same icons whose legacy he labored ceaselessly to destroy.

In 1974, Norquist entered Harvard. It was an era of scandal—Nixon had just resigned the presidency—and an era of upheaval. The late sixties saw the rise of the left on America's campuses. But the seventies would see a counterrevolution: the education of a group of conservatives who were repelled by the left and eager to work toward damping the sixties' excesses. Nowhere was this more true than at Harvard. William Kristol had finished his undergraduate work there the year before Norquist showed up and was now pursuing his doctorate in political theory. Future Chief Justice of the United States John Roberts was in his second year. Another future conservative activist, Peter Ferrara, worked with Norquist on the *Harvard Crimson*. Once on campus, Norquist joined the College Republicans. The national chair at the time was one Karl Rove.

He graduated in 1978. Graduation Day was brief. In the middle of the party his parents threw to celebrate the occasion, Norquist said his good-byes, got into the loaded U-Haul parked in the driveway, and started for Washington.[2]

Almost more than he despised Soviet communism, Norquist despised liberalism. He saw liberalism as an antecedent to socialism and then communism. He saw Washington as a gigantic monument to the pretensions of state power. According to his Manichaean worldview, Washington bureaucrats existed for the sole purpose of stealing money from the American people. The threat of violence accompanying such confiscation was implicit. It was no small leap for Norquist to liken the landscape of Washington to the landscape of Hitler's Berlin. "Neo American fascism," he told Easton when recalling the sight of the buildings. "Stuff that looks like Albert Speer designed it."[3]

Within a year of his arrival in Washington, he became executive director of the National Taxpayers Union, an antitax nonprofit. The goal of the National Taxpayers Union was to oppose tax increases whenever and advocate tax cuts when possible. The late seventies was a time of great victories for the antitax movement. In June 1978, California voters passed Proposition 13, which drastically reduced property taxes. Soon other states were mimicking California. Proposition 13 and its clones, Norquist told the *Washington Post* at the time, showed that "two shibboleths have been smashed. One said that paying taxes to government was like giving to the United Way, and the other said that you get it all back in services."[4]

The 1978 talk with the *Post* was one of Norquist's first on-the-record interviews with an influential publication. Reading the article today, one is amazed at the constancy of Norquist's beliefs. He's been on message for more than twenty years. "The facts are that government is not a benevolent charity—the poverty program didn't help the poor, it helped the bureaucrats—and government is not providing services efficiently," Norquist told the *Post*. "You go to city hall or the post office and what do you see? Bureaucrats pushing papers, drinking coffee, and harassing the people."[5] It is the same philosophy Norquist espouses today—government is always opposed to the people, bureaucrats leech off the public teat, taxes are the nourishment of the state. That decades of Republican dominance have continued to confirm parts of this worldview seems not to have shaken Norquist's partisan affiliations in the least.

After a few years as the head of the National Taxpayers Union, Norquist went back to Harvard—"at the behest of his father," the

New Yorker writer John Cassidy tells us—to get a graduate degree in business.[6] Here again, Norquist followed the trajectory of his fellow yuppies. The future leaders of the conservative movement were not so different from their opponents in background, in education, in aspiration. But there was a paradox. As members of the educated elite grew more alike in their postgraduate degrees and consumer preferences, they also grew further apart in ideology.

Shortly after Reagan won, Abramoff asked Norquist if he wanted to work on another presidential campaign: his run for head of College Republicans. Norquist agreed, and the two went to work. Norquist ran the campaign from his dorm room.[7]

The College Republicans is the oldest and largest student activist group, tracing its founding to the last decade of the nineteenth century. Officially called the College Republican National Committee, the group is incorporated under section 527 of the U.S. tax code, making it a nonprofit engaging in political activity. For almost a century, the College Republican National Committee enjoyed financial backing from the Republican Party (that ended in the 1990s). There are chapters at colleges and universities in each of the fifty states. Each state elects a chairman, and a national chairman is elected every two years at the College Republican convention. Some of those chairmen—Lee Atwater, Karl Rove, Jack Abramoff—went on to legendary political careers. But the bulk of those who join College Republicans, along with its affiliate, the Young Republicans, are activists; true believers who are content to toil behind the scenes. They exist in the background. Many of the people central to Abramoff's life, both his rise and fall, he met in College Republicans—people like Norquist and Ralph Reed, but also less famous people like Adam Kidan, a student at George Washington Law School, and Amy Moritz, who later married another College Republican, David Ridenour, and worked in the think tank industry.

Amy Moritz was Abramoff's chief opponent in the race for the national chairmanship. Norquist and Abramoff, we are told, saw Moritz as an establishment figure, unwilling to move the College

Republicans to a more conservative, confrontational posture. So they more or less bought her off. Abramoff told Moritz that if she withdrew her candidacy and threw her support to him, he would reward her with the title of "executive director." Apparently, the title pleased Moritz. She pulled out. Abramoff spent $10,000 on his campaign and won overwhelmingly.[8]

The College Republicans select their presidents at national conventions. The year Abramoff ran, 1981, the convention was held in Chicago. One of the delegates that year was a young conservative, Ralph Reed, the head of College Republicans at the University of Georgia.

Reed was just twenty years old. He had been born six weeks premature on June 24, 1961, in Portsmouth, Virginia, and to this day his frame is slight, his face preternaturally boyish. Although Reed would spend most of his adult life in Georgia, he did not move there until 1976, when his family settled in the small town of Toccoa, in the northeastern part of the state. Reed was in high school at the time. Georgia was the fifth state, and Toccoa the seventh town, he had called home. He entered the University of Georgia in 1979 and was quickly drawn to campus politics. Only a few months into his college career, Reed watched hundreds of students gather outside their dorm rooms to protest Iran's taking of U.S. hostages. The protesters sang the national anthem and shouted patriotic slogans, urging the use of deadly force to liberate the American prisoners. The expression of American nationalism struck Reed; though he was not part of the protest, he watched intently. He was fascinated by the architecture of the mob. Shortly afterward, he joined his school's chapter of College Republicans. He rose through the organization's ranks and spent the summer between his sophomore and junior years in Washington, as an intern on Capitol Hill.

One day during the 1981 College Republicans convention, Reed approached Abramoff while waiting for a hotel elevator and asked for a job.[9] Abramoff, flush with power, gave him one on the spot. Reed would work under Norquist.

The two became inseparable. When the group returned to Washington, Norquist and Reed would stay up throughout the night, planning rallies and protests, writing press releases, and talking about the threats the left posed to America. At times Norquist took a pedagogical turn. He taught his acolytes to learn about politics and leadership from historical examples. But the example he had in mind wasn't Reagan or Churchill but Stalin. Stalin "was running the personnel department while Trotsky was fighting the White Army," Norquist is quoted as saying in *Gang of Five*. "When push came to shove for control of the Soviet Union, Stalin won. Trotsky got a pick ax through his skull, while Stalin became head of the Soviet Union. He understood that personnel is policy."[10]

Perhaps to illustrate his point, Norquist worked with Reed to freeze Moritz, to whom Abramoff had promised the title of executive director, out of the College Republicans leadership. Moritz never became executive director. That title went instead to Norquist, and Moritz became "deputy director," a vague title that carried little weight. There is a famous anecdote in which Reed takes all of Moritz's belongings, puts them into a box, and writes "Amy's desk" on the side of the box. And that was that. "We probably made it very dictatorial," Abramoff would say years later. "But we wanted the College Republicans to remain conservative. That was our big concern."[11] Note again the strange mixture of libertarian politics with autocratic tendencies, the missionary zeal with which this small group of true believers faced down the opposition, even when the opposition was, technically speaking, on their side. Note, too, the romantic streak in Norquist's politics, the adulation and emulation given to larger-than-life leaders, even those who deployed violence and terror in their single-minded pursuit of power.

Under Abramoff, the College Republicans entered a period of rapid growth. When Reagan was elected in 1980, there had only been 250 chapters of the group. A year after Abramoff was elected chairman, there were an estimated 1,100 chapters.[12] With Norquist and Ralph Reed his top lieutenants, Abramoff brought the College Republicans media attention. The trio's conservatism imbued the organization. "It is not our job to seek peaceful coexistence with the left," Abramoff said in 1983. "Our job is to remove them from power permanently." They were romantics. They staged rallies and agitated against the left. They believed that they were living in the midst of a world war, and they were soldiers. And their seriousness and dedication to the cause earned them regard among their elders in the Reagan White House. By 1984, Abramoff could tell *National Journal,* "We're better trained for this election" and "We have stronger clubs, trained advisers, and more resources."[13]

What the trio at College Republicans was doing, in retrospect, was turning a backwater organization into a bastion of "movement conservatism"—a sort of School of the Americas for future conservative shock troops. This is not a glib analogy. There was always a paramilitary flavor to the three friends' politics. They had read the works of New Left authors such as Saul Alinsky. Abramoff and Norquist courted anti-Communist guerrillas—and "former" Maoists—such as Angola's Jonas Savimbi. And all three were self-consciously working toward a conservative revolution in America—albeit one that would be achieved at the polls.

Abramoff knew how to generate publicity. He had a knack for planning outsized events that would attract a reporter for the *Post* or the *Times.* And Reed and Norquist would appear alongside him, providing quotes whenever possible. The trio organized many rallies. In 1982, there was a rally in favor of a balanced budget amendment to the Constitution.[14] In September 1983, after Soviet military jets shot down Korean airliner KAL 007, Reed led a march of young conservatives through downtown Washington—"his tie knot loosened, his fists pumping, his face twisted in anger," according to Nina Easton. Reed's photo was published in *U.S. News & World Report.* On August 11, 1983, Abramoff was the first among a group of College Republicans to tear down a cinder-block, mock Berlin Wall constructed in Lafayette Park, across from the White House. The wall was five feet tall. About 100 kids showed up. "The Berlin Wall is a symbol of communist tyranny," Abramoff said. "We are showing that Americans will not forget the sin that one-third of the world

lives under communism." The activists tore down the wall and burned
Soviet dictator Yuri Andropov in effigy. "Someday," Abramoff went
on, "we will break down the real Berlin Wall."[15] In 1984, as president of Students for America, a nationwide group for religious conservative college students, Reed helped organize public celebrations
of the first anniversary of the invasion of Grenada. In 1985, he set
up a "mock Sandinista prison camp" on the west lawn of the Capitol Building. "Everyone who's going on the abduction, come over
here!" the *Washington Post* quoted him as shouting.

The trio organized petitions supporting unrestricted immigration from Communist dictatorships.[16] They launched an attack on
the left's student activists, distributing, in 1983, fifty-page packets
to College Republican chairs attacking state Public Interest
Research Groups (otherwise known as PIRGs) and other Naderite
organizations. The campaign spawned coverage in the *New York
Times*. Abramoff told the paper that the PIRGs were "instrumental
in leading anti-Reagan and anti–free market forces on campuses"
and had to be stopped.[17] They organized voter registration drives.
"We will go door to door in every dormitory, sorority, and frater-
nity house. We will distribute absentee ballots in cafeterias and student lounges," Abramoff said at a July 28, 1983, news conference.
"By January 1, 1984, two million young people will be added to
voter registration rolls in time to make their voices heard in the
presidential primaries." Appearing alongside Abramoff was a
third-term congressman from Georgia, Newt Gingrich.

The members of the gang were unafraid of criticism, even when
it came from members of their own party. In fact, they took it on
themselves to police their own party, purging it of refuseniks and
deviationists. In early January 1983, moderate Republican Jim
Leach held a press conference in which he charged that the Reverend
Moon's Unification Church was funneling money to the College
Republicans. Norquist attended the press conference and confronted
Leach during the Q & A. It was not a civil exchange. "This is not
just a lie, it's charging us with a federal crime," Norquist told the
Washington Post.[18]

The trio spent so much time together, in fact, that their social life was often dependent on other members of the group. Norquist had no personal life to speak of. Reed met his future wife, Joanne, through College Republicans. And Abramoff, in 1983, attending Ronald Reagan's seventy-second-birthday celebration at the White House, met his future wife, a young activist named Pam Alexander. Reed played matchmaker.

Norquist spent six months with Abramoff and Reed at the helm of College Republicans before taking a job at Americans for the Reagan Agenda, a nonprofit set up by the administration to lobby Congress. From there he worked briefly as an "economic analyst" and speechwriter for the Chamber of Commerce, one of the country's oldest pro-business special-interest groups. While he was working at the Chamber, the *Washington Post* featured Norquist in an article on young conservatives. The article's headline was "Young and Restless on the Right."

The interview is worth noting even today, as it captures well the attitude of young conservatives in the Reagan era, along with the anthropological attitude with which the mainstream press covers conservatives. The *Post* reporter, James Conaway, wrote:

> With his gray suit and matching tie, precise hand motions and well-rehearsed monologue, Norquist looks like a 60-year-old Rotarian three decades before the fact. At 21 he was executive director of and spokesman for the National Taxpayers Union. Today he makes speeches about free enterprise and fiscal responsibility for the Conservative Opportunity Society.[19]

"People under 25 remember only two presidents," Norquist told the *Post*. (He was twenty-eight.) "For them the Democratic party is not John Kennedy, real or mythical. It's not FDR. It's Jimmy Carter." Carterism leads—inevitably, in Norquist's view—to Reaganism. To the *Post*, Norquist had related two of his most deeply held beliefs: that the United States is inherently conservative, and therefore the more conservative party is destined to enjoy power;

and that the conservative movement requires ideological enforcers, gatekeepers to lord over the entryways to power. Norquist saw himself as such a person. All he needed was a gate to keep.

He got one in 1985. That was the year when the second Reagan administration, in the person of the presidential chief of staff, Don Regan, announced its tax reform plan. To assure that Reagan's bill passed Congress, the administration founded a nonprofit, Americans for Tax Reform, to lobby for lower tax rates and a simplified tax code. Regan asked Norquist to head the group. He was twenty-nine. Congress passed substantial tax reform the next year, but Americans for Tax Reform—ATR for short—lived on, mimicking, in its own way, those government programs that conservatives attack for outliving their usefulness.

ATR of course was still very much useful to Norquist, who used the group to lobby to shrink the government and to prevent Republicans, who should know better, from raising taxes. Norquist is fond of remarking that tax cutting is the Republican brand, and whenever a company betrays its brand—he gives the example of New Coke—consumers run away. Republicans who raise taxes are betraying the cause. They are ruining the brand. To prevent them from doing so, Norquist wrote a No Tax Pledge in 1986 and has cajoled lawmakers and candidates for office into signing it ever since. This is what the pledge says:

> I, [the undersigned], pledge to the taxpayers of the [blank] district of the State of [blank] and to the American people that I will:
>   ONE, oppose any and all efforts to increase the marginal income tax rates for individuals and/or businesses; and
>   TWO, oppose any net reduction or elimination of deductions and credits, unless matched dollar for dollar by further reducing tax rates.
>   Signed [blank]

Since its debut in 1986, 222 congressmen and 46 senators have signed the pledge, as well as countless state legislators. Just as

Norquist had hoped, the politicians who broke the pledge ended up paying dearly. The most famous example is, of course, George H. W. Bush, who signed the pledge in 1988 and broke it two years later when he agreed to a budget deal with congressional Democrats that raised taxes. Two years after that, he lost his job, the victim of a fractured Republican Party and an electorate in revolt against the establishment. In Norquist's eyes, Bush lost because he broke the pledge. He betrayed the brand.

The success of the pledge, and his prodigious networking, catapulted Norquist to the upper echelons of conservative grassroots politics. The pledge was one of two great achievements. The other was the construction, over many years, of what Norquist called the Leave Us Alone coalition, a group of activists and pamphleteers who congregate in ATR's downtown Washington offices each Wednesday to spread the word about their activities and grouse about the liberals' latest skulduggery. The Wednesday Meetings, as they were soon called by Washington's conservatives, began in 1993. Writes Nina Easton: "At first, a dozen seats filled constituted a decent turnout."[20] A decade later, with the Republicans in control of both houses of Congress and the presidency, more than 100 activists would show up every week, along with corporate lobbyists, Bush administration officials, and wide-eyed interns.

Talk to political professionals in Washington, and they will tell you that, for all the press attention it receives, the Wednesday Meeting has in fact little impact on our national life. These critics—and not all of them are personal critics of Norquist—are probably right. The Wednesday Meeting is a world unto itself, a collection of people for whom the victory of the conservative movement over that movement's enemies is the organizing principle of their everyday lives. Even though many of the attendees are full-time activists, they should be considered hobbyists instead, obsessives who can't imagine waking up in the morning without a battle to fight over school vouchers or school prayer or expanded broadband access or no-tax pledges.

But what the hobbyists lack in numbers they make up for in

zeal. And while the majority of Americans consider themselves "moderates" and "independents," the hobbyists have an overarching ideology, a worldview that explains human and government behavior—and that can be applied to almost any issue or interest.

As the eighties turned into the nineties, one politician in particular turned to Norquist for advice. This was Newt Gingrich. Norquist had met him in the 1980s, when Gingrich was still a backbencher dreaming of transforming American civilization. "It was the political equivalent of love at first sight," Norquist has said. "Newt walked into the room, and he wanted to do what I wanted to do. He wanted to build a movement to take over the House and the Senate, and he didn't consider this nutty talk."[21] Gingrich has repaid the compliment by calling Norquist "the single most effective conservative activist in the country."[22] This mutual admiration would result in mutual benefit.

In 1983, when Norquist left College Republicans, Reed succeeded him as executive director. Also in 1983—and of considerably more interest to his future biographers—Reed had a religious conversion. One Saturday night that September, he was at Bullfeathers, a bar on Capitol Hill, drinking and carousing, when he decided, "This isn't as fun as it used to be." He left the bar, walked to the nearest phone booth, opened the phone book, and found a listing for Evangel Assembly of God church, a Pentecostal congregation in Camp Springs, Maryland. He went to services the next morning. Abramoff later told the *Los Angeles Times:* "There were some real hard political hacks who were probably skeptical when Ralph went through this. . . . I thought it would be positive in his life, as it has been."[23]

Reed quit drinking. He quit smoking. He did not quit politics, however. His activism continued for another two years, until the fall of 1985, when he gave it all up to pursue a doctorate in history at Emory University. His dissertation, finished in 1991, weighs in at 515 pages and is titled "Fortresses of Faith: Design and Experience at Southern Evangelical Colleges, 1830–1900." As the title indicates, Reed's study examined the history of religious higher education in the South. Besides the fact that it was written at all, the dissertation is notable for the way in which Reed chastises the institutions of higher learning he writes about for their racism.

And yet Reed never pretended he was about to take up a career in academia. That he wrote the dissertation and completed his Ph.D. is evidence, in all probability, of an unquenchable ambition, a desire to prove himself in a liberal academic setting. (When people refer to him as "Dr. Reed," he doesn't seem to mind.) He continued to participate in Republican politics throughout graduate school. In January 1989, at a Students for America dinner in Washington, D.C., Reed met Christian broadcasting magnate Pat Robertson, who had just run a failed presidential campaign the year before.

Robertson's campaign wasn't a total failure, actually—he came in second to Bob Dole in the 1988 Iowa caucuses, scaring the daylights out of the Republican establishment—and he wanted to start an organization devoted to bringing social conservatives into Republican politics. After dinner, Robertson asked Reed if he wanted to run the group. At first Reed demurred; he returned to Georgia and his schoolwork, but soon found he couldn't support a wife and child on a doctoral candidate's income. In September, he accepted Robertson's offer and moved to southeastern Virginia, home of Robertson's television evangelism empire.

The Christian Coalition was incorporated as a nonpartisan, tax-exempt nonprofit. But its political allegiance was always clear. In October 1990, the National Republican Senatorial Committee gave the Coalition $64,000 in what Reed would later call "seed money." The seeds sprouted and grew like crazy. Within a few years, under Reed's leadership the Coalition became, as Nina Easton describes in *Gang of Five*, "a $12 million-plus lobbying machine" boasting "250,000 dues-paying members" and "1.6 million potential allies."

Read press accounts from the Coalition's early history and you find that, when he spoke to the press, Reed would use the same language he had used a decade earlier at College Republicans. In 1991, in a quote that has been hung around his neck ever since, he bragged to Norfolk's *Virginian-Pilot:* "I want to be invisible. I do guerrilla warfare. I paint my face and travel at night. You don't know it's over until you're in a body bag." In 1992, he told the *Los Angeles Times*: "It's like guerrilla warfare. If you reveal your location, all it does is allow your opponent to improve his artillery bearings. It's better to move quietly, with stealth, under cover of night."[24]

Grisly stuff. But such stuff stands out, a decade later, because it runs against the grain of Reed's actual accomplishment. Namely, he did bring social and religious conservatives into the mainstream of the Republican Party, and thus, in turn, into the mainstream of American politics. And he accomplished this, interestingly enough, by draining the Christian Coalition of much of its explicitly Christian, or even religious, content. Just look at the 1993 article Reed wrote for *Policy Review* titled "Casting a Wider Net." In Reed's essay the Religious Right becomes the "pro-family" movement—which movement, it seemed then to Reed, was "policy thin" and "value-laden." He wrote: "If the pro-family movement is not to suffer the same fate" as earlier conservative reform efforts, "the cluster of pro-family issues must now be expanded to attract a majority of voters."[25]

He expanded this message in his book *After the Revolution*, first published in 1994 under the title *Politically Incorrect*:

What we have in mind is not a Christian agenda or even a Republican agenda. It is not a special interest agenda of any kind. It is a pro-family agenda which restores autonomy to the two-parent family and provides sensible protections for this most basic and most essential unit of society.

And furthermore:

The American people need to know that we do not desire to exclude our political foes, only to gain our own place at the table. They cannot hear too often that our objective is not to dominate, but to participate, and that our vision of society includes protecting their right to speak and be heard as much as making our voices heard. We are not trying to elect Billy Graham to the presidency.[26]

Looking back, the Christian Coalition seems a uniquely nineties institution. Reed, like other politicians of that decade, appropriated the language of civil rights to describe Christians—in other words, the vast majority of Americans—as "victims." Conservative Christians became, in Reedspeak, "people of faith" and "religious folk." Attacks on "people of faith" were "grounded not in fact" but "in fear and bigotry." "People of faith" had become caricatures, mere stereotypes in the popular culture; they had become, Reed wrote, the new "Amos and Andy."

Under Reed, the Christian Coalition also embraced the multicultural politics that typified the 1990s. His "pro-family" movement embraced all denominations, all religions, all Americans. In 1995, he started the Catholic Alliance to recruit conservative Catholic voters, and he addressed the annual convention of the Anti-Defamation League and admitted to the audience that Christians had not always been the best friends of the Jews. In 1996, in his book *Active Faith,* he suggested that social conservatives ought to seek compromise on the abortion issue. (Needless to say, controversy ensued.) In 1997, he started the Samaritan Project to reach out to black churches. He gave money to help repair southern black churches destroyed by arsonists.

This wasn't the fire-and-brimstone politics of Jerry Falwell's defunct Moral Majority. This wasn't even the fire-and-brimstone politics of the Christian Coalition's founder, Pat Robertson. But it was a hugely successful electoral strategy. In 1994, Reed told the *Washington Post* that he had assembled a "data bank" of 1.3 million supporters.[27] A year later, he told *Time* magazine that the Coalition had 1.6 million "active supporters" and a $25 million budget.[28] A year after that, Reed said the Coalition had 1.7 million names in its "data bank." Reed used the collection of tools he had sharpened organizing students in the 1980s to build a home in the

Republican Party for religious conservatives. The party, and American politics, were changed irrevocably.

Though the Coalition's membership reached its high point in 1996, the group's political apogee came, of course, in 1994, with the election of the Republican congressional majority. Reed began the year organizing a $1.4 million campaign to stop the Clinton health care plan; a year later, on May 15, 1995, he appeared on the cover of *Time* magazine. The cover line read: "The Right Hand of God." Reed was thirty-three.

When Reed appeared on the cover of *Time,* however, Abramoff had given up on politics. In 1985, Abramoff had been asked to head Citizens for America, one of the many conservative nonprofits concerned with "grassroots organizing" that sprang up like wild mushrooms during the Reagan years. Citizens for America was the brainchild of Lewis Lehrman, who had made a fortune as the founder of the Rite Aid drugstore chain, and who had also spent a considerable amount of that fortune running for governor of New York in 1982. Lehrman lost, by two points, to Mario Cuomo. Citizens for America was a consolation prize.

As chairman, Abramoff relied heavily on his crew of College Republicans. He made Norquist field director. The two followed the playbook they had developed in the early Reagan years, characterized mostly by outsized rallies and cartoonish rhetoric. The Republican political consultant Jeffrey Bell, who worked with Abramoff and Norquist at Citizens for America, told reporter Andrew Ferguson that the College Republicans duo "were just wildmen. They always were willing to throw the long ball. Jack's specialty was the spectacular—huge, larger-than-life, almost Hollywood-like events."[29]

Abramoff did not last long. He was forced to resign. He had gone "hog wild," one Lehrman aide told Sidney Blumenthal, who wrote for the *Washington Post* at the time. "Apparently," Blumenthal reported, "Lehrman concluded that the organization's $3 million budget was being mishandled." For his part, Abramoff insisted that he was the victim of a power struggle. About Abramoff and Norquist's relationship with Citizens for America, Lehrman has said only the following: "I was recruited by President Reagan to set up Citizens for America in 1983. It was a voluntary, part-time position which I held for about three years. Among the paid staff, Jack Abramoff came in well after CFA was started, was there only for a short while, before his termination."[30]

Abramoff floated through the nonprofit world before moving back to Hollywood, where he and his brother started a production company, Regency Entertainment.[31] The two produced a few films, relying on questionable finances, before the company went bankrupt. Abramoff went into debt. He and his brother were forced to sell Regency to Performance Guarantees, a debt-management firm. He began practicing law in southern California.

The night Republicans took Congress, Reed, Abramoff, and Norquist were far apart. Abramoff was in Los Angeles. Reed was in Washington, D.C. And Norquist was with Newt Gingrich in Georgia, celebrating with the newly elected speaker. Together, he, Gingrich, and others spent that night drinking champagne, eating ice cream, and talking about the possibilities before the conservative majority.

It was a moment of great promise. The election results "signaled our political arrival," Reed would later tell political reporters Dan Balz and Ronald Brownstein. "Now we have to institutionalize. [Our goal] is not to reach the voters and turn them out. We've already done that. Now we want to make ourselves permanent. . . . It's what the social historians call professionalization."[32]

His language was revealing. The approach to politics forged during the years in College Republicans, the confrontational tactics and polarizing rhetoric, could be put to the use of other interests. The movement had begun as a cause. Now it was turning into a career. For Abramoff, it would soon become a racket.

CHAPTER TWO

THE K STREET PROJECT

THE REPUBLICAN TAKEOVER OF THE LOBBYING INDUSTRY

ON THE SATURDAY after Election Day, 1994, Jack Abramoff got a call from Preston Gates Ellis & Rouvelas Meeds, a Seattle-based law firm with offices scattered across the globe. (The Gates is Bill Gates's father.) The man on the other end of the line offered Abramoff a job, which he accepted. He was going to return to Washington, to work in the firm's "government affairs" division. He was going to become a lobbyist.

Abramoff embraced his new profession with gusto. He capitalized on his contacts inside the conservative movement, including his friends Grover Norquist and Ralph Reed. And he made new friends, most notably the soon-to-be majority whip, Rep. Tom DeLay.

It is unclear how Abramoff and DeLay met. A common story is that Rabbi Daniel Lapin, a conservative activist who cultivates ties between Orthodox Jews and evangelical Christians, introduced them at an event sponsored by his group, Toward Tradition, in October 1994. But the more likely story is that Abramoff was introduced to DeLay in Washington, D.C., shortly after Republicans took Congress, at a fund-raiser. The way some people tell it, DeLay's chief of staff, Ed Buckham, who later became a lobbyist himself, made the introductions. Abramoff was someone worth knowing, Buckham said. Abramoff would be working with them a great deal.

DeLay understood the necessity of working with lobbyists. By February 24, 1995, the House of Representatives would pass his deregulation package, Project Relief. After passage in the House, the bill went across the Capitol to the Senate, where it quickly became mired in parliamentary procedure. It was soon clear that Project Relief's proposals would not become law; after all, even if the Senate passed the regulation moratorium and sent it on to the president, Clinton was likely to veto it. And in any case, a veto proved unnecessary. Once again the Senate filled its traditional role, which is to frustrate the desires of the majority.

In one regard, however, Project Relief was a stirring success, because it provided DeLay an opportunity to grasp the possibilities of government by lobbyist. Money flows to views—and to success. Corporations fund the war chests of sympathetic lawmakers. And the corporations' hired hands—the lobbyists—also provide donations. There is a certain circularity to this idea—of course corporations will donate to candidates with similar ideas; everyone donates to candidates with similar ideas—but business has so much pull, and so many dollars, that its influence can grow out of control. Bank accounts filled to bursting with all that cash, it is all too easy for lawmakers to place private above public interest.

In the first six months of 1993, the political action committees that eventually became associated with Project Relief delivered $2.6 million in contributions to the GOP. But in the first six months of 1995, with Republicans in control of Congress and with Project Relief well under way, that number had risen to $5.36 million. In all, in the first six months of 1995, the amount of soft money—the unregulated, unlimited donations banned by the 2002 McCain-Feingold campaign finance reform law—flowing into GOP political action committees more than doubled. Together, financial firms, energy companies, and Philip Morris (a small sample of the myriad business interests scouring the capital for friendly faces) gave more than $20 million in the first six months of 1995.[1]

Before Republicans took power, if Tom DeLay had stood on the balcony surrounding the Capitol Dome, he would have seen a river of money flowing along K Street through downtown Washington—but with tributaries that stretched into both Democratic and Republican backwaters. His goal was to reshape that river's course and direct it straight into the pockets of Washington's Republican politicians. And he thought he knew how to do it. With Project Relief, he had hit upon a strategy.

That strategy came to be known as the K Street Project. And the project's goal was nothing less than the partisan realignment of the lobbying industry—to go along with the partisan realignment of Congress—and thus cause the reorientation of corporate America's political giving habits. The project's methods, though innocuous, disturbed many people. This was probably because the central method was compiling lists of names, a legal activity with considerable historical resonance.

According to reporter Nicholas Confessore, in early 1995 DeLay had his staff compile a list of the 400 largest corporate political action committees. Next to each name, DeLay's staff showed the amounts the PACs had given to both political parties in the past few election cycles. One by one, the top lobbyists for the industries associated with those committees were invited to DeLay's office in the Capitol to see the list. They saw their names. They got the message: In order to protect their interests, business PACs needed to stop giving to Democrats.[2]

Another list was started by Representative Bill Paxon of New York, the chairman of the National Republican Congressional Committee and one of the architects of the 1994 victory. Paxon's list focused on individual lobbyists. The original draft included about 1,000 names. Each lobbyist's partisan affiliation and political giving was written down and circulated among members of Congress and the larger lobbying community. Paxon had a sunny demeanor, but he was also a respected power broker. According to political writer Franklin Foer, as early as 1994 Paxon had warned "that lobbyists who contributed to Democrats would not be welcome" in the offices of the Republican House leadership.[3]

Grover Norquist compiled a third list. He assembled one of the largest lobbyist databases in Washington, tracking lobbyists' employment histories, partisan leanings, and, of course, donations. Norquist also provided the name "K Street Project." And he started a Web site with that name, incidentally, at www.kstreetproject.com. Visitors to the site encounter news on the lobbying industry, including lobbyists' latest comings and goings, job listings, and promotion announcements. The design is enlivened by clever graphics, and the whole atmosphere of the site is sunny and upbeat. But the reality behind the news postings can be quite different.

In addition to the lists, DeLay and his top lieutenants frequently held meetings with lobbyists in which they would discuss developments on K Street and recommend Republicans for lobbying jobs. On the House side, these meetings were held every Thursday morning in the offices of John Boehner of Ohio, a Gingrich ally and the chair of the Republican Conference. Attendees included representatives from the National Federation of Independent Business, the National Association of Homebuilders, the Chamber of Commerce, Americans for Tax Reform, and others—many of the same groups, and many of the same people, that worked on Project Relief. Other influential lobbyists—such as Gary J. Andres, Bruce A. Gates (again, of Project Relief fame), and Nicholas Calio, who would go on to oversee congressional lobbying for George W. Bush's first administration—also showed up. On the Senate side, Pennsylvania senator Rick Santorum held a similar meeting every Tuesday morning.

Lists, meetings, job postings, recommendations—these are the building blocks of Washington life, seemingly dreary and mundane. But meetings have power: the power to include and the power to exclude. Once he became majority leader, for example, DeLay refused to meet with Democratic lobbyists.[4] Other lawmakers behaved similarly. The message was that a new majority had taken power in Washington, and that the other loci of power in the city— the bureaucracy, the presidency, and K Street—would have to adjust. That was the plan, anyway.

And it was remarkably successful. The K Street Project placed so many Republicans in top lobbying firms that it was as though the old lobbying establishment, like a cicada, had shed its Democratic skin and revealed a shiny new Republican exoskeleton beneath. In fact, a new skin had been draped over the old. Pick a year after 1995 and you will find plenty of stories about Republicans making inroads into K Street. Toward the end of George W. Bush's first administration, the transformation was well under way. In 2003, for example, the *Washington Post* reported that a top "Republican National Committee official" had informed GOP lobbyists that "33 of the 36 top-level positions he was monitoring" on the Street had gone to Republicans.[5]

In the aftermath of Election 2004, one Republican e-mailed a reporter at *National Journal,* the Inside-the-Beltway political magazine, suggesting an article on "the devaluation of Democrats on K Street." It's "sort of like steel dumping from [the WTO] rulings of old, where the price drops through the floor from market flooding," the party flack continued, "but with people instead." And in 2005, a "former GOP leadership staffer turned lobbyist" told *National Journal* that lobbying firms no longer considered Democrats a valuable commodity. "I would say on average a Democrat could expect to make somewhere between 25 to 50 percent less than a Republican with the same skill set," the lobbyist said.[6]

One establishment replaced another. The "new order" Republicans had promised in the aftermath of the 1994 election looked more and more like one party assuming the majority status it had long sought, then taking on all of the old majority's bad habits. Little changed—besides K Street's new powers to write legislation in congressional offices and the partisan breakdown of corporate political donations. In 2002, the Center for Responsive Politics released a study of corporate giving. The center found that, while there had been only a slight difference between donations from "19 industry sectors"—defense, banking, health care, and the like—in 1992, before the Republicans stormed Washington, in the ten years since, the GOP had run up a two-to-one edge in donations.

Here are the numbers. In 1992, those "19 industry sectors" gave, in total, $128 million to Democrats and $135 million to Republicans—a difference of $7 million. But in 2002, those 19 sectors donated $121 million to Democrats and $213 million to Republicans—a staggering difference of just under $100 million. More striking: The amounts business gave to Democrats actually declined by $7 million in the decade after the December Revolution.

Break the numbers down further and the gap widens into a chasm. In 1992, the accounting industry donated $3.4 million to Democrats and $2.9 million to Republicans. But, in 2002, donations to Democrats had shrunk to $2.1 million and those to Republicans had ballooned to $5.7 million. In 1992, pharmaceutical companies donated $2.3 million to Democrats and $2.5 million to Republicans. By 2002, the Democrats' take had risen to $3.4 million, but the Republicans' had swollen to $10.8 million—over three times as much as was donated to Democrats.

In fact, by 2002, Democrats retained an outsized fund-raising advantage in just two sectors: lawyers and labor. Seventy percent of lawyers' campaign donations went to Democrats; labor favored Democrats nine to one. But those levels of support were congruent with giving patterns circa 1992. And both industries were under intense political pressure from Republicans, who hoped to pass right-to-work laws and class-action reform.[7] If successful, the Republicans would undercut lawyers' profits and labor's dues, thus further crippling the Democrats' ability to raise money.

One of the insights behind the K Street Project was that a realigned influence industry would not only affect the donations of the corporations that hired lobbyists; it would also affect the donations of the newly enhanced ranks of Republican lobbyists. Reaping huge sums, they would donate to—no surprises here—other Republicans.

If there was a surprise at all, it was that it would take several years for this shift to occur. According to research compiled by the Center for Responsive Politics, it wasn't until the 2000 election cycle that lobbyists and lobbying firms gave more to Republicans than to Democrats. And in 2000, the margin was small—$7.8 million to Democrats, $8.1 million to Republicans. Plus, in the 2002 cycle, lobbyists actually gave about $200,000 more to Democrats than to Republicans. That changed again in 2004, when lobbyists gave almost $1 million more to Republicans than to Democrats.[8]

It is likely this figure will only grow larger as the K Street Project continues. In any case, the underlying trend is clear. In a matter of years, lobbyists have become a financial pillar of the Republican Party. And the result is a machine—one of the most successful and grandiose political machines in American history.

For most of our history, the federal government was small in size and limited in powers. The real action was back in the states. Look through American history textbooks and you'll read that the corporations and trusts concentrated their political and financial power at the state level. They built towns. They employed vast swarms of men. They helped to write state charters, which created state legislatures, which they then influenced in turn. And because state legislatures appointed U.S. senators until the Nineteenth Amendment provided for direct elections, the financial interests also had a path to the federal government. But that path always began in the states. Pre-World War II, federalist principles of devolution and power sharing didn't just apply to American law. They applied to American corruption, too.

There were some dramatic punctuations to this trend of limited federal government. These tended to occur whenever the nation was at war. And yet the equilibrium was maintained, more or less, for a long while. But the staggering growth of the federal government in the mid-twentieth century—the result of World War II and

America's strategic posture during the Cold War—transformed the way politics was played.

The Cold War welfare state attracted many supporters. It also attracted more than a few critics. And yet these critics—conservatives included—accepted, for the time being, that the growth in government was necessary to fight the Soviet Empire. The only questions were how much growth, and what shape it would take. Overall, the consensus in favor of a mobilized society ruled the day. Remember that, of the four Republican presidents of the Cold War era, only one—Ronald Reagan—was a vocal critic of the growth of government, and then only rhetorically. *Even under Reagan,* the American welfare state shrank not one inch.

The Cold War federal government also attracted a third group of people: the representatives of the corporations, industries, and ideological or ethnic interest groups now under the purview of Washington. Those "representatives"—"agents" is probably a better word—are called lobbyists, and they have been around for as long as there has been a government to lobby. What's more, lobbyists, along with clergymen and journalists, bask in the privilege of a constitutionally protected vocation. No less an authority than the First Amendment says that "Congress shall make no law . . . abridging the freedom . . . to petition the Government for a redress of grievances."

Toward the end of the twentieth century, because of the Cold War, government became powerful, complex, and unwieldy. The number of interests petitioning the government metastasized. And lobbyists, as a group, became something more than agents. They became an unofficial fifth branch of government—more powerful than, but not unlike, the "fourth branch of government," the press. (You won't find any mention of either in the actual Constitution, of course.)

Through their campaign contributions, through their vigorous jostling for influence, through their constant buttering up of lawmakers and bureaucrats, lobbyists could dictate which issues rose to the top of the national agenda and which did not. Like the activist, the lobbyist was possessed of a narrow devotion to singular causes. But the lobbyist had two things the typical activist lacked—time and money. Plus, the lobbyist focused on matters that the public largely considered trivial: one megabank's annual tax depreciation on computer purchases, or one commercial farming company's quarterly mohair subsidy. Lobbyists do much of their work in the dark. Turn on the lights, however, and one encounters some incredible numbers.

Between 1961 and 1982, the number of corporations with branches in Washington increased by a factor of 10. Between 1970 and 1980, the number of trade associations operating in Washington doubled. In 1971, there were 175 businesses that had lobbyists in the capital. In 1982, that number had grown to 2,444.

In just 10 years, from 1973 to 1983, the total number of registered lobbyists in Washington tripled. Between 1981 and 1985, the number quadrupled. By the mid-nineties, Washington was home to about 10,000 registered lobbyists. By 2000, about 15,000. And by mid-2005, there were 36,135.[9] That's roughly 68 lobbyists for every congressman and senator on Capitol Hill. The number grows every day.

They come from a lot of places. Most are lawyers hired by corporate clients. A few work their way up through their firm to a high-paying lobbying gig. But plenty more enter the industry through jobs on Capitol Hill, and use the connections they established while working on a representative's or senator's staff to push their new employer's agenda. Still others are drawn from the ranks of the former representatives and senators themselves.

This last group is in the highest demand, and for good reason. A lobbyist thrives on access to the people who are in a position to do his client good or ill. In fact, access is the only discernible skill a lobbyist need possess to have a successful career—and recently retired congressmen have the greatest access of all. The colleagues they leave behind will be more than willing to catch up with an old friend. The staffs they abandoned will have likely gone on to jobs with other congressmen, and those other congressmen could help to secure favorable legislation. Prior to 2006, a former representative had access to the House floor at all times. Both former congressmen and senators had access to their respective chamber's gyms. Hence, ex-lawmakers have become the 600-pound gorillas of K Street. They command the greatest salaries and they receive the most desirable perks.

It's basic economics. Lobbying is just another market. Where there's demand, there will soon be supply, and on K Street there is considerable demand for lobbyists with former legislative experience. In 2005, Public Citizen, the Naderite "good government" group, studied the career paths of the 198 congressmen who have retired since 1998. Of that group, 43.4 percent have become registered lobbyists. When Public Citizen limited its sample to the 112 Republicans who have retired since 1998, they found that almost 52 percent had taken up jobs in the lobbying industry.

Appended to the report was a list of all the legislators, Republican and Democrat, who have left Congress since 1970 to become lobbyists. The list is long enough to comprise a shadow Congress, entirely composed of former lawmakers. Except that the shadow Congress's members would all be on the corporate dole.

The shadow Congress's members would also be better paid. Indeed, the salaries that corporations, Indian tribes, and foreign governments pay lobbyists have increased by as much as 100 percent in George W. Bush's first term *alone*. As of 2005, your average salary on K Street was around $300,000. But many lobbyists make much more. It's been said that a low salary on K Street is about $175,000.[10]

That does seem low, when one considers that lobbying firms average tens of millions of dollars a year in revenues. In the first six months of 2005, K Street's largest firm, Patton Boggs, had $17.91 million in revenues. Cassidy & Associates had $13.88 million. Akin Gump Strauss Hauer & Feld: $13.34 million. Van Scoyoc Associates: $12.78 million. Dutko Worldwide: $10 million. Williams & Jensen: $8.96 million.[11]

Those are midyear totals. The firms listed above were expected to earn over $150 million by the end of 2005. And that is only six firms. In 2005, there were 3,199 outfits with registered lobbyists in Washington. All told, lobbying the federal government is a $2-billion-a-year industry. The biggest industries spend many hundreds of millions of dollars a year in fees—and quite possibly more, if Congress is preparing a vote on a pressing issue.

Consider bankruptcy reform. In 2004, in the run-up to congressional passage of the "Bankruptcy Abuse Prevention and Consumer Protection Act," a law that made it more difficult for small debtors to declare bankruptcy, commercial banking interests in favor of the legislation spent over $36 million on lobbying fees.[12] Credit card companies spent an additional $13.75 million.[13] Accounting firms: $6.3 million.[14] Business associations (including the Chamber of Commerce): $98.85 million. All for one bill, which President Bush signed into law on April 20, 2005.

For ambitious politicians, lobbying has it all: money, power, influence, and a multitude of opportunities to trade favors for campaign contributions. It's as though someone dismantled the great urban political machines of Gilded Age America and shipped the parts to downtown Washington, where they lay dormant for years, scattered lazily among the glass-and-steel boxes that line K Street. All that the parts needed was an engineer.

Enter Tom DeLay.

There were always two sides to the K Street Project: a broad strategic vision appended to a narrow personal ambition. The vision was that of the Republican Party's leading strategists, who argued that conquering K Street would strengthen the party's grip on power. The ambition was that of DeLay, who sought also to move loyalists into key positions in the lobbying industry, and thus strengthen his own political hand through their connections and donations. And in this, too, as in so many other things—raising money, ascending the House ranks, passing conservative legislation—DeLay was incredibly successful.

Author and lobbying expert John Judis reports that since the late 1990s about twenty-nine members of DeLay's congressional staff have gone on to "major lobbying positions."[15] In contrast, Dennis Hastert, who as Speaker of the House is the most powerful Republican on Capitol Hill, has seen six of his staffers leave for jobs on

K Street since the late nineties. When one leaves DeLay's office, it's said, there are plenty of job opportunities waiting outside, in lobbying, in business, in consulting, at the White House, and in other offices on Capitol Hill.

Building a vast network of friends and protégés across several power centers in Washington is a time-tested way of winning prestige and influence. When DeLay became majority leader in 2003, for instance, top aide Mildred Webber remained behind to advise his replacement as majority whip, Missouri congressman Roy Blunt. When Brett Decker resigned as DeLay's speechwriter in 2000, he eventually wound up as senior vice president for communications at the Export-Import Bank. And when Dan Allen resigned as DeLay's communications director in mid-2005, he took a job with Scott Howell & Company, a Republican political consulting firm that cuts ads for Republican Senate candidates, including Norm Coleman of Minnesota, John Thune of South Dakota, and Saxby Chambliss of Georgia.

Yet K Street remains the top destination. Lobbyists who have entered the trade from a perch in DeLay's office are known as "graduates of the DeLay school," otherwise known as DeLay, Inc.[16] Not without reason.

Let's meet a few of the alumni. The most prominent is probably former chief of staff Edwin (Ed) Buckham, who with DeLay's help founded the Alexander Strategy Group in 1998. Buckham, a licensed minister, was also DeLay's pastor, so the lucrative Enron contract that DeLay helped Buckham land that year could perhaps be viewed as a form of tithing. The Alexander Strategy Group quickly became the DeLay standard-bearer on K Street: Karl Gallant, the former director of DeLay's PAC, set up shop there, as did Tony Rudy, a former DeLay staff counsel who had also worked as a lobbyist with Jack Abramoff. Before it was disbanded in January 2006, the Alexander Strategy Group had spent $16,894,500 in lobbying activities—$7.6 million in 2004 alone. Its clients included the Pharmaceutical Research and Manufacturers of America (who spent $360,000 in 2004), Freddie Mac ($390,000), drug maker Eli

Lilly ($240,000), the American Bankers Association ($190,000), and the Asbestos Study Group ($240,000).[17] The firm was drowning in money.

It was not alone. Former chief of staff Drew Maloney and former legislative assistant Chris Lynch lobby at the Federalist Group, whose clients include Altria, the National Rifle Association, and Verizon Communications. In 2004, the Federalist Group reported spending $12.3 million in lobbying activities.[18] When he went freelance, former press secretary Michael Scanlon, after a brief stop working with Abramoff, made millions as a "public affairs" specialist.

Former DeLay policy analyst Tom Pyle is director of government relations at Koch Industries, an oil, gas, and chemicals conglomerate with annual revenues in the ballpark of $35 billion.[19] Former deputy chief of staff Bill Jarrell was a registered lobbyist at Preston Gates, then joined the public affairs firm Washington Strategies. Former policy director Ralph Hellmann is senior vice president for government relations at the Information Technology Industry Council, a trade association that, according to its Web site, "helps member companies achieve their policy objectives through building relationships with Members of Congress, Administration officials, and foreign governments; organizing industry-wide consensus on policy issues; and working to enact tech-friendly government policies"—one of the most treacly but on-target definitions of lobbying you are likely to find. Members of the Information Technology Industry Council, incidentally, include, among others, Dell, Microsoft, Apple, eBay, Honeywell, Hewlett-Packard, Panasonic, and Sony. Together those eight companies spent about $20 million in lobbying activities in 2004.

The list goes on. Policy analyst Geof Gradler went on to "government relations" jobs at the Cincinnati Stock Exchange and Charles Schwab. Former floor assistant Glenn LeMunyon went on to become senior lobbyist for Chicago law firm Winston & Shawn, then returned to Washington to start Tate-LeMunyon. Tate left, and the firm became the LeMunyon Group, which lobbies for Verizon, Lockheed Martin, and other aerospace companies. Former district office chief Jill Dowell lobbied for United Distillers, then Motorola, and then took a post as director of legislative affairs at the American Association of Health Plans—a special-interest group that spent $2.7 million on lobbying activities in 2004—and its subgroup, America's Health Insurance Plans, which spent $3 million in 2004.

When former DeLay chief of staff Susan Hirshmann left her job in 2002, she had so many offers from so many lobbying firms that she hired superlawyer Bob Bennett to act more or less as her "agent."[20] Eventually, she took a job at the firm Williams & Jensen; *National Journal* called it "the biggest hiring coup of the year." Williams & Jensen is the twelfth-largest firm on K Street, with more than 100 corporate clients, including Time Warner ($460,000 in 2004), Continental Airlines ($280,000), the quasi-government agency Fannie Mae ($140,000), and the city of New Haven, Connecticut ($80,000).[21]

Hirshmann offers proof that DeLay protégés are vaunted commodities on K Street; that the closer one was to DeLay, the higher one's salary will be; and that lobbyists, their pockets overburdened by heavy wallets, make excellent sources for campaign contributions.

One day in late summer 2005, I spent some time tracking the political donations of former DeLay staffers who became lobbyists. I was surprised with what I found. There was a great divide between small-time donors, who have given a few thousand dollars over the past six years, and big-money donors, who have given tens of thousands.

It turns out that Hirshmann, for all her prestige, is one of the small-time donors. (Of course, she hasn't been on the Street for long, so that may change.) According to the Center for Responsive Politics, Hirshmann gave $2,500 worth of contributions in the 2004 cycle—the only cycle in which she's on record as providing donations. All but $500 of that was to Leadership Political Action Committee. The remaining funds went to House Republican Conference chair Deborah Pryce of Ohio. Other alumni who were small-time donors as of midyear 2005 include Tom Pyle, who has donated $7,300 in contributions over the last three election cycles; Geof

Gradler, who has donated $5,000; Drew Maloney, who has donated $5,250 (including $1,500 to his old boss); and Jill Dowell, who has donated, by comparison, a paltry $750.

Then there are the big-money donors. Ralph Hellmann, living in the no-man's-land between small-time and big-money contributors, has delivered $9,750 in contributions over the last three election cycles. This is a large sum, but it doesn't hold a candle to those given by Ed Buckham, who has donated some $43,800 (including $2,000 to his old boss); his partner, Karl Gallant, who has donated some $29,050 (including $2,000 to his old boss); or his other partner, Tony Rudy, who has donated $48,090 (including $3,000 to his old boss). Bill Jarrell has donated $56,250 (including $1,000 to his old boss). Glenn LeMunyon has donated $71,342 (including $9,000 to his old boss). In all, then, since 2000, DeLay staffers on K Street have provided about $279,000 in political donations to the Republican Party and its affiliate political action committees in the past three election cycles, including $18,500 to DeLay. Sounds like a lot. But it pales in comparison with the amount of money DeLay himself has raised: over $11 million since 1989.

Think of the 1994 elections as a great surge of water that crashed as it hit the nation's capital. At the front of this wave are all the newly elected politicians—the Gingriches, the DeLays, the Armeys, the Kasiches, the Walkers, the Coburns, the Sanfords, the Flakes, the Frists—that the surge brings to power. But right behind them are the flotsam and jetsam that a wave picks up in one place and deposits elsewhere. In this case, the flotsam and jetsam were the grassroots activists, organizers, journalists, think tank fellows, lobbyists, and establishmentarians often grouped together as the "conservative movement." If it were not for these people, the politicians likely would not have the ideas or the arguments to enact programs such as the K Street Project. The "movement conservatives" helped lend the new era of machine politics ideological cover.

Consider the contributions of Grover Norquist.

Norquist has long been an advocate and facilitator of Republicans' attempts to take over the lobbying industry. But there is something curious about his interest in the project. Norquist is a liber-tarian, and his goal, which he pursues with singular and ferocious devotion, is the elimination of much of the federal government. But Norquist's star has risen at a moment when government continues to grow under a Republican Congress and a Republican president. At a moment when the number of "earmarks"—federal appropria-tions devoted to a congressman's pet projects, otherwise known as pork-barrel spending—are at an all-time high. At a moment when Norquist is doing all he can to link the Republican majority to K Street firms, which feed off government like a remora attached to a great white shark. Lobbyists *need* big government. Otherwise, they would have no way to make money.

Yet Norquist continues to help make more Republican lobby-ists—who, in turn, continue to agitate for an ever-more-intrusive federal government. In effect, then, he's undermining his own goals by advancing the interests of firms like Patton Boggs and Greenberg Traurig. Why?

Partisanship is probably one reason—Norquist is as Republican as he is conservative, which is to say that his conservatism has never been at odds with his support for the GOP. Lucre is undoubtedly another—Americans for Tax Reform benefits from lobbyists' largesse just as much as Tom DeLay's political action committee. No one can know Norquist's motivations for sure, of course. But if we turn to *Rock the House,* a collection of his columns for conservative publications released shortly after the 1994 elections, another, more intriguing, answer suggests itself.

Rock the House was published in 1995. Norquist acknowledges "Jack Abramoff," whom he credits with "instigating the whole pro-ject." The book's tone is celebratory. "On November 8, 1994," Norquist begins, "the American people went to the polls and made the Republican party the majority party of the United States."[22] The prospect of Republican rule thrills Norquist, as it would any conservative, though he sees it as inevitable: Prior to '94, he writes, "something" was "rotten in Washington."

Norquist is also thrilled at the idea that the "liberal Establishments of Washington D.C. and previously Democrat-controlled state capitals are similarly shaken."[23] He writes:

> Fortune 500 companies that had hired almost all former Democrat[ic] staffers as lobbyists will now find it prudent to have at least 50-50 Republican-Democrat[ic] registration in their Washington and state capital offices. There are now more than 10,000 business lobbying groups that will be making this adjustment. Only as this shakeout occurs over time will it become clear how thoroughly and completely the Democrat[ic] party has controlled the entire Washington establishment over the past four decades.[24]

The "shakeout," then, is a way for Republicans to assert control and embed themselves in Washington's power structure: the first step in a long process that will presumably result in Norquist's long-term goal of halving the federal government by 2025 and halving the remaining portion by 2050.[25]

It's a splendid term. When you shake an apple tree, you have no control over which apples will fall to the ground. You have only the power to shake the tree. In Norquist's view, voters shook the tree of government in 1994, and thus it was entirely natural for the Democratic apples to fall to earth.

But the loss of a few apples does not change the character of the tree. Lobbyists for trial lawyers and racial and sexual grievance groups and agriculture and unions fell to earth; lobbyists for credit card companies and energy traders and Wall Street bond barons remained secure. And among the flora of special interests, a new species emerged: the lobbyists themselves.

Again and again, Norquist has said to anyone who would listen that Republicans and conservatives should encourage the development of lobbyists as a distinct group, that they should begin to think of lobbyists *as a constituency*. He told *National Journal:* "It makes no sense for the business community to have a Democrat [lobby for them] . . . If you're in the business community, you want the exact opposite of what the AFL-CIO and the trial lawyers want." He told *Washington Post* writer Thomas B. Edsall: "Just like the Democrats get a 90-10 split from the trial lawyers and labor, we will have a 90-10 split in the staffing on K Street and 90-10 business giving." He told journalist Elizabeth Drew: "There should be as many Democrats working on K Street representing corporate America as there are Republicans working in organized labor—and that number is close to zero."[26]

And so the GOP has come to adopt the theory of interest group politics, which dictates that politicians should seek to please the specific interests that brought them to power, and not promote national goals that affect diverse groups. This is a good theory to have if you are a machine politician—punish your enemies; reward your friends—and it's definitely enough intellectual backbone to prop up Tom DeLay's K Street Project. But it is bad for the Republican Party. It's bad because it makes it seem as though the GOP is nothing more than a grab bag of favoritism and greed, and it's bad because no political party should become too beholden to the interest groups that populate it.

Consider the fate of the party that the Republicans defeated.

The Democrats have suffered loss after electoral loss because they have jettisoned any sense of national purpose, or greater good, or overarching ideology in favor of the needs of narrow special interests—civil rights groups, feminists, and organized labor. Look at how the Democrats held up the creation of the Department of Homeland Security in 2002, simply because they would not abandon their allegiance to the public-sector unions—then look at how they suffered for it at the polls. Republicans, in a remarkably short span of time, have become similarly beholden to corporate cash. It is not that difficult to see a moment when they, too, will reap the whirlwind.

The lobbyists are already out of control. In his definitive piece on the rise of Tom DeLay's K Street machine, Nicholas Confessore argues that the GOP has "disciplined" the capital's army of lobbyists—that the party "controls" K Street activities. But this is incorrect. In fact, Confessore undercuts his own argument when he reports that, at a 1996 meeting with corporate executives, GOP leaders demanded that the CEOs purge their businesses and lobbying teams of Democrats. The executives refused. Corporations might agree that they need a few more Republicans on their side, especially if the majority leader of the House of Representatives refuses to meet with Democrats. But they will not—do not—take marching orders from the GOP. Quite the contrary.

There have been hiccups, tremors, signs of resistance. In 1998, for example, former Oklahoma Democratic congressman Dave McCurdy was offered a job as chief lobbyist for the Electronic Industries Alliance (EIA). The alliance is a trade group. Its staff numbers in the hundreds; its budget is several tens of millions of dollars.[27] When DeLay heard that McCurdy had been offered the job, he did everything in his power to stop it. He ordered that all Republican leaders be banned from meeting with McCurdy; he called the outgoing president of the EIA, Peter McCloskey, to urge the group to reconsider; he even pulled the Digital Millennium Copyright Act, a property-protection bill that would save the industry billions of dollars, from the House calendar. The bill was a top priority for the EIA. To have it pulled from consideration was a blatant insult.

The Electronic Industries Alliance hired McCurdy anyway. Yes, the group also hired Republicans, namely former congressional aide Adrien MacGillvray and former congressman—and DeLay opponent—Bob Walker. But the essential point remains: K Street did not back down. DeLay's attempts to "control" big business failed.

Something similar happened in 2002. That year, Republican congressman Michael Oxley of Ohio, the chairman of the House Financial Services Committee, suggested he would soon look into how the mutual fund industry set its prices and user fees. Through back channels, however, Oxley aides let industry representatives know that the congressman would back off if the industry's trade group, the Investment Company Institute, fired its chief lobbyist, Julie Domenick. Domenick is a notable Democrat. Oxley wanted a Republican in her place. Once again, the price the industry would have to pay, Oxley's aides threatened, would be both financial (possible government regulation) and political (heightened public scrutiny of industry practices).

But the Investment Company Institute never fired Domenick. Oxley's threats never became reality. And when the *Washington Post* reported on Oxley's attempts at intimidation, the House Ethics Committee flirted with an investigation and rebuke. Oxley's reputation—not the mutual fund industry's—was damaged. Eventually, the trade group hired a Republican. But it refused to give in to Oxley's demands.

A third example occurred in 2004. That year the Motion Picture Association of America hired Dan Glickman, the former Democratic congressman and Clinton's secretary of agriculture—to replace Jack Valenti. Once again, Republican leaders were outraged. Once again, they threatened retribution. And this time, they actually did retaliate. The House Republican leadership eliminated $1.5 billion in tax incentives for Hollywood that had been prominently featured in upcoming legislation. But the MPAA never fired Glickman. They just hired a Republican as well.

Whenever liberals talk about Republican intimidation of K Street, they always bring up the above examples. But they persistently ignore the fact that the intimidation didn't work. The Democrats weren't fired. Business responded by simply increasing its lobbying footprint—not by bowing before its Republican masters. Grover Norquist and Tom DeLay are both misguided if they think the K Street Project works to the Republican party's advantage. It doesn't. By giving corporations unprecedented access to a governing majority's internal operations, the project works to big businesses's advantage.

Republicans and conservatives don't seem to realize this. If they do, they show no signs of changing their behavior. The GOP's infatuation with K Street increasingly resembles a love affair in which affection makes one partner blind to the other's faults. In some cases Republican pols are literally in bed with lobbyists. Roy Blunt's wife, for example, is a lobbyist for Altria. But the Republican party's love affair with K Street seems to be unrequited. One partner pursues another. And what does he get in return? A broken heart.

CHAPTER THREE

THE PETRI DISH

HOW A TINY ISLAND COMMONWEALTH CORRUPTED THE CONSERVATIVE MOVEMENT

On Friday, December 26, 1997, at the invitation of Jack Abramoff, Tom DeLay and his entourage left for the Commonwealth of the Northern Mariana Islands—a U.S. territory in the Pacific acquired after World War II—on an all-expenses-paid junket. The trip lasted through January 1. DeLay, his wife Christine, their daughter, Ed Buckham, and others stayed in Saipan. Though the junket was billed as "educational," it was clear in the weeks before departure that the Republican whip had already made up his mind about what was at stake in the Pacific. DeLay spokesman Tony Rudy told the *Houston Chronicle* the week before the trip that "we still believe that the federal government shouldn't come in and dictate economic policy on a U.S. territory 12,000 miles away," because "the reality is they're bettering the lives of those people who are able to send money home and improve the lives of their families." Rudy went on to parrot Abramoff talking points. "I think the vast majority of Republicans view what they're doing as a noble experiment," he said. The Marianas, he continued, were "the economic success of the Pacific."

While in Saipan, DeLay attended a reception with the Chinese businessman Willie Tan, a local tycoon. He played two full rounds of golf at the Lao Lao Bay Golf Resort. He visited Managha Island, where a few people snorkeled. On December 31, New Year's Eve, a banquet was thrown in his honor. DeLay delivered remarks in which he praised governor Froilan Tenorio: "You are a shining light for what is happening in the Republican Party, and you represent everything that is good about what we're trying to do in America and in leading the world in the free-market system." The audience whooped and cheered. A video of the occasion shows DeLay and Abramoff, both wearing native caps, embracing. DeLay called Abramoff one of his "dearest and closest friends."

Back in Washington, DeLay took on the Marianas' cause as his own. On January 5, 1998, he declared he was opposed to any legislation that interfered with immigration to Saipan. Then he took things a step further. He said he thought the United States should adopt the *Northern Marianas'* immigration laws—specifically, a "guest worker program" that provided one- or two-year visas to foreign laborers. The program, DeLay said, would allow "particular companies" to "bring Mexican workers in" for jobs in America. And those workers, DeLay continued, would be paid "whatever wage the market will bear."[1]

Back in Saipan, there was great rejoicing. The celebratory feeling was greatest among the archipelago's tycoons. On May 24, 1999, ABC News's *20/20* aired a report on the Marianas that included an undercover interview with Willie Tan. "DeLay will never let it go," Tan told human rights activist Steve Galster, who was secretly taping the conversation. "Do you know what Tom told me? He said, 'Willie, if they elect me majority whip, I make the schedule of the Congress, and I'm not going to put it on the schedule.' So Tom told me, 'Forget it, Willie. No chance.'"

A promise was a promise. Later, in an on-the-record interview, DeLay would tell the *Washington Post* that CNMI "is a perfect Petri dish of capitalism. It's like my Galapagos Island."

That a small group of Pacific islands could be the subject of such passion on the part of the majority whip of the United States House of Representatives can be traced back to Abramoff, who registered as a lobbyist on the Marianas' behalf in 1995. The government of the archipelago was one of Abramoff's first clients. He had been introduced to interests there by his father, who had once tried to open a casino on the islands. In 1995, the Republican Senate passed the Insular Development Act, which would have extended, over several years, U.S. immigration and minimum-wage laws to the Marianas. The bill's sponsor, Alaska senator Frank Murkowski, was a Republican, though not a conservative. Dismayed, and concerned that the application of U.S. law to the U.S. territory would quiet the islands' economic boom, governor Tenorio hired a Washington lobbying firm, Preston Gates Ellis & Rouvelas Meeds LLP, to ensure that the bill failed to pass the House of Representatives. Tenorio's chief contact at Preston Gates was Abramoff. From 1995 to 2000, the government of the CNMI paid Preston Gates more than $8 million.[2]

The Commonwealth of the Northern Mariana Islands, or CNMI for short, sits between the Philippine Sea and the northern Pacific Ocean, some 9,000 miles from the United States. It is an archipelago composed of fourteen islands, and its capital, Saipan, occupies a small patch of land on an island of the same name.[3] For most of recorded history, the islands were little more than a sparsely populated backwater, and then a refueling stop for transpacific air traffic. During World War II, however, the islands had the dubious honor of becoming strategically important. The United States took the islands from the Japanese in 1944. Once the war was over, the archipelago was put under the control of the U.S. Navy, which ruled until 1962. That year the U.S. Department of the Interior took over administration of the islands. The islands had little sovereignty of their own. But the islands' inhabitants did not seem to mind.

In 1972, the Marianas' local government began negotiations with the United States for eventual incorporation as a U.S. territory. After a referendum, the archipelago became a commonwealth "in political union" with the United States in 1975. Congress approved the "Covenant to Establish a Commonwealth of the Northern Mariana Islands in Political Union with the United States" in 1976. Marianas natives became U.S. citizens.

Like many U.S. territories, the Marianas were a strange mix of native custom and Anglo-American republicanism. The Marianas were not truly the United States, but they were not truly apart from it, either. As if to confirm that disjunction, in 1986, President Reagan issued a proclamation that exempted the Marianas from large swaths of the U.S. code.

Pursuant to that proclamation, the commonwealth is not subject to the U.S. customs regime; it is not subject to U.S. federal minimum-wage laws; it is not subject to U.S. immigration law; the commonwealth has the freedom to create its own tax regime; it need not ship goods to U.S. ports on U.S.-registered ships. In short, the commonwealth is a semisovereign entity. It has also become an economic powerhouse.

For most of its history, the population of the Marianas was small. In the early seventies, there were only about 14,000 people living there. But after the 1986 deal, the population exploded. A congressional investigation reported that in April 1997 there were 58,000 people living there. The same year, the Environmental Protection Agency put the number at 63,000. According to the EPA, the population had ballooned by 275 percent from 1980 to 1997.[4] Immigrants outnumber the natives. Besides being foreign-born, the population is overwhelmingly young. A 1995 Department of the Interior study said that the median age was 17.2 years.[5] The 2000 census reported a population of 69,221 people.[6] Most of the immigrants are Filipino. Others are Chinese. All are guest workers who travel to the Marianas to work for a specific amount of time in the islands' garment industry. They are not natives, they are not Americans, and they are not accorded the same rights as natives or Americans.

Labor conditions in the Marianas resemble those one might encounter in a third-world country. In the summer of 1996, the Occupational Safety and Health Administration sent agents to inspect conditions in the 5,000 labor camps on Saipan, the main island. The camps are home to about 40,000 foreign laborers. The OSHA agents inspected 64 camps and found 178 violations of U.S. labor law—"including blocked exits, fire hazards, nonworkable and unsanitary restroom facilities, no refrigeration for food storage, and exposed and frayed wiring," according to a report written by members of the House of Representatives—and sent 20 referrals to the Department of Labor.[7] The OSHA inspectors also looked at some of the garment factories that make up the islands' largest industry. They found 63 violations among the 26 manufacturers they looked at, and recommended over $100,000 in penalties. They looked at the commonwealth's construction industry and ended up recommending more than $280,000 in penalties against a single company.

Immigrants enter the Marianas on a one-year contract. There are few unions. The territorial government refuses to recognize collective bargaining agreements. Grievances filed by employees of the Sako Corporation, one of the major garment manufacturers in Saipan, include allegations that they have been locked in barracks. (Sako is now defunct.) Minimum wage on the islands is set between $2.90 and $3.05. In the United States proper, the minimum wage is $5.15 an hour. The Department of Labor regularly files suit against CNMI companies for recovery of back wages. Crime—prostitution, drug abuse, corruption—is a feature of everyday life. In 1992, the U.S. Labor Department leveled the largest fine in its history— $9 million—against five garment factories owned by Willie Tan. According to the Labor Department, the fine was restitution for 1,200 employees who, we learn in Lou Dubose and Jan Reid's *The Hammer*, "had been locked in worksites and barracks and obliged to work 84 hours a week with no overtime pay."[8] In response to these and other abuses, in March 1995 the Philippine government declared a moratorium on all emigration to the Marianas. It was the first time such a thing had happened in U.S. history. However, the ban was quickly lifted, and Filipino immigration accelerated. Working conditions remained the same, however.

Here is one of the conclusions of a report prepared by Democratic staff members on the House Resources Committee:

> Because of its Commonwealth status, CNMI garment factories are allowed to sew "Made in the USA" labels into its products. However, the men and women who labored to produce these products are being denied the protections of the laws of the United States . . . the CNMI Government has failed to implement adequate minimum wage increases as pledged to the U.S. Congress, has refused to enforce accurately and actively its immigration policy and has vocally refused to give a voice to the foreign workers it has recruited.

There is no sales tax in the Marianas. There is no estate tax. There is no property tax. There is talk of introducing a flat tax. There is talk of introducing a school-choice program, including publicly financed vouchers students can use to attend private schools. Where does the Marianas government find the revenue to finance such programs? The short answer is that it doesn't need to. The Commonwealth of the Northern Marianas is a welfare state. Between 1976 and 1986 alone, the U.S. government gave more than $500 million to the CNMI government.[9] Another $500 million was delivered between 1986 and 1996. At least another $500 million has been delivered in the decade since. Cash payments to dependents is the very definition of welfare. Cash payments that encourage dependency are something that conservatives are supposedly against.

Yet the commonwealth is also an extremely rich welfare state. In 1985, the garment factories in the CNMI earned $224 million in total revenues. In 1995, those revenues had grown to $1.5 billion. The revenues continue to increase and show no sign of slowing down. This staggering economic growth has inspired copycats. In the late nineties, the government of Guam began to lobby to have the same sort of exemptions from U.S. law as the commonwealth.[10]

When territorial governments look at the Marianas, they see a place where businessmen have built labor camps to attract business and generate revenue and make local politicians rich. They see a place where immigrants flock in order to make a decent living, earning U.S. dollars that they can send back to their families in their native countries. They see the way of the future. When human rights activists and pro-labor groups look at the Marianas, they see a place where workers are routinely abused. They see a place where workers are paid unfairly. They see a place where modern-day corporate giants have built a system of sweatshops and labor camps.

When Jack Abramoff looked at the Marianas, he saw a conservative paradise, a free-market utopia, and a test case for the principles of K Street Conservatism.

In 2001, in an eight-page memo to a different governor of the Marianas, Abramoff explained his strategy:

> With strong ties to the new Republican majority in control of Congress, we launched an intense education and public relations effort that served and continues to serve the CNMI very well. In 1995 alone, we began educating Members of the House Resources Committee and committee staff. We actively lobbied the House leadership to prevent full House consideration of the Senate bill. We cultivated relationships with think-tanks and public policy organizations with invaluable public relations contacts.

Abramoff went on to explain what happened next:

> All of our tactics produced enormously positive results. Our efforts with the House Resources Committee allowed us to transform two congressional hearings that promised to be embarrassing to the CNMI into platforms to express local opposition to federal takeover schemes. We worked with the House leadership to assure the bill would not move to the House floor, even if the committee did act. It also allowed us to acquire some very powerful allies, such as Majority Whip DeLay. Perhaps most importantly, our

dedication to the public relations aspect of the lobbying campaign helped the CNMI develop a reputation for freedom and local autonomy, two virtues that were very attractive to the new Republican majority.[11]

Abramoff's strategy had three components. The goal of each was to establish that the Commonwealth of the Northern Mariana Islands was an experiment in libertarian ideology. The first component was rhetorical. Abramoff urged members of his staff and CNMI officials to couch their arguments in conservative rhetoric. In 1996, in the pages of Marianas Variety—"Micronesia's leading newspaper since 1972"—Governor Tenorio argued that the mainland should "leave the territories alone," a phrase that brings to mind Grover Norquist's "Leave Us Alone" coalition, which, in turn, brings to mind conservative principles of federalism and limited government. This was a consistent theme in the governor's rhetoric. Thus, in December 1996, Tenorio told the Pacific Daily News, "All I want from Congress is to leave us alone." In his eyes, the commonwealth's enemies were the conservative movement's enemies: nosy, busybody bureaucrats and enterprise-squelching labor activists. "The CNMI is no place for labor unions," Governor Tenorio said on April 11, 1997. In 2000, Abramoff told the Post that attempts to regulate the archipelago were "immoral laws designed to destroy the economic lives of a people." The fight over the Marianas was "a microcosm of an overall battle." On one side, according to Abramoff, were the forces of economic control. On the other were "these guys in the CNMI," who were merely "trying to . . . build a life without being wards of the state."

The second component of Abramoff's strategy was a series of junkets for Republican (and some Democratic) lawmakers to showcase the commonwealth's potential. Most trips lasted about five days. Guests stayed at the Hyatt Regency in Saipan. According to the resort's brochure, the hotel "lies on 14 acres of lush, tropical gardens, lagoons and magnificent microbeach."[12] The visitors enjoyed the tropical climate and the clear blue water. They played golf at the Lao Lao Bay course. Each trip cost thousands of dollars. One of Abramoff's trips, from October 21 to November 4, 1996, cost $13,000. But that amount of money was understandable, Abramoff explained to the *New York Times* on January 20, 1998. The junkets were for "educational" purposes. "They don't have a congressman or a delegate to the United States," Abramoff said. "It's the farthest territory from the United States. Nobody knew anything about it. And the federal bureaucracy, which for so long had a paternalistic and almost colonialist rule over these guys, said let's make a move on their economy."

By December 1997, more than 150 congressmen and staffers had made the trek to the Marianas.[13] Each voyage cost between $4,000 and $6,000 per person. In the twenty months between April 1996 and December 1997, six House members went to the CNMI. Each brought an entourage—"Representatives Ralph Hall, Brian Bilbray, and John Duncan brought their wives along," Ken Silverstein has explained in *The Nation,* "while Representative Dana Rohrabacher was accompanied by his fiancée."[14] In those same twenty months, the *Washington Post* reported, more than "60 VIPs" were invited to the archipelago. The "educational" component of the trip involved touring several factories owned by Willie Tan. Because Abramoff and his lobbying team were behind them, the junkets were often subject to scrutiny. In December 1996, Abramoff wrote his Marianas contact: "I . . . expect to receive a call tomorrow or Tuesday from the House ethics committee, asking for an update as to the reimbursement situation and, possibly, our outstanding bill. They are watching the trips very closely."

They should have been. House ethics rules forbid a lobbyist from paying directly a lawmaker's travel fees. But there are ways around the rules. And in this, Abramoff's Marianas lobbying was a prelude of things to come.

Consider the manner in which Abramoff financed a January 24, 1997, junket.

Two Democrats were on the 1997 trip: Jim Clyburn of South Carolina and Bennie Thompson of Mississippi. According to a billing memo Abramoff sent on May 20 that year, the trip cost more than $15,000. The question is who paid for it. Abramoff seems to have organized the trip through the National Security Caucus Foundation, a project of the American Security Council Foundation, a conservative nonprofit. The disclosure reports of the two Democrats, Clyburn and Thompson, both said that the National Security Caucus Foundation paid for the travel. But this was incorrect. These lawmakers, like many who traveled with Abramoff, were unaware of, or unconcerned by, the details of who paid what, when. The National Security Caucus Foundation is now defunct. Its parent group, the American Security Council Foundation, lives on, however, and its director, Gregg Hilton, went on the trip, too. Hilton denies that the foundation paid the lawmakers' travel expenses.

Preston Gates' billing memos prove the law firm paid for Thompson's and Clyburn's—and Hilton's—travel expenses. And the money, it seems, was put to good use. In the summer of 1997, DeLay and Dick Armey sent a letter to Governor Tenorio extolling the islands' virtues. Members of the Republican caucus who had visited the commonwealth under Abramoff's junket program, they wrote, have returned to the United States and described "a very different place than the one the administration has portrayed." The two went on: "Furthermore, we have been greatly encouraged by your administration's tough approach to labor abuses and law enforcement. Most impressive has been your commitment to eliminate labor problems in the CNMI, while at the same time adhering to, and advancing, the principles of free markets, enterprise, education choice, tax reform, and other innovative approaches to governance."[15] After his visit, Dana Rohrabacher took to the House floor in September 1997 and said that the Marianas "have had a great deal of reform, free enterprise reform, in the last five years that has totally turned around their economy."[16] There was some criticism, however, mostly from Democrats. California Democrat George Miller sought to draw attention to the islands' unfair labor practices whenever he could. And sometime during 1997, President Clinton sent a letter to Governor Tenorio in which he wrote that "certain labor practices in the islands . . . are inconsistent with our country's values."[17]

The majority of the Republican caucus supported Abramoff's position: that the Marianas were victims of large-scale government interference; that the island territory was a laboratory of free-market economics; that the guest workers populating the archipelago's labyrinthine factories were lucky to be there. The Republicans were taking cues from their leader, DeLay.

The first two components of Abramoff's strategy—rhetorical repositioning and congressional junketeering—seemed to be going smoothly. Yet, in 1997, Marianas citizens elected a new governor, who wrote a new budget, one that cut the amount of money the government planned to pay Abramoff.

The budget cuts took Abramoff by surprise. On January 31, 1998, he wrote a four-page memo to Willie Tan and two other Marianas officials. "I composed this email before receiving Willie's email concerning the budget for the representation," he began, "so please understand that if the budget is significantly curtailed, it will be hard, if not impossible, to do many of these things." Then Abramoff sketched out exactly how the astronomical fees he was charging the Marianas government paid for themselves:

> There is no doubt that trips to the CNMI are one of the most effective ways to build permanent friends on the Hill and among policymakers in Washington. In light of the recent spate of publicity and the end of the congressional recess, the trips will be curtailed for a while. It is likely, furthermore, that the upcoming congressional elections will keep many Hill people in the states; however, the importance of bringing congressmen and senators to the CNMI cannot be overstated.[18]

Recall that most of the money in the Marianas budget comes from the U.S. government. The CNMI, in other words, was paying U.S. tax dollars to Patton Boggs to lobby the government to give more money to the CNMI.

Marshall Wittmann witnessed the birth of the third component to Abramoff's Marianas strategy. Today, Wittmann is a senior fellow at the centrist Democratic Leadership Council, but back in 1995, he was a scholar at the conservative Heritage Foundation. Later, he would take a job with Ralph Reed at the Christian Coalition, then the Hudson Institute, and then with Arizona Republican John McCain. One becomes dizzy studying Wittmann's political résumé.

One day in 1995, as he sat in the back of one of Grover Norquist's Wednesday Meetings, Wittmann's curiosity was piqued. "All of a sudden the Marianas shows up as one of the number-one priority issues," Wittmann said. "And people talked about how this is a great free-market paradise. Lobbyists would speak, and then representatives from the Marianas." When this happened, Wittmann would shake his head and chuckle. "What's this about?" he asked his friends.

It was about co-opting conservative journalists and intellectuals. As outlined in his retrospective memo, Abramoff knew from the start that a good lobbyist not only targeted lawmakers, he also targeted opinion makers. So representatives were dispatched to Norquist's Wednesday Meetings to preach the gospel of guest-worker programs. And some of Washington's premier conservative journalists and think tank scholars went along on special "journalist junkets" to the islands. You may recognize the names.

Marlo Lewis, the head of the Competitive Enterprise Institute, went on an Abramoff junket in 1996.[19] On March 22, 1997, Patrick Pizzella, a member of Abramoff's team at Patton Boggs, hosted a "think tank" trip to the Marianas that included John Liu, Philip Terzian, Robert Holste, Ed McDonald, Helle Bering-Jensen, Jason Bertsch, and Greg Peek. Airfare on this trip cost over $33,000. Another 1996 junket included libertarian journalist Ron Bailey, Republican pollster Kellyanne Conway, and libertarian activist Clint Bolick. *Wall Street Journal* editorial board member John Fund, who paid for his own travel, attended meetings with government officials alongside members of the group. There were many others. According to the *Washington Post*, "Among those who visited the Marianas at the government's expense were officials from conservative groups such as the Heritage Foundation, the Cato Institute, Citizens for a Sound Economy, the Institute for Justice, and the Traditional Values Coalition." Add to that representatives from Citizens Against Government Waste and Americans for Tax Reform. An army of right-wingers descended on the Marianas in the late 1990s, all at Jack Abramoff's bidding.

Jason Bertsch was the managing editor of the *Public Interest* when he went to the Marianas. Though he never wrote about his trip, this is what he later told journalist Ken Silverstein: "I took a moped ride around Saipan and saw workers' barracks that were pretty bad. It looked like public housing in D.C. They didn't show us that side of the island."[20] Helle Bering-Jensen was the deputy editorial page editor of the *Washington Times*. Shortly after she returned, editorials in support of the CNMI began to appear in that newspaper's pages. Reading what she wrote about the Marianas, it is unlikely she ever traveled to the seedier parts of Saipan. Consider just one of her bylines, from the paper's April 24, 1997, edition. It was titled "Keeping Uncle Sam out of Saipan." Bering-Jensen did not disclose who had paid for her trip. But she did praise Froilan Tenorio, whom she called "a Democrat unlike any you are likely to meet in Washington."

> He wants school choice, believes food stamps "only create unemployment," and is mulling over a flat tax to substitute for the present complex tax system, which, in the end, rebates most of the local taxes anyway (there are no federal taxes levied out here), as much as 95 percent. Mr. Tenorio does not even want a nonvoting representative on Capitol Hill. "We pay no tax, why should we have representation?" he demands.

One marvels at the honesty with which Tenorio acknowledges that the Marianas is a rentier state—meaning that it derives its income from Washington—and therefore will happily give up any claims to political rights.

The pages and pages of conservative scribbles that resulted from

Abramoff's junkets were not nearly as forthright. Few, if any, of the writers acknowledged that they had traveled to the far Pacific at the request and on the dime of a third-party lobbyist. And few, if any, of the articles mentioned the downside of a commonwealth in which capitalism has run amok: the poverty, the alienation, the potential abuse. On June 11, 1997, the *Washington Times* published "Sticking It to Saipan." And while the editorial admitted that "labor abuses do occur" in the archipelago—actually, the editorialists wrote, "they were rampant some years ago"—they focused instead on the idea that "the progress that has been made in addressing these problems has been extraordinary."

"The surest way to destroy economic development on the CNMI and force its citizens to become dependent on the federal government," the *Times*'s editorialists concluded, "is to destroy the industries that have generated that growth, which has been the source of the explosive rise in living standards."

The championing of economic growth at all cost, the advocacy of autonomy and sovereignty for the islands without the acknowledgment that the federal government was sending half a billion dollars a year there, is a common theme of the articles resulting from trips to the Marianas. On September 17, 1997, Clint Bolick, vice president of the Institute for Justice, praised Froilan Tenorio in a Heritage Foundation report on school choice. Tenorio's system, Bolick wrote, "would transform a portion of the state's education budget into child-centered funding that would allow each child in the CNMI to [attend] the public or private school of the family's choice. Significantly, funds going to public schools in the program would be placed under the control of the particular school." The plan, Bolick went on, "would foster decentralization, autonomy, and competition in the public schools. It would also create a system that is entirely neutral, as between religious and secular educational options." Never a mention of the working conditions in the Marianas or of the lobbying campaign that had paid for Bolick's trips to the islands.

On May 5, 1999, Heritage Foundation scholar Daniel Mitchell published another op-ed on the Marianas in the *Washington*

Times, this one titled "Modern Siege of Saipan." "In World War II, the United States fought fiercely to capture Saipan and the rest of the Northern Mariana Islands from Japan," Mitchell began. But "in a strange twist of fate, America once again has targeted this tiny set of islands in the northern Pacific. Only this time, instead of Marines, gunboats, and aircraft, the attackers are using laws, regulations, and bureaucrats." The immigrants from China and the Philippines are "lucky, not exploited." The federal minimum-wage regulations "violate freedom of contract and harm less-skilled workers."

On June 27, 2001, Michael Cantanzaro, a reporter for the Evans-Novak Political Report, wrote an op-ed for the *Washington Times* attacking Alaska senator Frank Murkowski. Murkowski supported Allen Stayman, who as head of the Clinton Interior Department's Office of Insular Affairs campaigned vigorously for extending U.S. labor law to the Marianas. Murkowski and Stayman, Cantanzaro wrote, are "both . . . allied with powerful forces trying to straight-jacket CNMI's free-market economy."

On October 17, 2001, conservative columnist Doug Bandow wrote an op-ed for the *Washington Times* in support of Marianas autonomy. At issue was S.507, another iteration of the Murkowski bill that would have extended U.S. immigration law to the Marianas. Bandow argued that lax immigration policies were unacceptable in an age of terror—but that there was no need to get tough on the Marianas. "The islands have grasped the essentials of development: open markets and foreign investment," he concluded. "New federal controls would shut off the economic growth that offers those at the bottom the most hope." Furthermore: "Fighting terrorism is no excuse for economic meddling: Washington should respect the Commonwealth's independent policies, which have allowed the islands to rise above the poverty evident elsewhere throughout Micronesia."[21]

Bandow is a special case: In December 2005, he admitted that Abramoff had paid him $2,000 per article favorable to the Marianas, among other clients. He further implied that he was not alone.

There were in fact conservative critics of the Marianas. In a 1998 article for *National Review,* the immigration restrictionist Mark Krikorian singled out the CNMI for special rebuke. Republicans, Krikorian wrote, were rallying behind an "emerging consensus" that was "pro-immigration, anti-immigrant." For confirmation, one need look no further than the Marianas. The CNMI, Krikorian went on, was nothing less than a "Kuwait in the Pacific."[22]

Harsh words. And yet one cannot help wondering whether Krikorian would have felt the same way if he had ever been invited by Jack Abramoff to spend a week in the Marianas.

In the late 1990s, the Marianas confronted a rash of bad publicity. In February 1998, the Occupational Safety and Health Administration sent investigators to the commonwealth to conduct another round of inspections. According to a report prepared by the staff of Rep. Miller, OSHA staff found that "workers' barracks are unhealthy, with overcrowding, unsanitary facilities, dirty and inoperable toilets, dirty kitchens, and electrical hazards." On March 11, 1998, a month after the inspectors had returned home to the United States, the *Marianas Variety* reported that in the course of their inspections the federal bureaucrats had found factory exits nailed shut and smoke detectors covered in tape.

That year, of course, the capital's political professionals were consumed by the investigation into President Clinton's affair with Monica Lewinsky. Stories involving a president mired in scandal drowned out stories involving corporate malfeasance on a small group of islands thousands of miles away. But every now and then a story on the Marianas bubbled to the surface. On March 13, 1998, ABC News's *20/20* aired a segment titled "Is This the USA?" The reporter, Brian Ross, opened the piece this way: "Clothing manufactured on an island in the middle of the Pacific called Saipan, in factories—as we saw with our hidden cameras—jammed full of low-cost workers brought in from China, putting in fourteen-hour days under often miserable conditions, making clothes under contract for the American market." At one point, Ross interviewed the human rights activist Eric Gregoire, who told him, "I've seen people locked in barracks, locked behind barbed wire."

Then James Lin, the president of the Saipan Garment Manufacturers Association—another Abramoff client—took Ross on a tour of one of his factories. What follows is a transcript of their exchange. It reads like something out of Monty Python.

ROSS: Isn't it awfully hot?

LIN: No comment.

ROSS: No comment? Mr. Lin, isn't that a pretty simple question?

LIN: It's not hot to me.

ROSS: It's not hot to you. You're sweaty. I'm sweaty.

LIN: I'm not.

ROSS: What is the moisture?

LIN: It's oil. I'm oily-faced.

Whereupon Lin simply stopped answering Ross's questions.

A March 26, 1998, report issued by the Democratic staff of the House Committee on Resources only compounded the damage. The U.S. economy, it turns out, was not the sole beneficiary of a boom fueled by lax immigration policies and substandard wages. Instead, Congressman Miller's report drew attention to the fact that "of the 29 operating garment factories in CNMI, at least 19 (nearly 70 percent) are owned by foreign interests, and only 9 have any U.S. shareholders." In other words, in his capacity as a flack for the government of the CNMI, Abramoff was also flacking for "interests in Korea, Hong Kong, Japan, Thailand, and China." And those interests in China included "the Chinese government."

Not that U.S. companies weren't making a profit from what increasingly looked like a modern form of indentured servitude. Miller's delegation, which toured the garment factories on a fact-finding mission, saw Chinese and Filipino immigrants making clothes that would eventually be sold in shopping malls across the United States, in stores like The Gap, The Limited, Gear, Old Navy,

Tommy Hilfiger, Nordstrom Inc., JC Penney, Ralph Lauren, Aber-crombie & Fitch—even Brooks Brothers, where Jack Abramoff bought his suits. Clothes from the Marianas could also be found at—where else?—Banana Republic.

"Indentured servitude" is a phrase that should not be used cava-lierly. And yet that phrase remains a good description of the type of labor Miller encountered in the Marianas. Often immigrants to the Marianas were "recruited" by headhunters canvassing swaths of the north Pacific and South China Sea. Upon accepting a job in the Marianas, a recruit was required to pay a transportation fee "as high as $7,000," a sum that would plunge the poor recruit immedi-ately into debt. Many recruits thus spent most of their yearlong stay in the Marianas clawing their way back to solvency. But the dream of a better life—and perhaps anything *is* better than condi-tions in parts of China or Malaysia or the Philippines—ensured that most recruits were eager for any chance they had at escaping their native lands. When Miller's delegation traveled to the Mari-anas, they encountered "more than 20,000 foreign workers in the garment industry," a number that was less than half of the "approximately 42,000" guest workers "in the CNMI overall." And in many cases workers didn't want to—perhaps they couldn't—leave. In 1997, the government in Saipan issued more than 37,000 work permits. The number continues to rise.

In his report, Miller and his staff told of several encounters the congressman had with immigrants eking out a living in the archi-pelago:

Congressman Miller met also with several young Chinese women who had paid $5,000 apiece in recruitment fees to work in restau-rants in the CNMI. None reported being shown a contract prior to arriving in Saipan, as is required by law. They were admitted to the CNMI in June, 1997, and were told there were no restaurant jobs available. Instead, they were sent to work at karaoke bars and told to follow the manager's instructions, which included drinking and engaging in sexual activities with customers, often in small cubicles in the club or in hotels. Destitute and with no way home, the young women had little alternative but to comply with the demands of their new employers.[23]

Here is another sample:

After working for five months without a day off and with no pay other than occasional tips, living in rooms supplied by the employer where they had to purchase their own food, they sneaked out of the club with an unsuspecting customer. Despite threats, they filed a complaint . . . Congressman Miller was told that the agency reportedly investigated their complaint, met with the owners of the club, and took no further action.

Reports of such conditions spawned a massive lawsuit—three, actually. In 1999, two firms—Milberg Weiss Bershad Hynes & Lerach and Altshuler, Berzon—filed three separate complaints against twenty-eight companies who housed factories in the Marianas. Named in the suit were major American apparel manufacturers such as Donna Karan, Liz Claiborne, Calvin Klein, Brooks Brothers, and so on. The ins and outs of tort law worked to the workers'—and the lawyers'—advantage. By September 2001, nineteen of the companies had settled. Almost two years after that, in April 2003, a Marianas judge okayed settlement at $20 million.

All this criticism, however, merited little attention in the Marianas themselves. If anything, the attacks confirmed the official line that the islands were under siege, surrounded on all sides by bureaucrats and liberal congressmen and ambulance chasers and hostile journalists. Money has a way of numbing one's troubles, however. Typical of the sentiment in the Marianas was an article that appeared in the *Saipan Tribune,* a daily newspaper owned by Willie Tan, on November 26, 1998—Thanksgiving Day. The byline was that of one John Del-Rosario Jr. The headline: "There's a lot to be thankful for, Friends."

DelRosario knew exactly whom to thank. "In 1995," he wrote, "former Governor Froilan C. Tenorio retained the services of Preston Gates, one of the nation's leading legal and lobbying firms, to carry loads of unheard messages from the NMI to key members of Congress about our aspiration to retain the integrity of the Covenant Agreement, specifically, the provision that guaranteed our rights to self-government." The governor's concern, DelRosario informed his audience, was ideological, not economic. "However strange it may seem," he went on, "freedom, friends, is an issue that one must constantly guard and defend with real heavyweights on Capitol Hill."

DelRosario ended with a holiday wish:

> Please join me in extending our most profound thanks to Jack Abramoff, Congressman Tom DeLay, his colleagues and key staff people who now have a clear understanding of the islands; the garment industry, who, despite all the unjustified bashing, now stands as the strongest economic pillar amidst the tourism industry having gone deep south; Governor Pete P. Tenorio; Willie Tan; David M. Sablan; Bishop Tomas Camacho and Fathers Gary and Isaac and all the clergy; and most importantly, you, my brothers and sisters. Let us give thanks to Divine Providence for all our blessings. Happy Thanksgiving!

The thanks were genuine, but the cost to the Marianas had been high. The government had paid millions to Preston Gates, and in 1999 Abramoff's contract was once again due to expire. Renewal was not assured.

Abramoff made certain that the contract would be renewed by meddling in the elections of a territorial government. In December 1999, Ed Buckham, the former DeLay aide turned lobbyist at the Alexander Strategy Group, and Michael Scanlon, then still one of DeLay's top aides, visited the Marianas. The two were there to help Ben Fitial win a race for speaker of the commonwealth's House of Representatives.

The Marianas' legislature has eighteen members. Its main function is to lobby the federal government for aid, and to manage the budgets that make up the archipelago's relatively small public sector. The next speaker of the CNMI House of Representatives would be elected in January 2000. There were two major candidates. One was Fitial, who, before he decided to enter politics, had been chief deputy to garment tycoon Willie Tan. The other candidate was businessman Heinz Hofschneider (one of the major immigrant groups in the Marianas, believe it or not, is expatriate Germans). Hofschneider had no Tan connection.

When Buckham and Scanlon arrived in Saipan, Fitial was losing the race. He was two votes behind Hofschneider. During a strategy discussion, Fitial suggested to DeLay's men that they meet with Reps. Alejo Mendiola and Norman Palacios. The two lawmakers were the likeliest candidates to shift their support. A meeting was arranged. Mendiola and Palacios later told reporters that they had each discussed switching their votes in exchange for federal appropriations to the island. Palacios wanted the federal government to pay for the repair of a breakwater on Tinian, one of the smaller islands in the archipelago. Mendiola wanted to build an airstrip on his island. He would need federal aid for that project, too. Buckham and Scanlon listened intently and returned to Washington shortly thereafter. Soon after that, the mayor of Rota, Benjamin Manglona, wrote a letter to Scanlon. The letter was gracious, and at times effusive in its praise. Manglona thanked Scanlon for "visiting our island." He also thanked Scanlon's boss, DeLay, for the "great many supports . . . he has given us over the years."[24]

Shortly after *that,* a few weeks before the January 2000 election, Manglona and Palacios, along with several other local officials, declared their support for Fitial. He was elected speaker in January 2000.

Now it was time to fulfill the other half of the bargain. On January 13, Manglona sent another letter to Michael Scanlon. "We hope that the action of our leadership would please" the House Republican leadership, he wrote. "We hope we can now work together as a real good team to enhance and improve our CNMI/Federal relationship."[25] Meanwhile, another DeLay aide, Brett Loper, traveled to the islands to investigate possibilities for federal aid. In April 2000, Scanlon resigned his position in DeLay's office and went to work for Abramoff. In May 2000, the Congress passed an appropriations bill instructing the bureaucracy to make the Rota airport a priority. Soon after, the FAA delivered $900,000 to the island for its airport. And in October 2000, Congress passed yet another appropriations bill. This one included $150,000 for the breakwater project on Palacios's island.

A few months earlier, in June 2000, the Commonwealth of the Northern Mariana Islands had renewed its contract with Preston Gates and Jack Abramoff—whom the islands had now paid $6 million in fees—for $1.6 million per year.

He had a lot of work to do. Early in 2000, Alaska senator Frank Murkowski had once again pushed for his immigration standards bill. And once again it passed the Senate. But the bill imploded when Don Young, chairman of the House Resources Committee, declared his opposition. Two of Abramoff's former lieutenants were on Young's staff at the time. The road to K Street runs both ways.

Also in 2000, Representative Bob Franks of New Jersey and Senator Spencer Abraham of Michigan, Republicans both, led a bipartisan effort to pass a bill that would have barred factories in the Northern Marianas from using the "Made in the USA" label, and would also have made imports from the archipelago subject to duties and tariffs. According to the *Washington Post,* as of August 2000 the bill had 220 cosponsors in the House and 24 in the Senate. On August 4, 2000, Pedro Tenorio, the CNMI's governor, said the bill would bankrupt his government. "This bill would have a devastating impact on our economy," he said. DeLay made sure that it never passed.

For Abramoff, such episodes held two lessons. One was that politics never ends; people never give up. The other was the importance of having the right friends in the right places at the right time. The year 2000 saw further attempts to extend the full U.S. code to the Marianas, which meant that that year also saw Abramoff work to thwart such an extension. Another year, another lobby.

That was also a presidential election year: an opportunity for patronage, an opportunity for prestige. Throughout the summer of 2000, Abramoff worked on language to be inserted into that year's Republican Party platform favorable to the Marianas. Here is what he came up with:

> We welcome greater participation in all aspects of the political process by Americans residing in Guam, the Virgin Islands, American Samoa, the Northern Marianas, and Puerto Rico. Since no single approach can meet the needs of those diverse communities, we emphasize respect for their wishes regarding their relationship to the rest of the Union. We affirm their right to seek the full extension of the Constitution, with all the rights and responsibilities it entails.[26]

"In the case of the Republican platform," Abramoff wrote to his clients later that year, "the team reviewed and commented on sections dealing with insular territories to ensure appropriately positive treatment. This was successful." So was the Republican convention. Abramoff was treated like royalty. Preston Gates threw lavish parties, including a private reception where members of the firm toasted their ally Don Young.

Abramoff had ties to the presidential campaign of George W. Bush, for whom he raised campaign money. As early as 1997, according to documents obtained by the Associated Press, Abramoff had billed his clients for obtaining a letter written by the then Texas governor. In the letter, Bush expressed his interest in the Marianas' school choice initiative. "I hope you will keep my office informed on the progress of this initiative," Bush wrote. The letter was cc'd to a member of Abramoff's lobbying team.

Early 2001 was a time of transition for Abramoff. He had decided to leave Preston Gates for Greenberg Traurig and wrote his Marianas contacts in January 2001 to persuade them to switch firms as well. "Our standing with the new administration promises to be solid," he wrote, "as several friends of the CNMI will soon be taking high-ranking positions in the Administration, including within the Interior Department."[27] He was right. The new administration was both antiregulation and pro-immigrant. For those reasons and others, the Marianas joined Abramoff at Greenberg Traurig. In October 2001, in his annual report, Abramoff wrote: "We have worked with WH Office of Presidential Personnel to ensure that CNMI-relevant positions at various agencies are not awarded to enemies of CNMI." And sure enough, two of Abramoff's deputies at Preston Gates, David Safavian and Patrick Pizzella, won political appointments in the new administration. Safavian was placed in the Office of Management and Budget. Pizzella was appointed assistant secretary of labor. It was just like Grover Norquist used to say about Stalin, back in the days of College Republicans: Personnel is policy.

To study Abramoff's work for the Commonwealth of the Northern Mariana Islands is to see, in outline, all the hallmarks of K Street Conservatism. It is as though the archipelago were not only Tom DeLay's perfect petri dish of capitalism but also a petri dish for all of Abramoff's subsequent lobbying endeavors. It is all here. The dressing up of clients' causes in ideological clothes. The courting of sympathetic lawmakers via lavish junkets. The tempting of sympathetic conservative elites. The outrageous fees.

The final distinct culture in our petri dish is a willingness to limit one's favors to a small circle of intimate friends. When Marianas functionaries visited the United States, Abramoff would make sure not only to shepherd them to Grover Norquist's Wednesday Meetings. He also billed them thousands of dollars for "discussions" with Norquist. He billed the Marianas for the airfare to send staff members of Americans for Tax Reform to Saipan. From *National Journal*: "According to sources familiar with ATR's finances, the group sent Marianas officials a bill for $10,000 at least once in the mid-1990s for attendance at Norquist's tax policy dinners."[28]

It paid to be a friend of Jack Abramoff's. Consider the case of

Rabbi Daniel Lapin and his brother David. Abramoff met the Lapin brothers on one of his many trips to South Africa in the 1980s. While he was working on *Red Scorpion* and defending the Botha apartheid government, the three men became close friends (like Abramoff, the Lapins are Orthodox Jews). In 1996, at Abramoff's urging, the Marianas awarded a $1.2 million contract to David Lapin to promote "ethics in government." In a subsequent audit, the Marianas government said it was unable to determine what work, exactly, Lapin performed for such a fee. For his part, Lapin said he fulfilled his part of the contract. And the CNMI cautioned that they were not impugning the rabbi's integrity. Lapin never gave the money back.[29]

In 1999, energy giant Enron Corporation entered negotiations with the Commonwealth of the Northern Mariana Islands to build an eighty-megawatt power plant. Enron felt it wasn't getting a fair hearing from island officials. So Enron asked its Washington lobbyist, one Ed Buckham, to see what he could do. On May 18, 1999, DeLay sent a letter to Marianas officials in which he said that the commonwealth "desperately needs a fair hearing in far-off Washington, D.C., which at least some of us here have been able to provide." It was only fair, DeLay argued, that the Marianas should give Enron a fair hearing as well. Not only *fair*—the Marianas government was "*obligated*" (my emphasis) to "provide the same opportunity to" Enron. In 2000, after Buckham and DeLay had eased his ascent to the speakership, Ben Fitial introduced a bill in the Marianas legislature that reopened bidding on the power plant. It passed. Governor Tenorio signed it into law. And then, on May 26, 2000, the Commonwealth Utilities Corp.—the Marianas' power company—voted 3-2 to grant the $120 million power plant contract to Enron.[30] (Enron's own legal and financial troubles later forced it to back out of the deal.)

In 2001, congressional Republicans again defeated an attempt to extend the U.S. minimum wage to the Marianas, saving Willie Tan and other garment manufacturers millions of dollars. The factory owners were not the sole profiteers. The 2001 federal budget also contained an additional $2 million in aid to the Marianas. The circuit was complete. As Greenberg Traurig lobbyist Kevin Ring wrote to his island clients, and to his boss Abramoff, in October 2001: "We believe that this additional funding—along with other funds we expect to secure by the end of the year—will make clear to even our biggest critics that we pay for ourselves."

CHAPTER FOUR

ROGUES' GALLERY

EVEN BAD GUYS NEED A LOBBYIST

AFRICAN DICTATORS. Islamic fanatics. Russians with ties to military intelligence. Israeli guerrillas. Small-time mobsters. They are all parts of the world that the K Street Conservatives inhabit. At first these rogues were sketchy allies, "our sons of bitches," tools necessary to achieve the ultimate goal: the end of the Soviet Empire. The rogues were means to an end, but, as tends to happen, the means became ends in themselves.

Consider Tom DeLay's trip to Moscow.

It was 1997, and Jack Abramoff had been elected to the board of the National Center for Public Policy Research. The National Center, as it was called, was run by Amy Ridenour, formerly Amy Moritz, a friend of Abramoff's since his College Republicans days. Abramoff's election to the board provided him new opportunities to bend the rules governing congressional travel. For Abramoff, the

National Center became an indirect means to achieve the same result.

The collapse of Soviet communism brought dramatic changes to Russia's economic and political institutions. Russia was characterized by corruption and turmoil. In such an atmosphere, there were ample opportunities for former apparatchiks, as well as Western businessmen, to make a quick buck, trading in political connections for market advantage. Abramoff, an expert influence peddler, was drawn, like a bird of prey, to the scene.

Sometime in early 1997, Abramoff registered as a lobbyist for Chelsea Commercial Enterprises Ltd. Chelsea was incorporated— here the documentary record is contradictory—either in the Bahamas or in Jersey, an island in the English Channel that is known for its lax financial disclosure laws. In his registration, Abramoff specified that Chelsea was paying him to build "support for policies of the Russian government for progressive market reforms and trade with the United States." To that end, he was paid $260,000 in 1997 and, according to the *Washington Post*, "less than $10,000 in 1998." Chelsea also paid a New York law firm, Cadwalader, Wickersham & Taft LLP, $180,000 in 1997 and about $30,000 between 1998 and 2001 to work on its behalf.

"Another source" handed the *Post* reporters a memo taken from Cadwalader, Wickersham & Taft dated May 6, 1997. In the memo, Ellen S. Levinson, then a lobbyist for Chelsea at Cadwalader, outlines a yearlong schedule of junkets to Russia. The six junkets mentioned in Levinson's memo, the *Post* reported, included a trip for an "advance team" in May 1997, a visit by conservative journalists and foreign policy wonks in June, and a trip by Tom DeLay in August. Abramoff was cc'd on the memo.

Ed Buckham was part of that "advance team." In a January 21, 1998, AP story (headline: "You Won't Find Congressional Travelers in Coach"), Buckham said he had taken the Concorde from Paris to Washington in July 1997, after visiting Russia in advance of his boss. Buckham said his Concorde ticket, like the August 1997 junket, was paid for by the National Center for Public Policy Research.

"We told the travel agent to just find the best flight," Amy Ride-nour told AP at the time. "Ed took the Concorde. I didn't realize that's what the travel agent picked."

But where did the National Center get the money? The *Wall Street Journal*'s David Rogers provided an answer on April 13, 2005. "The Russia trip was covered from an estimated $165,000 payment [to the center] from an international law firm seeking to promote exchanges with Russian businessmen," Rogers wrote.

Wherever the money ultimately came from, the trip was a success. DeLay, his wife, and his top staff were joined in Moscow first by Ride-nour, then Abramoff, then Julius Kaplan, a lawyer on the Chelsea account at Cadwalader. They golfed, met with Russian religious leaders, visited tourist attractions, and spoke with Prime Minister Viktor Chernomyrdin. The trip cost over $57,000. When the delegation stayed for two nights at the Le Meriden Moscow Country Club, Abramoff had the room next to the DeLays'.[1] The hotel bills show that the group made extensive use of the minibar. One night they attended a sumptuous dinner party hosted by the heads of NaftaSib, a Russian energy company. DeLay met NaftaSib's president, Alexander Koulakovsky, and its executive vice president, Marina Nevskaya. NaftaSib was another client of Abramoff's at Preston Gates.

Little is known about NaftaSib's executives. Alexander Koula-kovsky "graduated from Odessa Technological Institute in 1975," according to his company's literature, and left the Russian oil giant SibNeft in 1993 to start NaftaSib. Other than that, there is only an October 26, 1994, dispatch from Tass, the Russian news agency, which reported that an Alexander Koulakovsky was "arrested by authorities of Hatichohe, Northern Honshu, Japan, . . . for illegal storage of a handgun and 150 rounds of ammunition." (There is no evidence that Koulakovsky was ever convicted on these charges.)

Even less is known about Marina Nevskaya. The NaftaSib promotional material says she "taught at the Military Diplomatic Academy and lectured at Moscow State University" until 1991, when the Soviet Union collapsed. Apparently, she is "the author of several publications on the economy of Southeast Asia, economic cooperation between the USSR and Asian countries and textbooks on oriental languages." She is fluent, we are told, "in English, Vietnamese and French." There is no record of her in the Nexis news database prior to 2005.

Except for this. The August 23, 2004, issue of the *Russian Oil and Gas Report* had an article on NaftaSib's bid to buy the remnants of YUKOS, the giant Russian oil firm run by Mikhail Khodorkovsky until he became a prisoner of the Russian government. The article contains this aside:

> The names of Koulakovsky and Nevskaya, not very well known in Russia, are sufficiently well known in the U.S. Thus, in 1997 NaftaSib paid for the Moscow part of the visit of leader of the house of representative [sic] of the US Congress Tom DeLay. Nevskaya accompanied DeLay on that visit to Moscow.

Although the National Center for Public Policy Research paid for most of the junket's expenses, Abramoff used his credit card to cover some expenditures, as did Alexander Koulakovsky. NaftaSib denies having paid for the trip.

One thing is clear. Nevskaya and Koulakovsky sold more than energy products. Russia's energy industry is a sick parody of free-market capitalism. Success depends on one's contacts inside the government. Nevskaya and Koulakovsky have such contacts. And they sought similar contacts inside the American government. At the Moscow dinner party, Koulakovsky reportedly asked DeLay "what would happen" if he and his wife awoke one day "and found a luxury car in their front driveway." Koulakovsky was quickly informed that "the DeLays 'would go to jail and you would go to jail.'"[2] The conversation moved on to another topic.

Yet Abramoff had brokered a warm relationship between the House majority whip and Russian energy interests—which interests, not incidentally, were being looked at by both the FBI and CIA. "Even the CIA didn't know much about them," Michael Waller, a conservative writer on Russia, told NBC News reporter

Lisa Myers in the spring of 2005. When Nevskaya and Koulakovsky visited Washington, they met with DeLay in his offices on Capitol Hill. And though it wasn't a luxury car, on June 25, 1998, a London-based law firm, James & Sarch Co., issued a $1 million check to the U.S. Family Network, a nonprofit associated with DeLay and Buckham. In December 2005, former employees of the group told the *Washington Post* that Koulakovsky and Nevskaya had routed the check through the London firm to draw attention from themselves. Nevskaya denies any involvement. (Other contributors to the U.S. Family Network, it should be noted, included Abramoff clients like the Commonwealth of the Northern Mariana Islands and the Mississippi Choctaw Indian tribe.)

The relationship lasted several years. One day in November 1998, Abramoff met Sergei Kiriyenko, a Russian foreign minister, at Dulles Airport and spirited him to the Four Seasons hotel in Georgetown for several days of meetings with conservative lawmakers and policy wonks. Attendees recall that NaftaSib representatives were present throughout the visit. In 2000, when Abramoff arranged a ten-day junket for DeLay to play golf at the fabled St. Andrews course in Scotland, Koulakovsky, along with Marianas tycoon Willie Tan, came along. The National Center for Public Policy Research covered many of the expenses associated with that "educational" trip as well.

In Russia, the line between criminal and "legitimate businessman" is extremely thin. When Nevskaya and Koulakovsky are in Russia, they travel alongside guards armed with machine guns. Abramoff enjoyed the company of his Russian friends. And he began to ask them for favors.

On October 15, 2001, "VADIM," identified as an "assistant to Mrs. Nevskaya," wrote Abramoff the following e-mail:

Dear Mr. Abramoff,

The unit TN-4604MT will cost 28000 US dollars and higher that depends on the number of functions and options:

1) The basic set of units with the objective:

Focus = 18—$28635

Focus = 25—$28204
Focus = 50—$31051
2) Additional (changeable) objectives:
Focus = 18—$4115
Focus = 30—$4274
Focus = 50—$5862
Focus = 75—$7046
Focus = 100—$8230
Focus = 18 . . . 100—$15511
3) Stand—$176
4) Case—$200
5) Additional Accumulator—$212

Besides, delivery on terms of customs, delivery, insurance increases the cost by 30–35%.

Doesn't sound like they are discussing a camera, does it?

Abramoff forwarded the e-mail to his friend Shmuel Ben Zvi, under the subject line "thermal vision."

"I say that we should go with the larger objective lens," Abramoff wrote. "If it's standard Russian optics, we'll need the added light coming into the objective lens." Some of the other items, Abramoff went on, probably weren't necessary.

Ben Zvi responded: "We went back into Beit Jalla, my boys that you see in my class set up sniper positions and covered the rest of the g'dud (battalion) going in. . . .

The paratroop officer in charge of the area, that you see in the photo with me that I sent you is very happy that we'll have the thermal imager. When I told him about all the possibilities that we looked into, he told me that if it looks like it will take a long time to get the Russian model, then we can actually use our army address to buy the U.S. made thermal imager and have a colonel or higher sign for it, but I told him that it is taking so long for us to arrange this, and I need it so badly that instead of rocking the boat we'll just go with Marina.

Shmuel Ben Zvi is an Israeli settler living in the West Bank. He is also a high-school friend of Abramoff's, and the two enjoyed a close relationship over e-mail. NaftaSib says it never sold Abramoff or Ben Zvi weapons and only provided price information to them. For his part, Abramoff provided Ben Zvi—who also ran a sniper school and apparently performed paramilitary operations—with a monthly stipend, as well as money for weapons and other military equipment.

On October 19, 2001, Ben Zvi wrote another e-mail to Abramoff. "I just got this letter from Vadim," he wrote.

Vadim had written Ben Zvi to say that the "thermal visor" would be delivered "about half a year" after the contract was signed. "I will fax you a letter stating that I am purchasing this equipment for the IDF," Ben Zvi wrote, "and at the same time get a signed letter from the commander of a Paratroop brigade 890 to 'who this may concern.' Mr. Shmuel Ben Zvi is purchasing this thermal device for us . . . And we can go both to RAYTHEON and FLIR (near Boston) who sells the better MILCAMEXP."

Abramoff replied: "Oh boy. Get me the letter from the army! Good shabbos."

Ben Zvi wrote Abramoff again on August 13, 2002:

The reason I got the digital camera in the first place was to be able to take a photo of the arabs shooting at us or cutting into the security fence and then send the photo off to the police right away. . . . And now that I'll have wheels, I'll be so much more effective. You did this for me my brother. It really breathes new life in me. I feel like the tank commanders in the Yom Kippur war, who when hearing over the radio that reenforcements were coming, felt so great that they raised their seats higher out of the tank hatch and went forward.

Abramoff replied the next day: "Thanks brother. If only there were another dozen of you the dirty rats would be finished."

But soon money became a problem. On September 19, 2002, Alison R. Bozniak, Abramoff's assistant, wrote to Abramoff and Gail Halpern, his tax accountant:

I spoke with Shmuel and he is a little afraid to begin changing things with the bank since they set up the loan for the jeep based on the 2K payments each month for the last year. They regarded the 2K as a sign that the transfers were stable and felt that these consistent payments, plus the letter from Jack, made the loan a good risk.

He studies half a day at a place called "Kollel" but he doesn't think that they even have a bank account as it really doesn't pay its members. He also has no way to set this up with a Yeshiva at the moment.

He did suggest that he could write some kind of letter with his Sniper Workshop Logo and letter head. It is an "educational" entity of sorts.

Abramoff replied an hour later: "No," he wrote, "don't do that. I don't want a sniper letterhead."

The money still didn't come. On November 6, 2002, Halpern e-mailed Abramoff: "Please don't get too upset w/me asking you this, but is it at all possible for you to suspend your kindness and generosity until we have this Eshkol matter under control, ie, can we cut the Shmuel spy equipment and his monthly stipend ($3,560)."

Abramoff replied, in all caps: "I CAN'T SUSPEND SHMUEL ON SHORT NOTICE. . . . WE WILL JUST HAVE TO MAKE MORE MONEY."

Ben Zvi e-mailed Abramoff later that week:

My brother I am really happy that the ERT in Efrat has turned to me for their training this coming winter, spring, and summer. Last night one of their guys who was in the army when I did the workshop for the snipers in his unit said that they need the workshop badly (duh) . . .

The army for the most part creates soldiers, not WARRIORS. Unless one is very fortunate and gets into a recon unit, like I did . . . It is not in the interest of any government to create warriors that they feel will one day become a fifth columb [sic], and the previous labor governments have always expressed those sentiments. Shulimit Aloni, the labor blabber mouth, has always expressed fears that the Miszrachi movement will one day make a call to arms and announce "MEDINAT" Yehuda. So they have always been leery about arming the Ishuvim properly . . . But they don't really understand the Jews. They are really flipped out if [they] think that it is morally correct to leave us to the vicious arab fundamentalist muslim fanatic wolfs.

Abramoff forwarded this e-mail to Gail Halpern with the note: "This is why it is so hard for me to cut off his funding. Who will fund this? He has no one else."

Halpern replied: "Understood. . . . I actually had chills reading the 2 emails you forwarded me. However, we need to work this into the tax exempt purpose of the Foundation. More to come on this subject in an email tomorrow or so. May and B. is finishing the 2001 return and read me the riot act on some of the stuff that we are doing. We need to 'fix' the holes."

On December 24, 2002, Abramoff forwarded another of his exchanges with Ben Zvi to Halpern. "I cannot cut him off from the stipend and the jeep payment. I just cannot do it."

Halpern replied:

I agree w/you. If you know him and trust him, he certainly is a fellow Jew in trouble, and to quote Pam (well, she is referring to Eshkol) "there is a reason why hashem gave Jack the ability to earn so much money."

But let's try to figure it out in a way where we don't screw up the foundation. We need to get the money to a 501c3 or an educational institution, not directly to him. Can you ask him if he can

work something out w/ the kollel so the money goes from the kollel to him?

    If he can't, then I need to sit down [REDACTED] and have him
make amendments and Grant procedures and all kinds of other
stuff to make this legit, from a tax point of view. I already need to
talk w/Mac about the skating rink, so let me know what shmuel
says about getting money to a kollel, and if it won't work, then
I'll add this to the [REDACTED] list.

Abramoff wrote Ben Zvi: "Brother, please set up an account for
a kollel and get me the info so we can send the $ there from now on.
Thanks."

Then Abramoff wrote Halpern: "He said he can do the kollel."
Halpern:

Good. He needs to give us back the name and bank account info,
and can the jeep payments go to the kollel as well, as well as all
the other military expenses that don't look good on the Foundation's books? At the end of the year, he'll need to write us a letter
on Kollel stationery thanking the Foundation for the money to
promote their educational purpose.

Abramoff: "ok."

They set up the account.

Between January 23, 2002, and June 4, 2002, Abramoff's "charity," the Capital Athletic Foundation, issued $15,000 in checks to
Shmuel Ben Zvi's account at the "Israel Discount Bank." Another
$2,000 in July. Another $2,000 in August—plus over $27,000 for a
"new Jeep." Another $3,560 in October. Over $8,000 in November.[3]
Anything for a friend.

    Why did Jack Abramoff introduce Tom DeLay to Russians traf-
ficking in the accoutrements of war? Because the Russians were
Abramoff's clients. And Abramoff had a history of disregarding his
clients' moral compasses. There were reasons for this besides

money, however. There's a certain thrill that comes with flaunting convention, disobeying the rules, rubbing shoulders with men and women who move in shadow. The only danger is that you may start to feel more comfortable in the dark.

Abramoff's compromise with his religious and cultural values was long in the making, and reflected not just his own corruption but certain compromises undertaken by the conservative movement itself over a decade before. In his 1985 State of the Union, Ronald Reagan articulated a set of principles that would later be termed the Reagan Doctrine. "Support for freedom fighters," Reagan said, "is self-defense." Thus his administration would support to its utmost the anti-Communist insurgencies in Afghanistan, in Nicaragua and El Salvador, in Southeast Asia, and in Africa. In many instances, the support would be overt. In others, it would not.

Jack Wheeler was the embodiment of the Reagan Doctrine. A Californian who had worked on Reagan's gubernatorial campaigns, he had decided to leverage his New Right connections into a full-time job as an adventurer. He traveled the world, fought in guerrilla armies, and mentored both Jack Abramoff and Grover Norquist. "Just got out of Cambodia with the KPNLF," Wheeler once wrote Abramoff. "Went to their three main command posts . . . almost got my ass blown away by a Vietnamese mortar barrage . . . Again, I realize it gets people in the door, but go lightly on this 'real life Indiana Jones' stuff. I've been doing these things for a quarter of a century now. . . . It is a better argument (perhaps true for all I know) to say that the character was based somewhat on my life, not the other way around. . . ."[4]

To demonstrate the strength of the Reagan Doctrine, Wheeler helped Abramoff and Norquist organize, under the auspices of Citizens for America, a conference of worldwide insurgent leaders called the Democracy International. The meeting was held in June 1985, in Jamba, Angola, the base camp of Jonas Savimbi's UNITA (pronounced ooh-nee-tah) movement. UNITA received direct assistance from the United States, and had been waging a ten-year-long war against the Soviet-backed government in Luanda. Savimbi had created a ministate—called "UNITA-land"—that included a stadium large enough for the gathering.

It was quite a scene. Representatives from the mujahedeen, the contras, an anti-Communist Laotian army, and UNITA all attended. Abramoff and Norquist arranged American media to fly into Angola from South Africa. They arranged for Citizens for America's president, Lew Lehrman, to hand out framed copies of the Declaration of Independence, as well as other gifts. The capstone to the event was a speech that Lehrman delivered to a stadium packed with guerrillas and mercenaries from around the world. Lehrman read from a letter that Ronald Reagan had sent him. He told the crowd that Reagan had meant the letter for them. "Around the world," Lehrman read, "we see people joining together to get control of their own affairs and to free their nations from outside domination and an alien ideology. It is a global trend and one of the most hopeful of our times."[5]

Then the leaders of each of the armies—Savimbi of UNITA, Ghulam Wardak of Afghanistan, Adolfo Calero of the Nicaraguan Democratic Force, and Pa Kao Her of the Ethnics Liberation Organization of Laos—put their names to a "Declaration of the Democratic International," which read, in part, "Our common goals of liberty and constitutional democracy lead us to form this Democratic International." And yet Alan Cowell, who covered the conference for the *New York Times*, seems only to have been struck by the amount of time it took for his plane out of Angola to arrive:

The chartered Dakota aircraft had been scheduled to fly in from South Africa at 7 A.M. on Tuesday. So, in the cold hours before dawn framed stunted trees against ribbons of gold, the participants rose early and trundled from Jamba to an airstrip two hours drive away, and scanned the skies. And waited.

The sun rose, approached its zenith, and passed it, and began to dip. And still they waited. Trucks arrived bearing beds and mattresses, ominous omens. Table was set, with vintage Portuguese wine, for lunch and dinner. The fire was lit as evening's chill curled cold fingers around the impromptu encampment, and the Afghan visitors turned to the east to pray. And still they waited.

While he was waiting, Cowell might have taken the opportunity to tell his readers a little about Jonas Savimbi—the host, and star, of the Democracy International. It's not a pretty story.

"He was the most articulate, charismatic homicidal maniac I've ever met" is how Don Steinberg, President Clinton's ambassador to Angola, once described Savimbi. Steinberg forgets to mention that Savimbi was also a Maoist. He had been schooled by the Chinese Communists, and he had been friends with Che Guevara. The initial funding for UNITA came from the Chinese Communist Party.[6] It grew to 50,000 soldiers. Many of them were children.

Yet American conservatives embraced Savimbi, who was cultured, charming, and debonair. Jeane Kirkpatrick called Savimbi a "linguist, philosopher, poet, politician, warrior."[7] Conservatives believed it was important to support anyone—*anyone*—who was fighting the surrogates of the Soviet Empire. But when the topic turned to Savimbi, conservatives took things one step further. In 1986, for example, the conservative activist Howard Phillips said that "if Jonas Savimbi was an American citizen, he would be the presidential candidate of the conservative movement in 1988." Savimbi was a regular at the Heritage Foundation. The Republican lobbying team of Black, Manafort, Stone & Kelley spent hours painting him in a favorable light. For this the firm was paid $600,000 a year.[8] When the political scientist Williamson M. Evers wrote an op-ed in the *Journal* that pointed to the many instances in which Savimbi identified himself as a socialist, Jack Wheeler wrote an irate letter to the editor.

No conservative embraced Savimbi more than Norquist, who ghost-wrote an article under Savimbi's byline—"The War Against Soviet Colonialism"—that appeared in the January 1986 issue of *Policy Review*. The essay bears rereading. Savimbi (which is to say, Norquist) is forthright about his Communist education: "From

Mao and the Communists, I learned how to fight and win a guerrilla war. . . . We are using Communist military and propaganda principles in order to defeat the Soviets and their political ideology." He expounds on the "five central principles of guerrilla warfare," the second of which, "a clear political program," is "key to the success of a revolutionary movement." However, the content of Savimbi's political program depended on the audience he was addressing—and who was writing the address.

Six months after the *Policy Review* essay, Norquist ghost-wrote a similar op-ed for Savimbi—"Don't Sacrifice Angola on the Altar of Socialism"—that was published in the *Wall Street Journal*. Beginning in 1985, when he traveled to Jamba to plan the Democratic International, Norquist visited Savimbi a dozen times over the course of a decade. He often told stories of his adventures in the jungle. "One time I was at a forward base camp," he told Nina Easton, "and all of a sudden the sky lit up and there was a huge amount of shooting and heavy machine-gun fire. I was wearing a UNITA uniform, so I ran over and changed out of it to see if that would buy me [safety]."[9] Listening to Norquist describe his relationship with Savimbi, reading the articles that Norquist penned under Savimbi's name, it is difficult to tell where the libertarian activist ends and the African "freedom fighter" begins.

In fact, Savimbi seems unfit to have been called a "freedom fighter" in the first place. In 1989, the conservative writer Radek Sikorski—now Poland's defense minister—visited Jamba and wrote about his experiences for *National Review*. This is what he found:

Where ten years ago elephants and gazelles roamed virgin bush, today vast logistics bases sprawl, with broad avenues, electricity, and some of the best repair shops in Africa. UNITA doctors and paramedics can successfully perform advanced surgery; UNITA's intelligence service can chart dozens of enemy moves every day; while dozens of UNITA bush schools, though usually with only a blackboard and an enthusiastic teacher for assets, turn out graduates with more determination for self improvement and greater academic qualifications than most American high schools do.[10]

Impressive. But Sikorski wasn't finished. UNITA officers were "compulsive liars," he wrote. The territory under Savimbi's control was in the grip of a politics of "extreme centralization" that "would impress a Ligachev or a Honecker." There was no currency. There was a cult of personality instead. Bottom line: "UNITA's structure is overtly Leninist."

Evidence began to mount that Savimbi was a killer. A former UNITA activist, Sousa Jamba, took to the pages of the London *Spectator* to describe a series of killings that took place in September 1983: "Twelve women and three children who were accused of practicing witchcraft were burnt to death," Jamba wrote. "Savimbi and his phalanx of generals witnessed the burning; and when one of the women tried to escape Savimbi pulled out his famous ivory pistol and tried to shoot at her." By 1991, it was clear that Savimbi had ordered the killing of Wilson dos Santos, his ambassador to the United Kingdom.[11] In 1992, the British journalist Fred Bridgland, who had written a hagiographic biography of Savimbi, described a conversation he had had some years earlier with Pedro "Tito" Chingunji, a longtime UNITA activist and the group's envoy to the United States. Chingunji had known Bridgland for many years. This is what he said:

Each time I return to Jamba I do not know whether or not I will come out again, or whether or not I will be killed. My parents [were] beaten to death on Savimbi's instructions. I have now confirmed that that is true. My sisters and brothers and their wives and husbands are under arrest and have been severely beaten. One of my sisters, Xila, has been executed. My father was a strong character and he never hesitated to criticize Savimbi. He became increasingly disapproving of Savimbi's callous treatment of women. Savimbi took "wives" from everywhere and everyone, and his children from many women are scattered throughout southeastern Angola. For a long time there had been rumors that four of my brothers had been killed on Savimbi's orders. Then I learned that my surviving brothers and sisters had been arrested, and they got reports out to me saying that the strongarm men who surround Savimbi had beaten our parents to death.[12]

In 1992, having lured him back to Angola, Savimbi murdered Chingunji, his wife, and their small children.

Four years later, in 1996—*after* the Cold War was over, *after* Savimbi's true self had been revealed—Norquist registered as a lobbyist for UNITA. His stipend, he disclosed to the Justice Department, was $5,000 per month.

The rogues' gallery goes on and on. Back in July 1985, a month after the Democratic International came to a close, Abramoff and Norquist were out of a job. They would have to seek out other opportunities.

The night that Abramoff was purged from Citizens for America, Norquist was in Johannesburg, South Africa, attending a conference put on by the National Student Federation, a South African students' group that supported free-market economics. According to Nina Easton, speakers at the conference "included a Taiwanese military intelligence officer, a former NATO intelligence officer who served in Hitler's Navy, and a South African naval officer." Botha, the hard-line South African prime minister, couldn't make it. Instead he a sent a letter, read aloud to great applause.[13]

College Republicans like Norquist had always had a tenuous relationship with South Africa, reflecting the tortured position of the Reagan administration and the distorted politics of the Cold War. On the one hand, no American conservative would have said that he supported South Africa's apartheid caste system. But, on the other, conservatives recognized that the only hope for a Communist-free Africa was found in the arms of the South African military. They had to choose.

In 1984, under Abramoff's leadership, the College Republicans adopted the following resolution on South Africa:

Whereas the pretense of Soviet proxy forces in Southern Africa threatens not only the interests of the RSA and the USA but all western interests in the region;

Whereas the Soviet-backed terrorists in Southern Africa are a vital link in the world-wide chain of Soviet aggression and furthermore that aggression is a continual re-affirmation of long standing communist designs for world domination;

Whereas the socioeconomic and political developments in South Africa are resulting in the betterment of the lives of all the peoples of South Africa;

Whereas the RSA suffers from deliberate planted propaganda by the KGB and their operatives, concerning its action in the region;

Whereas it is important for visionary student leaders to cooperate insofar as they are the moderating factors in the moulding of our future;

Be it resolved that: We as College Republicans offer our moral support and cooperation to the Student Moderate Alliance of South Africa for the general pursuit of our common world security interests.

Be it further resolved that we join in solidarity with the peoples of the RSA in their struggle against Soviet expansionism in that region and that we place a primary emphasis on supporting the South African initiative to better their situation.

The National Student Federation supported apartheid. It was a vocal ally of the South African Defense Force. Members of the National Student Federation had studied political organizing at College Republicans seminars. A brochure for the group displayed prominently a photo of Abramoff. In 1991, the Manchester *Guardian* reported that it had discovered documents from the early eighties revealing South African security services' influence on student groups, including the National Student Federation. Specifically, the government sought to foster ties between the Federation and Zulu chief Mangosuthu Buthelezi, whose Inkatha political party supported the racial caste system. Norquist also had met with Buthelezi.[14] On August 1, 1991, the president of the Federation, Danie Kril, admitted that the group had received secret funding from the government, and the NSF disbanded forever.[15]

The ties between Abramoff and the South African regime were more than superficial. In 1986, after graduating from Georgetown Law, Abramoff got a job as director of the International Freedom Foundation, a pressure group meant to combat the Comprehensive Anti-Apartheid Act, a South Africa sanctions bill under consideration in Congress. Abramoff held events, published pamphlets, met with lawmakers—all the things your typical special interest does to get by. What no one knew at the time—and what Abramoff to this day denies any knowledge of—was that the group's funding ultimately came from the South African Defense Force.[16]

Abramoff did not stay long at the International Freedom Foundation. He moved back to Hollywood, where he and his brother started a production company, Regency entertainment.[17] In the space of only a few months, the Abramoffs managed to raise $16 million to produce a movie about a Red Army officer who is sent to the fictional African nation of Mombaka to quell an anti-Communist rebellion and ends up siding with the rebels. To this day, no one knows where the money came from.

The movie was *Red Scorpion*. If the movie is still known at all, it's because it has the dubious distinction of launching the film career of action "star" Dolph Lundgren. Abramoff served as executive producer. But the circumstances surrounding the film's production are what make it interesting. *Red Scorpion* was filmed in Namibia, which was then occupied by South Africa. The South African Defense Force contributed men and matériel to the film. And a *Red Scorpion* producer, Russell Crystal, was a known adviser to F. W. DeKlerk—and the Johannesburg chief of the International Freedom Foundation. In 1995, a former South African intelligence agent, Craig Williamson, told *Newsday* that *Red Scorpion* was "funded by our guys." Abramoff denies this.

Red Scorpion was released in 1989 to miserable reviews. "The movie's reflective moments," wrote the reviewer in the *New York Times,* "belong to Mr. Lundgren's sweaty chest." It is pretty easy to understand where this reviewer was coming from. Consider some sample dialogue: "As a matter of fact," one character tells another, "in America, an American can swear whenever, wherever, and however much he or she fucking well pleases! A little something called freedom of speech, which I'm sure you Russians aren't real familiar with!"

Red Scorpion flopped. But it found a second life in the strange netherworld of television syndication and home video rentals— enough of a life, in fact, to occasion the production of a direct-to- video sequel, *Red Scorpion 2.* Lundgren is absent from the sequel, having gone on to star in the film adaptation of the Marvel comic *The Punisher.* Abramoff was credited as *Red Scorpion 2*'s pro- ducer—but it has since been reported that his actual connection to the film was minimal. Which would make sense, because the bad guys in *Red Scorpion 2* aren't Marxists but antigovernment militia groups.

Abramoff and Norquist were close to the butcher Savimbi. They had connections to South Africa's apartheid state. But that's not all. The two seemed willing to flack for any African insurgency, as long as it was fighting Communists—and once the Cold War was over, they were just as happy to flack for African dictators.

Consider the work Norquist performed for the Renamo.

Mozambique is the poorest country in the world. Like Angola, it won independence from Portugal in 1975, and the government in the capital of Maputo was quickly dominated by Soviets. But, unlike Angola, Washington did not support Mozambique's anti- Communist insurgency. In 1985, the country's dictator, "President" Samora Machel, began to make overtures to the West. He opened the country to direct foreign investment. He joined Western, capi- talistic institutions like the World Bank and International Mone- tary Fund. He refused to allow the Soviets to build permanent bases. He was killed in October 1986 when his private plane slammed into a mountain. As Richard Grenier put it in *National Review:* "The great debate over Mozambique is whether the United States can, for the first time in history, entice a Communist country out of the Soviet Union's orbit."[18] Grenier didn't think so. He thought the Reagan administration should support instead the Mozambique National Resistance, or Renamo.

The Renamo was a creature of the Rhodesian government. When that government was toppled in 1979, the Renamo moved to South Africa, which provided logistical and financial support. The Renamo were nearly as brutal as UNITA. In April 1988, the State Department issued a report claiming that "100,000 civilians may have been murdered" at the hands of Renamo.[19]

Just as with Jonas Savimbi, however, when conservatives looked at the Renamo, they saw what they wanted to see. An article in *National Review* described Renamo leader Alfonso Dlakama as "young and happily married, a devout Catholic, and an admirer of Ronald Reagan and Margaret Thatcher."[20] Inconvenient facts were dismissed. And sometimes convenient facts were invented.

In 1987, Norquist traveled to Mozambique. He spent six days in the country, touring the capital as well as territories under Renamo control. He met the Marxist president Chissano. When he returned, he wrote a summary of his findings for the Heritage Foundation. "Renamo repeatedly calls for free, internationally supervised elections," Norquist wrote. Renamo supports "freedom of religion." The movement "operates freely in more than 85 percent of Mozambique, has grown to more than 22,000 men under arms, and has limited the government's control to little more than narrow perimeters around the major cities." All of which was true. But then Norquist added this startling observation: "Anti-Semitic posters . . . grace the capital's walls. One depicts 'Zionists' strangling blacks."[21]

Norquist's Heritage report caught the attention of Senator Jesse Helms. And Norquist made sure a copy got to the Simon Wiesenthal Center and its dean, Rabbi Marvin Hier. Hier sent letters to then-Secretary of State George Shultz: "Since it cannot be missed by anyone driving in from the airport," he wrote, the mural "serves as an outrageous anti-Semitic statement which reminds one of the banners and portraits that once were displayed in the cities of Adolf Hitler's Nazi Germany."

The Mozambicans were a little shocked. It should have been plain, they said, that the person depicted in the mural was a member of the Portuguese colonial police. The mural was anti-imperialist, not anti-Semitic. Norquist told the American media, according to the *Times*, that this was "an evasion."

It wasn't. It turns out the artist had made a mistake. From the *New York Times*: "The Mozambicans, assisted by the Portuguese embassy here, produced evidence that the star on the official's cap in the mural was that of the Portuguese colonial police, not a Zionist figure."[22]

Yet this did not stop Norquist from telling his story to President Reagan himself on September 22, 1987. The administration had invited a group of conservative activists and thinkers, including Columbia University professor Robert Jastrow, to the White House. Norquist was included. He wanted to grab the president's attention—and further the Renamo's cause.

Peggy Noonan describes the scene in her memoir. Norquist, Noonan writes:

> captivated the president with a kind of show-and-tell on Mozambique—that the governing party is Marxist-Leninist; President Chissano is a communist. You may have been given the impression by the State Department, which tends in its worldview to assume a black African is too dumb to be a Communist, to think that's only for white Europeans—you may have been given the impression that the people of the Mozambique government are not serious. But they are.

Then Norquist showed the great man a photo he had taken of the mural in Maputo. Noonan writes: "At that point, for the first time in the meeting, Weinberger, Carlucci, and Howard Baker picked up their pencils and wrote on their white White House pads." Reagan, too, seemed interested.

Yet Norquist's meeting did little to change the administration's position. Eager to find allies in Africa, Reagan's State Department viewed the postcolonial Mozambican regime with suspicion, but also believed that it would be willing to compromise. The administration saw an opportunity to tear a hole, through diplomatic means, in the Soviet sphere of influence. Reagan met with Chissano on October 6. He said the United States would assist Mozambique "in any way that we can."

That same day, Norquist appeared at a Renamo press conference on Capitol Hill and described his September 22 meeting with Reagan. According to Norquist, Reagan told him, "You have certainly changed my agenda for when I meet Chissano."[23] On November 3, 1987, Norquist was at a meeting with Frank Carlucci, Reagan's national security adviser. Six conservative lobbyists were there. They brought along a representative from the Renamo. The meeting lasted an hour. Administration officials said that they had not been told someone from Renamo was going to show up.[24] "We are with Mozambique today where we were with Savimbi and Angola three years ago," Norquist told the Washington Post. He was wrong. The Renamo never received support from the United States. Their human rights record was just too dismal.

The Cold War ended, but Norquist's trips to Africa did not. In 1992, he visited the Seychelles, a group of East African islands. Norquist's travel companion on this occasion was Sir James Mancham, whom the Marxist-Leninist France-Albert René had deposed in 1977. Upon his return, Norquist organized a pro-Mancham campaign to restore democracy to the Seychelles. Editorials supporting Mancham appeared in the Washington Times. Mancham delivered speeches at Heritage. Norquist introduced him to lawmakers. And the pressure seemingly worked. In 1993, the Seychelles held "free" elections. "I had spent five or six years to move René out of power," Norquist has said.

Except France-Albert René is still in power. What's more, in September 1995, in the first year of the Republican Congress, René hired Norquist to lobby on his behalf for $10,000 per month. When journalists asked him how he could work for a Communist strong-man, Norquist said simply that René was "a guy who preferred not to have elections for a number of years."[25] When journalists asked him how he could work for someone accused of multiple human rights violations, Norquist said simply that "there were one or two people who people suspected were done in. But it was always fairly murky."[26] Norquist terminated his contract with the government of the Seychelles in March 1999—by which point he had received several hundred thousand dollars for his work. Norquist continues to have good relations with the government of the Seychelle Islands. In 2005, he and his newly married bride visited the archipelago on their honeymoon. Lobbyists at Norquist's firm, Janus-Merritt, also represented the government of Pakistan, the government of Gabon, and Pascal Lissouba, the corrupt former president of the Republic of Congo. (Lissouba is still alive, living in exile in France.)

Abramoff, for his part, had ties to his own set of African dicta-tors. There was for example Mobutu Sese Seko, the dictator of Zaire. Mobutu, of course, was one of Africa's most infamous and nasty tyrants. He seized power in 1965 and proceeded to plunder his country's wealth, dying with a personal fortune valued at a bil-lion dollars. He was banned from the United States. But, in 1995, André Soussan, a Mobutu ally based in France, began paying Republican lobbyists to pressure the Clinton administration into granting the dictator a visa.[27] Soussan paid $30,000 to Paul Erick-son, a former Buchanan political aide, who then subcontracted the work out to Jack Abramoff's team at Preston Gates. Abramoff asked Norquist to help. Norquist told the Legal Times that he played only a "minor" role in the lobbying effort—but that he would also, as journalist Sam Skolnik paraphrased it, "provide eco-nomic advice to Zaire if Mobutu is allowed in the United States."[28] The targets of Abramoff's campaign were members of the Con-gressional Black Caucus—all of whom were Democrats.

What a spectacle: A Republican lobbyist targeting Democrats to support the unrestricted travel of an authoritarian. But there's worse. Abramoff claimed to be working pro bono.

That would not be the case with another potential Abramoff client. Documents released by the Senate Committee on Indian Affairs include a three-page letter that Jack Abramoff sent to Omar Bongo, "president" of Gabon since 1967. The letter is dated July 28, 2003. It is printed on Greenberg Traurig stationery—the law firm where Abramoff worked at the time. It is worth excerpting at length:

> Our firm is one of the very top lobbying and public affairs law firms in the nation. We have a wealth of powerful corporate and governmental clients who keep our team of lobbyists very active. Our success rate is exceptional. Based on my friendship with Roger, and without advance resources, I have been cautiously working to obtain a visit for the president to Washington, to see President Bush, the Congress and policy and opinion makers in the United States. . . . I explicitly told [Roger] that I was not telling him this as a way to get Gabon to match any offer, but rather that I would engage in this representation, and when it was concluded, revert to our efforts. . . . I suggested that I visit Gabon after my trip to Scotland in mid-August, but that in order for me to preserve this and be able to turn down the neighbor's offer, we had to commence the representation, even in small part, perhaps ten percent of the representation. Please bear in mind that the neighbor's proposal was to pay the entire amount up front. . . . I am willing to visit after my visit to Scotland with the Congressman and Senators I take there each year. It is possible that they will want to join me in Gabon, which would be an extra bonus. . . . With high regard and much admiration, I am sincerely yours, Jack Abramoff.[29]

What sort of man earns Jack Abramoff's "high regard" and "admiration"?

From the State Department's Country Reports on Human Rights Practices for Gabon 2003—the year Abramoff wrote his letter:

> The Government's human rights record remained poor; although there were some improvements in a few areas, serious problems

remained. The Government continued to limit citizens' ability to change their government. Security forces reportedly beat and tortured prisoners and detainees, prison conditions remained harsh, and security forces sometimes violently dispersed demonstrations. Arbitrary arrest and detention were problems. Authorities routinely infringed on privacy rights. The Government continued to restrict freedom of the press and movement. Violence and societal discrimination against women and noncitizen Africans continued to be problems. Forced labor, child labor, and trafficking—particularly in children—remained problems.

Abramoff included with his letter a lobbying contract for $9 million. The money was to be routed through Grassroots Interactive, a shell company that Abramoff had set up in suburban Maryland. Bongo didn't accept the offer. One wonders which was the more corrupt partner in this aborted deal.

It is hard to say what, other than greed, would motivate Abramoff to send his letter to Omar Bongo. This makes Bongo unique. An ideological element was always present when Abramoff represented a client. Everything was subsumed by a singular devotion to the conservative movement and the maintenance of the Republican majority. But this pursuit of a grand cause can lead to some unexpected, and dangerous, places. Consider Grover Norquist's attempts to broaden the Republican coalition to include American Muslims.

In 1997, Norquist opened a lobbying firm of his own. The new company was called the Merritt Group, then renamed Janus-Merritt Strategies—Janus, the Roman god of access, of entrances and exits, has two faces—then finally sold to the Richmond-based firm Williams Mullen in 2002. As with any Norquist venture, the tenor of the firm was fiercely ideological. Some of Janus-Merritt's most prominent clients were American Muslim activists. Here, too, the firm's choice of clients complemented its politics. Lassoing American Muslims into the Republican coalition has been a long-standing goal of Norquist's.

To that end, he established the Islamic Institute in 1998. Officially titled the Islamic Free Market Institute Foundation, the group, according to its Web site, seeks to "create a better understanding between the American Muslim community and the political leadership" and "provide a platform to promote an Islamic perspective on domestic issues." The institute also produces numerous pamphlets explaining how Islam is compatible with the free market. Norquist is chairman of the board.

A prominent American Muslim attorney, Khaled Saffuri, was for a time the executive director of the Islamic Institute. Saffuri is also a friend of Jack Abramoff's. His previous job had been at the American Muslim Council, or AMC, an Islamic interest group with a controversial past. That past caught up with him, the Islamic Institute, and Janus-Merritt sometime in October 2000, when the company submitted forms to the Senate registering Omar Nashashibi—one of the firm's partners—and several others to lobby for Abdurahman Alamoudi, the then-head of the AMC.

A naturalized U.S. citizen born in Eritrea, Alamoudi is now serving a twenty-three-year term in federal prison for conspiring to assassinate then-Crown Prince Abdullah of Saudi Arabia. Alamoudi, it turns out, is a radical Islamist and terrorist sympathizer who openly supported Hamas and Hezbollah while a client of Janus-Merritt's.

In 1996, Alamoudi told an audience that the United States will inevitably "become a Muslim country." But he first entered the public eye on October 28, 2000, when he took the mike at an anti-Israel rally outside the White House and chanted: "I have been labeled by the media in New York to be a supporter of Hamas. Anybody supporters of Hamas here?"

The crowd reportedly cheered, and Alamoudi went on: "Hear that, Bill Clinton? We are all supporters of Hamas. Allah akbar! I wish to add here I am also a supporter of Hezbollah. . . . My brothers, this is the message that we have to carry to everybody. It's an occupation, and Hamas is fighting to end an occupation. It's a legal fight. Allah akbar! Allah akbar!"[30]

Abdurahman Alamoudi inhabited the world of international Islamic terrorism. The *Jerusalem Post* has reported that he attended a conference in January 2001 in Beirut that released a communiqué saying, "America today is a second Israel." On August 11, 2003, while trying to fly to Damascus with $340,000 in cash stuffed in his luggage, he was detained by Scotland Yard at Heathrow International Airport. He told authorities the cash had been given to him by a Libyan intelligence agent and that the Libyan government had paid him between $10,000 and $20,000 on several occasions. Just like that, Alamoudi had revealed that he was an asset of the Libyan government, and, as he later admitted in a plea agreement, he had been plotting to murder Crown Prince Abdullah for some time.

In early 1999, Alamoudi delivered $20,000 in checks that helped the Islamic Institute gain its financial footing.[31] Saffuri says that the institute distanced itself from Alamoudi after the controversial 2000 rally, and that all parties were unaware of Alamoudi's alleged criminal activities. Other donors to the Islamic Institute: the Safa Trust ($35,000) and the International Institute of Islamic Thought ($11,000). In 2002, the offices of both groups were raided by the FBI. In 2003, the FBI served warrants to both their officers. All those involved denied any connection to terrorism.[32] In 2000, thanks to the strenuous lobbying efforts of Saffuri and Norquist, Abdurahman Alamoudi had his picture taken with then-presidential candidate George W. Bush.[33] Between 2000 and 2001, he paid Janus-Merritt Strategies about $40,000 in lobbying fees.

Or did he? In 2004, Janus-Merritt partner David Safavian told the U.S. Senate, "To my knowledge, neither I nor Janus-Merritt did any work for Mr. Alamoudi. I do not know why Mr. Alamoudi was erroneously listed in the client's lobby disclosure forms." Furthermore, "I do not believe Janus-Merritt received any funds from Mr. Alamoudi."

But, according to Senate disclosure reports, this was incorrect. For years Janus-Merritt registered as a lobbyist for Alamoudi. And then, on December 17, 2001, Janus-Merritt resubmitted its disclosure forms.[34] This time Alamoudi had been replaced by one Dr.

Jamal al Barzinji. Why the firm changed its registration is unknown. For his part, Safavian told the Senate, al Barzinji, not Alamoudi, was his client. "Dr. Jamal al Barzinji," he said, "should have been listed as the client retaining the firm for work related to Malaysian political prisoner Anwar Ibrahim." In fact, Barzinji had been listed as a contact, not a client, on all the prior disclosure forms. The matter remains unresolved.

Let's say, though, that al Barzinji was Janus-Merritt's client. That, too, is not really something to be proud of. Al Barzinji, unlike Alamoudi, is a free man. He is a Saudi, and he is the chairman and CEO of Mar-Jac Poultry, which, according to its Yahoo! Finance company profile, "slaughters and processes chickens for sale to foodservice businesses" and "processes 1.5 million pounds of poultry, making 250,000 fast-food products and 100,000 boneless products, per day."

Mar-Jac is located in Gainesville, Georgia, but al Barzinji lives in Herndon, Virginia, where he also serves as the director of the International Institute of Islamic Thought. He is the author of a book, *Working Principles for an Islamic Model in Mass Media Communication*, and he has appeared at numerous panels and conferences, including two at Virginia Tech's "Islam Awareness Week" in the spring of 2003, where he lectured on the "Islamization of Knowledge" and "Islam in America."

Last, but certainly not least, Dr. al Barzinji is a defendant in a massive, several-hundred-plaintiff civil suit against the planners and financial supporters of the September 11, 2001, attacks on the World Trade Center and Pentagon. The affidavit in that case, clocking in at 259 pages, alleges that al Barzinji was, among other things, an officer of the SAAR Foundation, a now-defunct Saudi-financed "charity" that allegedly "financially supports terrorism." The foundation was composed, the affidavit goes on, of "more than one hundred affiliated organizations registered or doing business at just one of SAAR's addresses in Herndon, Virginia." In 1998, SAAR reported $1.7 billion in revenues, the largest charitable take in history—most of which funds were subsequently diverted to Islamic fundamentalist organizations. "People associated with the SAAR Foundation and its network are also implicated in . . . the United States Embassy bombings in Kenya and Tanzania," the affidavit alleges.[35]

The affidavit further alleges that Mar-Jac Poultry and its holding company, Mar-Jac Investments, were subsidiaries of the SAAR Foundation. On March 20, 2002, the company's offices, along with the homes of al Barzinji and others, were raided by a federal task force investigating terrorist finances, Operation Greenquest. Al Barzinji was named in the warrant authorizing the search as an "officer or director" of the SAAR Foundation, "controlled by individuals who have shown support for terrorists or terrorist fronts."[36] Again, those involved deny any connection to terrorism.

One hastens to note that all the disclosure forms were filed appropriately. No wrongdoing can be traced back to the lobbyists, who are paid, after all, to put the best face possible on their client's case. And not even the best advocate knows everything about his client's background and beliefs.

When Abdurahman Alamoudi traveled to Austin, Texas, to have his photo taken with Governor Bush, he was not alone. Traveling alongside him was Dr. Sami Al Arian, a computer science professor at the University of South Florida. Also along for the ride was Agha Saeed, the founder of the American Muslim Alliance. Saeed attended several conferences put on by Al Arian's group, the Islamic Association for Palestine, which investigators suspect is linked to Hamas.[37] The association denies a Hamas link.

Al Arian, of course, was later indicted for his leadership of the American branch of the Palestinian Islamic Jihad. The indictment against Al Arian and his coconspirators runs 118 pages. It explains, in excruciating detail, how Al Arian assembled a network of Islamic Jihad operatives in the United States, how he wired money from the United States to bank accounts used by Islamic Jihad in the Middle East, and how he said, loudly and repeatedly, "Let us damn America" and all countries allied with America "until death," and sent fund-raising letters requesting "support to the jihad effort in Palestine so that operations such as these"—a February 1995 suicide attack in Israel that killed twenty-two innocents—"can continue."[38]

Yet, for a time in the late 1990s, Al Arian was known primarily because his brother, Mazen Al Najjar—a Palestinian who arrived in the United States in 1991—had been arrested in 1997 and held for several years on secret evidence. Al Arian began to speak out against the use of "secret evidence" in immigration and terrorism cases—more than a little self-interestedly, it would later turn out. He started the National Coalition to Protect Political Freedom. And he got to know Khaled Saffuri.

In April 2001, the National Coalition to Protect Political Freedom—identified the world over as a "far-left" group—gave Grover Norquist an award for his efforts to combat secret evidence. And in June 2001, a few months before radical Islamist terrorists flew planes into the World Trade Center and Pentagon, killing 3,000 people, Al Arian visited the White House.[39]

After September 11, Norquist, an avowed civil and economic libertarian, continued to oppose the use of secret evidence in terrorism trials. He also opposed the Patriot Act. He told *Salon* in 2002: "I don't think it's broke for the Bush people and the Republicans, but they need to refocus and speak to the [Muslim] community."[40] Al Arian reportedly visited Norquist's offices in July 2002. He cc'd Norquist on an e-mail he sent to the *Wall Street Journal* protesting an editorial that had pointed out his terrorist connections.[41] There is no evidence that Al Arian was a paying client of Norquist's, Saffuri's, the Islamic Institute's, or Janus-Merritt's.

On February 20, 2003, Sami Al Arian was arrested for conspiracy to commit acts of terrorism. The Justice Department had followed his activities for years, but had been unable to bring charges against Al Arian due to certain restrictions on the use of foreign intelligence in domestic criminal cases. The Patriot Act ended those restrictions. In December 2005, a Florida jury acquitted Sami Al Arian on conspiracy to murder people overseas, and deadlocked on three other charges. Shocked, the Justice Department considered moving for a retrial or just deporting him. But the underlying truth remained: By the end of his trial, even Al Arian's attorneys admitted that their client was an avowed member of the Palestinian Islamic Jihad.

While Norquist's firm represented Islamist advocates for human rights in Malaysia, Jack Abramoff worked for the government stomping on those rights. Among the documents released by the Senate Committee on Indian Affairs is an invoice from one of Abramoff's shells, the American International Center, dated June 15, 2001. The invoice is addressed to Dr. Fauziah Mohamed Taib, the Malaysian ambassador to the United States. It is a request for a $300,000 payment in return for "services" performed by Abramoff. The invoice instructs Dr. Taib to make his check payable to the American International Center. What "service" Abramoff performed for Dr. Taib is unknown.

Abramoff was also in business with Khaled Saffuri. On October 8, 2001, Abramoff's American International Center issued a $90,000 "subcontractors" check to Khaled "Saffyri." On January 3, 2002, the center issued another $45,000 check to "Saffyri" for "professional services."[42] Later Abramoff set up another shell, the Lexington Group, a lobbying firm that lasted from May to August 2002. Abramoff made Saffuri the group's president. But the group never registered any clients and its (now defunct) Web site never named the "major U.S. corporations" it represented.[43] Saffuri has since moved on, becoming a "government adviser" at the firm Collier Shannon Scott. Abramoff, of course, has had a different fate.

CHAPTER FIVE

THE HIT

JACK ABRAMOFF'S CORRUPT CASINO DEAL

*Gambling doesn't destroy people. People destroy people.
The gentleman or gentlewoman who decides to gamble makes
that decision of his own free will. It's a free-market industry,
and that appeals to conservatives.*
—MICHAEL SCANLON

THE NIGHT OF the murder, February 6, 2001, Gus Boulis had two meetings, one at 5 P.M., the other a few hours later. The first was in Hollywood Beach, where Boulis had a few business properties. He sat and talked with Joe LaBarca inside LaBarca's restaurant, Ruffy's Restaurant and Marina. LaBarca wanted a buyer; Boulis wanted to bulldoze the restaurant and use the land as a parking lot for a hotel he was hoping to build. Noncommittal, Boulis left Ruffy's, right along the water, and drove to Fort Lauderdale, to an office building he had purchased some time before. There he had his second meeting. It lasted a few hours.[1]

By the time that meeting was over, around 9:15 P.M., night had fallen, and Boulis was ready to go home. He said good-bye to his business associate, left the office, and walked outside to where his BMW was parked. He took out his keys, unlocked the door, and got behind the wheel. He pulled out of the lot and turned south, heading home. It was a cool night. There was a breeze off Lake Mabel, and Boulis rolled down his window.

A few blocks later, at the corner of Miami and Twentieth, a car pulled in front of Boulis, so he had to slow down, then stop. The car in front of Boulis didn't budge.

He waited. And as he waited, another car—a black Mustang in the oncoming, northbound traffic—pulled alongside him. The Mustang's driver had opened his window, too. Boulis turned to look at the driver, and made the grim discoveries that the man in the Mustang was pointing a gun at him and that raising his hand in front of him was not enough to stop three hollow-tip bullets—the man in the Mustang fired many more, forensic evidence shows— from burrowing deep into his chest.

Suddenly, the car in front of Boulis sped away. The black Mustang was gone into the night. Bleeding, in horrible pain, and barely conscious, Boulis pressed the accelerator, headed south a few blocks, turned a corner . . . and then, midblackout, lost control of his car—spinning across the median into oncoming traffic, and finally crashing into a tree next to a Burger King.

The first ambulances arrived in minutes. They took Boulis— who, the paramedics determined, was in cardiac arrest—to nearby Broward General Medical Center, where he died on an operating table. It was 10:20 P.M.

Boulis probably did not know when he was shot that those who allegedly plotted and executed his murder were on his company's payroll.

Jack Abramoff was traveling overseas when he first heard about Boulis's murder.[2] He and Boulis were never close, but for the past several months they had been partners in the casino cruise business. They, along with two other men, Adam Kidan and Ben Waldman, owned and operated the SunCruz Casino line out of Fort Lauderdale. The story of how they got to know one another, and what resulted from that meeting, illustrates the ways in which Abramoff manipulated power centers in Washington for his own financial gain.

It is an important story, because in the course of the narrative Abramoff transformed himself from a lobbyist into a criminal. It also foreshadows Abramoff's imminent dealings with the Indian tribes. Leading players in that Washington saga make cameo appearances. In both stories, the action unfolds against the backdrop of casino politics. And the moral of both is the same: the blinding allure of money; the black depths of human avarice and greed.

Konstantinos Boulis was born in Kavala, Greece, in 1949. His father was a fisherman and his family was poor. In 1968, the young Boulis joined the Merchant Marine. It was an escape route. Boulis jumped ship in Nova Scotia that year. He settled in Toronto, where he took a job as a dishwasher at a Mr. Submarine sandwich shop. Within five years, he had bought the shop and had become Mr. Submarine's CEO. Eventually, under Boulis's leadership, the chain grew to more than 200 stores. The sale of the company in the mid-1970s made Boulis a multimillionaire. He was twenty-five.[3]

In 1978, Boulis moved to Florida. At first he thought he was moving south to retire; but by 1983 he had put his fortune to work, buying another sandwich franchise, Miami Subs, and also buying property throughout South Florida, including apartment buildings and hotels and restaurants. (Boulis sold Miami Subs—which had grown to more than 150 franchises throughout the United States—to Nathan's fast-food company in 1998.)[4]

Then he got into the casino business. In 1994, Boulis bought a luxury yacht, turned its interior into a casino, and began to operate "cruises to nowhere" in which passengers would ride the refitted vessels into international waters where Florida state gambling prohibitions did not apply. There, out at sea, passengers would spend millions at poker and blackjack and slots. Boulis called his fleet of eleven ships the SunCruz Casino line. By the time he sold the company in 2000, SunCruz Casinos was earning tens of millions of dollars in annual profits and employed more than 1,000 people. The price: $4.2 million. That sum probably seemed like small change to Boulis, whose net worth then hovered around $40 million.

His was, needless to say, a success story, an example of the plasticity of American life. Boulis could reinvent himself at will, from Greek to Canadian to American, from restaurateur to Fort Lauderdale Donald Trump to casino impresario, rising from dishwasher to power broker in a few decades.

But there was a problem. Boulis was not a U.S. citizen. On August 3, 1998, he was indicted on charges of violating the U.S. shipping code, which forbids foreign nationals from owning American commercial vessels. Boulis had clashed with the authorities before. SunCruz boats had been raided by police, who charged that gambling had occurred in Florida waters. And community activists in Hollywood Beach, Florida—midway between Fort Lauderdale and Miami, where Boulis had a home—fought the basing of a SunCruz boat in their community. Boulis had won those battles.[5]

Not this time. It took more than a year to reach a settlement with the government, but Boulis was able to work out a deal in which he would pay a fine, sell his interest in SunCruz, and thereby escape a jail sentence. So that Boulis's selling position would remain uncompromised, the deal with the feds would be kept a secret. It was January 2000. Boulis needed a buyer.

He discussed possibilities with his attorney, Art Dimopoulos. Dimopoulos worked at Preston Gates, the megafirm in Washington, D.C. One day in the winter of 2000, Dimopoulos discussed his client's plight with the firm's star lobbyist, the vice president for government affairs, Jack Abramoff. Abramoff mentioned to Dimopoulos that he might know someone who would be interested in purchasing the casino line.[6]

That person was him. Abramoff had represented Indian gaming interests for some time; why not get in on both ends of the action? After all, casinos held a lot of profit for little work, and Abramoff had many contacts in the industry. Besides, his most recent venture, Potomac Outdoor Advertising, a small company that placed ads on Potomac River water taxis, had sunk like a rock. The casino line seemed much more promising.

But there was a catch. Preston Gates ethics rules prevented employees from entering into business deals with entities represented by the firm. SunCruz Casinos was such an entity. Abramoff's solution was not to tell his employer about the deal. Instead, he floated the idea to his partners on the water taxi venture, Adam Kidan and Ben Waldman. Both had known Abramoff since his days as national chairman of the College Republicans, and both were enthusiastic.

Abramoff got started. He went back to Dimopoulos and told him that Adam Kidan was interested in buying SunCruz. Dimopoulos and Kidan flew to Fort Lauderdale to meet with Boulis. Though he was not present at this initial meeting, it was always understood that Abramoff would be an equal partner with Kidan. Waldman's share would be minor.

The three began negotiations. They agreed on a price early on: $145 million. This was far more money than Abramoff and his friends could produce. They would have to seek outside financing. Meanwhile, Boulis began making demands of his own. He was behaving like a businessman, not a man under investigation by the U.S. Attorney's Office. At this, according to Susan Schmidt and James Grimaldi's reporting in the *Washington Post,* Abramoff and Kidan were annoyed. It became necessary for them to pressure Boulis, to show him that he had the weak hand.[7]

One day in March 2000, Michael Scanlon, who had moved on from his job in Tom DeLay's office to a job with Abramoff at Preston Gates, approached the office of Ohio congressman Bob Ney. Would Ney mind inserting some comments into the *Congressional Record*? Scanlon asked. Ney agreed. This is what Ney entered into the *Congressional Record* on March 30, 2000:

Mr. Speaker, you hear many arguments surrounding the gaming industry in America. Some have merit, some do not. Some criticism is deserved, some is not. Mr. Speaker, before I make my statement today I want to make it abundantly clear that while I am not an ardent proponent of the gaming industry nor an ardent foe of the gaming industry, I am an ardent foe of illegal activity in the gaming industry. Furthermore, I am an ardent supporter of consumer rights and consumer rights is exactly what I intend to discuss today.

At the heart of my comments today is how certain gaming companies treat their patrons and how they conduct business. I believe that the vast majority of casino owners play by the rules, treat their patrons fairly, and provide quality entertainment for individuals and families. I have talked with many of these businessmen over the years who have conducted themselves in such a professional manner. However, there are a few bad apples out there who don't play by the rules and that is just plain wrong.

One such example is the case of SunCruz Casinos based out of Florida. Florida authorities, particularly Attorney General Butterworth, have repeatedly reprimanded SunCruz Casinos and its owner Gus Boulis for taking illegal bets, not paying out their customers properly, and has had to take steps to prevent SunCruz from conducting operations all together. In fact, a few years ago the Broward County Sheriffs Office, under the supervision of Mr. Butterworth, raided SunCruz ships, seizing their equipment.

Mr. Speaker, how SunCruz Casinos and Gus Boulis conduct themselves with regard to Florida laws is very unnerving. But the consumer rights issue is even more disheartening. On December 1, 1998, the Broward County Sheriffs department announced that they had uncovered evidence that dealers on SunCruz ships were "cheating passengers by using incomplete decks of cards." This type of conduct gives the gaming industry a black eye and should not be tolerated.

Mr. Speaker, I want to repeat myself again. The vast majority of casino owners and operators are good honest people, but when an owner or operator stoops to this level to make a buck it hurts the public and it hurts the industry as a whole. I believe we can strike a balance here and our first step is to ensure that the average citizen is not hoodwinked by a dishonest casino operator.

There should be clear codes of conduct that are adhered to by every casino owner and operator. On the Ohio River we have gaming interests that run clean operations and provide quality entertainment. I don't want to see the actions of one bad apple in Florida or anywhere else to affect the business aspect of this industry or hurt any innocent casino patron in our country.

Mr. Speaker, I hope that steps will be taken by the industry, and in the case of lawbreakers by the appropriate authorities, to weed out the bad apples so that we can protect consumers across the country.

In early November 2005, I called Representative Ney's office to ask how these comments came to be, why an Ohio congressman felt it necessary to comment on a Florida casino, and what, exactly, Ney stood to gain from entering this speech into the record. Ney's staff declined to speak on the record. They referred me instead to past statements the congressman has made in which he regrets his association with Jack Abramoff and says he has been "duped." Ney's apologists—there aren't many—claim he was unaware that Abramoff had anything to do with SunCruz when Scanlon approached the congressman with the prefabricated speech. That it might be questionable for a congressman to enter into the record whatever a lobbyist hands him is a possibility left unmentioned. Congressmen do this all the time, I was told. It's perfectly ordinary.

The Ney speech was meant to demonstrate to Boulis both the seriousness with which Abramoff treated the purchase of SunCruz Casinos and the power of Abramoff's connections in Washington. It seems to have worked on both counts. In June 2000, Abramoff and Kidan—Waldman, it would seem, was more or less passive in the deal—approached Foothill Capital, a lending company based in California, to provide financing. Foothill, in turn, brought in Citadel Equity, another lender based in the Cayman Islands. The parties began to work on a financial arrangement that would allow Abramoff, Kidan, and Waldman to purchase SunCruz without getting into too much debt.

In the meantime, Abramoff continued to use his political connections to gain favor with his new targets, Boulis and Foothill Capital. Congressional records show that on June 9, 2000, six days after House Majority Whip Tom DeLay returned from a golf junket to Scotland with Abramoff, the whip's office sent an American flag that had flown atop the Capitol to Boulis. Less than a week later, on June 15, Abramoff, Kidan, DeLay's deputy chief of staff Tony Rudy, and Joan Wagner, Boulis's chief financial officer at SunCruz, flew on SunCruz's private jet from Fort Lauderdale to Pebble Beach, California, to watch the U.S. Open golf tournament. (Rudy never mentioned the trip in his congressional disclosure reports.)[8]

To obtain a loan, Abramoff and Kidan would have to meet a certain financial threshold. On June 20, Abramoff faxed a financial statement to Kidan, who by this time had moved to Florida. A month later, on July 25, Kidan sent his own financial statement to Foothill offices in California. According to the indictment later filed against Abramoff and Kidan, both statements were riddled with errors. Abramoff said that he was worth $13 million and provided a list of references including California Republican congressman Dana Rohrabacher. ("I don't remember it, but I would certainly have been happy to give [Abramoff] a good recommendation," Rohrabacher told the *Washington Post* in the spring of 2005. "He's a very honest man.")[9] Kidan said that he was worth $26 million. But Kidan specifically accounted for only about $874,000, and said the rest of his money was in "closely held corporations."[10]

Such errors seem to have been intentional. The indictment alleges that Abramoff and Kidan repeatedly misled representatives from Foothill Capital and Citadel Equity. The indictment specifically mentions an August 8, 2000, meeting in New York City at which Abramoff told the bankers that he was a partner at Preston Gates (he was not) and Kidan claimed to have had experience in running a casino (he had none).

But none of the moneylenders knew that. On September 18, there was another meeting in New York. There, Foothill Capital and Citadel Equity agreed to extend a $60 million loan if Abramoff and Kidan put up $23 million of their own money. Everyone seemed pleased by this arrangement. To celebrate, Abramoff, Kidan, and Foothill Capital vice president Greg C. Walker flew to Washington, where they watched the Redskins play the Dallas Cowboys from Abramoff's skybox at FedEx Field in Landover, Maryland. The sky-box that night had been reserved for Tom DeLay. Walker later told the *Washington Post* that he had met the majority whip at the game. DeLay's office says the congressman doesn't remember the encounter.[11]

Three days later, Abramoff and Kidan signed an Asset Purchase Agreement that outlined, in detail, how they would buy SunCruz for $147.5 million. Here, according to the agreement, is how the deal was supposed to have been structured:

> At the Closing, Buyer shall pay to Seller the amount of Buyer's financing plus Buyer's equity contribution in the sum of Twenty Three Million Dollars ($23,000,000), reduced by Buyer's closing and acquisition costs, by means of a cashier's check or wire transfer . . .[12]

Abramoff and Kidan then put their names to a Loan and Security Agreement containing similar language:

> agent [Foothill Capital] shall have received evidence satisfactory to it that Adam Kidan and Jack Abramoff have made an equity contribution to [SunCruz] in cash in an amount no less than $23,000,000 on terms and pursuant to documentation satisfactory to the lender group.[13]

This was the deal—before Abramoff, Kidan, and Boulis began to alter it.

On September 22, in secret, Abramoff and Kidan convinced Boulis to accept IOUs for $20 million in exchange for a 10 percent interest in the newly reorganized SunCruz Casinos. The deal was doubly illegal: Abramoff and Kidan were violating the terms of their purchase agreement with their financiers, and Boulis was violating the terms of his settlement with the government, which required that he separate himself entirely from his company.

They would have to move quickly to escape detection. According to the indictment, there was a flurry of activity on September 22. That day, Abramoff and Kidan put their names to an "Equity Contribution" document, which stated, "They have made a cash equity contribution to SunCruz Casinos LLC . . . in an aggregate amount of not less than $23,000,000." They sent a fax containing "closing documents" signed by Abramoff to their lenders' offices in New York. And they couriered the hard copies of these documents to their lenders' offices in New York. Finally, Kidan created two promissory notes, one for $5 million and another for $15 million, and sent them, via fax, to Boulis's representatives, who were also in New York.

On September 26, Kidan drew up another "closing statement" that read, in part, "CASH FROM BUYERS in the amount of $23,000,000 . . . has been received by the Sellers." Kidan then faxed this to New York City. It was only one part of an elaborate fraud. The next day, according to the indictment of Abramoff and Kidan, "the defendants" forged a document purporting to show evidence of a $23 million wire transfer from an account at Chevy Chase Savings Bank in suburban Maryland to Boulis's account at Ocean Bank in Miami Beach, and faxed that forgery to Foothill representatives in Boston. The forgery was titled, clumsily, "Funds Transfer Notification."

But no such transfer occurred. No such funds existed. Nothing had happened—nothing, that is, except the transmission of forgeries and two flimsy IOUs.

Upon receipt of the forged documents, Foothill Capital and Citadel Equity released a $60 million line of credit toward the purchase of SunCruz Casinos. Jack Abramoff was in the casino business.

It is hard to say how much involvement Abramoff had in the day-to-day operations of SunCruz Casinos. He remained in Washington while Kidan moved to Florida, and he and Kidan began to pay themselves salaries of $500,000 a year. With that money, Kidan bought a thirty-foot boat and a Mercedes S 500 and moved into a condo for which he paid $4,300 a month. SunCruz quickly hired Michael Scanlon as its "public affairs specialist" and spokesman, and the company began to pay for Abramoff's $230,000-a-year sky-box at FedEx Field. Kidan soon fired many of Boulis's hires, members of the Boulis family and the larger South Florida Greek community who depended on their benefactor's success. "We fired his friends, we fired his family, and he wasn't happy with it," Kidan would later tell the South Florida *Sun-Sentinel*.[14]

Boulis and Kidan did not get along. Boulis loudly voiced his opposition to his new partners' way of managing the business, and on October 24, 2000, he wrote a letter demanding that those partners pay him the $20 million they had promised. The letter was a flop. Boulis never saw any money.[15]

But he did see, a few days later, the following statement, which Rep. Bob Ney entered into the *Congressional Record* on October 26:

Mr. Speaker, a few months ago I felt it necessary to speak out against alleged abuses in the gaming industry. I did so not to express disapproval of the gaming industry as a whole but to express my frustration with those in the gaming industry who may unfairly take advantage of their patrons. My earlier statement was related to the previous actions of SunCruz Casino at the time and based on the findings of Florida Attorney General Robert Butterworth and several news reports.

I was concerned that some individuals who participate in gambling for entertainment and recreation can unwittingly fall prey to unethical practices by a few rogue casino owners. I said then and will repeat now that I am not anti-gaming, and I would not call myself pro-gaming either. I do, however, strongly believe in the concept that those who choose to gamble should be able to do so in the establishments of respected gaming interests who treat their customers and their communities fairly.

Given the Attorney General's findings and the record of Sun-Cruz under the previous owner, I did not believe that the casino was operating a fair and responsible establishment.

But things change:

Since my previous statement, I have come to learn that SunCruz
Casino now finds itself under new ownership and, more impor-
tantly, that its new owner has a renowned reputation for honesty
and integrity. The new owner, Mr. Adam Kidan, is most well
known for his successful enterprise, Dial-a-Mattress, but he is
also well known as a solid individual and a respected member of
his community.

While Mr. Kidan certainly has his hands full in his efforts to
clean up SunCruz's reputation, his track record as a businessman
and as a citizen leads me to believe that he will easily transform
SunCruz from a questionable enterprise to an upstanding establishment that the gaming community can be proud of.

Mr. Speaker, the purpose of my statement is not to criticize or
promote the gaming industry or to favor one casino owner over
another, but rather stand by the consumers who patronize casinos
as a form of entertainment. I believe that every individual who
visits a gaming vessel in Florida should know that they are gaming in an establishment that represents the community well, and
gives every individual a fair shot. I hope that all casino owners
and operators share in this philosophy. I look forward to the positive changes Mr. Kidan is more than capable of bringing to the
gaming industry and I hope that others will follow his lead when
he brings positive changes to SunCruz.

Once again Michael Scanlon had approached Representative
Ney's office with a statement that he wanted entered into the *Congressional Record*. And once again Ney had done exactly what
Scanlon asked him to do. And yet at no point did anyone think it
necessary to ask: Just who is Adam Kidan?

Kidan was born in 1964. He grew up in New York and went to
college at George Washington University in Washington, D.C. At
GW he joined the College Republicans, where he met Jack Abramoff.
The two became friends.

After graduation, Kidan returned to New York and began taking classes at Brooklyn Law School. He seems to have known exactly what he wanted to do in life: go to school, get good grades, work in politics, make a whole lot of money. He volunteered on George H. W. Bush's presidential campaign before getting his law degree in 1989, after which he took a job as president of the Four Freedoms Foundation, a New York City-based nonprofit, or "private sector initiative," meant to "assist Eastern Europe and other democratically emerging nations around the world." The foundation claimed to be an exercise in conservative benevolence. "Government cannot be expected to bear the financial burden of assisting countries that have chosen to adopt democratic principles," Kidan said in the February 14, 1990, press release announcing the venture. "The private sector must assume some responsibility if these countries are expected to compete in today's world market."

Kidan's association with the foundation was short-lived. In the early 1990s, he went into business for himself, starting a chain of bagel joints in ritzy neighborhoods on Long Island. Kidan's partner in the bagel business was Michael Cavallo, now deceased. In October 2005, NYPD officials told the *Miami Herald* that Cavallo was "an associate" of known gangsters. In all probability, one of them was Anthony Moscatiello, aka Big Tony, who began to frequent Kidan's bagel shops. "I had advice from him occasionally because he was in the food business," Kidan told lawyers for the Boulis estate in a 2001 deposition. Moscatiello owned a catering company, Gran-Sons Inc., in Queens.[16]

"This is someone I know who has experience in feeding large groups of people," Kidan has said of Moscatiello. In fact, some of these large groups of people were members of the Gambino crime family, including legendary mob boss John Gotti, who would often hire Big Tony to cater family weddings. Moscatiello has a relationship with the Gambinos going back at least two decades. On August 23, 1983, he was indicted on charges of heroin trafficking, along with several others, including Gotti's brother Gene. Gene went to jail. The charges against Moscatiello were dropped. In 1989, the

New York Times printed excerpts of a phone conversation between Moscatiello and Gotti recorded eight years earlier by the FBI:

> GOTTI: Listen, I called your [expletive deleted] house five times yesterday; now if your wife thinks you are a [expletive deleted] dunsky or if she's a [expletive deleted] dunsky and you're gonna disregard my [expletive deleted] phone calls, I'll blow you and that [expletive deleted] house up.
>
> MOSCATIELLO: I never disregard anything you . . .
>
> GOTTI: Well you call your [expletive deleted] wife up and you tell her, or I'll get in the [expletive deleted] car and I'll go over there and I'll [expletive deleted] tell her.
>
> MOSCATIELLO: All right.
>
> GOTTI: This is not a game. I'm not gonna have to reach for you for three days and nights here. My [expletive deleted] time is valuable.
>
> MOSCATIELLO: I know that.
>
> GOTTI: And you get your [expletive deleted] ass down here and see me tomorrow.

Moscatiello said he would be there tomorrow.

> GOTTI: Yeah, never mind you'll be there all day tomorrow. And don'ma, [*sic*] let me have to do this again, 'cause if I hear anybody else calls you and you respond within five days I'll [expletive deleted] kill you.[17]

It was a stormy friendship. But the two persevered. In 1991, Moscatiello was photographed accompanying Gotti into court.[18]

Kidan denies ever having known about Moscatiello's involvement in organized crime. Whether that is true or not, the mob is a recurring motif in Kidan's life. Consider his mother, Judy.

Remarried to one Samuel "Sami" Shemtov, she lived with her husband in a stately home on Staten Island. Shemtov was a businessman with interests in New York and Miami. He had fought in the Israeli Army. Although Judy didn't know it, a substantial part of his fortune was in pornography and sex shops, including a chain of stores called Sensations. ("It's very clean, very nice," Shemtov told the *Miami Herald* in 1995.)[19]

One night in February 1993, a Mercury sedan sat outside the Shemtovs' house, the engine running. The driver, Chris Paciello, aka "Binger," aka Christian Ludwigsen, was a low-level associate of the Bonanno crime family. A few weeks earlier, he had heard from a friend, Joe Eisenberg, who had heard from a former girl-friend, Carol—former wife of Sami Shemtov—that the pornographer kept thousands and perhaps hundreds of thousands of dollars in a safe in his house. Shemtov had not told his second wife about the safe, where he kept the money he had made in his sleaze shops.[20]

Paciello and a few of the boys from his crew wanted to break into the house and find the safe. But the job went horribly awry. While he waited outside, three of Paciello's associates stormed the house. In the chaos that followed, a member of Paciello's gang shot Kidan's mother in the face. She died on the spot. Her murder made the front page of New York's *Daily News*. The headline: "Death at the Door."

At her funeral at New York City's Temple Emanu-El, according to Michele McPhee's *Mob Over Miami,* Kidan delivered the eulogy:

> My sisters, our stepfather, and I are all completely emotionally distraught by all this. It's getting worse rather than better. It's bad enough losing someone close, but then to lose them in this way, and even worse, not to know why it happened. . . . If there was one aspect of my life that I always relied on to be there for me, it was my mother. She was very happy with Sami. She had a great marriage and great friends. She was never happier.[21]

Shemtov put up a $15,000 reward for information leading to the arrest of his wife's killers. But the killers remained free until 1999. By the time of his arrest, incidentally, Paciello had become semifamous for co-owning and operating a series of Miami Beach nightclubs with one-word names like Liquid and Joia. He had dated Madonna and MTV-veejay-turned-model Daisy Fuentes and was once seen with his hands on Jennifer Lopez's behind. He is now in prison.

Within a few months of Judy Shemtov's death, Kidan's bagel business had gone under. He looked for other opportunities. In 1992, he had started to do legal work for Dial-A-Mattress, the famous New York City company that rush-delivers bedding to people's homes. The company wanted to expand.

On February 14, 1994, less than a year before the Republicans took over Congress, Dial-A-Mattress announced the opening of its first Washington, D.C., franchise—Adam R. Kidan, proprietor. The press release marking the occasion is notable mainly for Kidan's use of exclamation points and lame puns. "I went to school at the George Washington University and always dreamed of coming back to D.C. to work. Now, I'm actually helping other people dream a little easier with a good night's sleep!" Kidan said. "We knew the D.C. area was a great choice. This was a decision we didn't have to sleep on!"

Kidan did his best to become a local celebrity. He cut his own radio advertisements, thirty-second-long exercises in commercial sadism in which Kidan would holler at potential customers and repeat, mantra-like, the Dial-A-Mattress slogan: "Leave off the last 'S'—that's for 'Savings'!" He made philanthropic contributions, donating $25,000 to southern Virginia charities. ("We like to help the shelters as often as we can," he told the Norfolk *Virginian-Pilot*. "We do this on a regular basis.") And he became a fixture of D.C. nightlife, attending, for example, the 1995 Bartender's Ball, a charity event noted mainly for its trashiness. A February 7, 1995, *Washington Times* article on the ball reported that Kidan had offered a "great" pickup line—"I can have a mattress here in two hours"— and then told a story about the Clintons: "The Clintons ordered a mattress and then didn't pay us for six months, but things are picking up with the new Congress. We sold 34 new Republican congressmen mattresses, and they all paid on time. Sonny Bono bought four!"[22]

Kidan liked this story so much that he told it to the *Washington Times*'s "Inside the Beltway" columnist John McCaslin two weeks later:

"A funny thing about the Clintons," [Kidan] disclosed. "The White House told us we could not use their purchasing a mattress from us for press purposes, and we agreed. But when six months went by and I didn't get paid I called the White House and said not only will I tell the press the Clintons bought our mattress, but that we didn't get paid. The next day I got a check."[23]

That this story was in all likelihood apocryphal was beside the point. It satisfied a dual need: Kidan's need for press, and the press's need for stories that made the Clintons look cheap. He reappeared in McCaslin's column on March 14, 1997, peddling another fiction:

Adam Kidan, the chairman and chief executive officer of Dial-A-Mattress, tells us that the queen-size Serta Perfect Sleeper his company sold to the White House in January 1993 for $549 is obviously holding up well for all the wear and tear.

"When the White House called our 800-number, they told us it was for the Lincoln Bedroom and Mr. Clinton's mom would be sleeping on it," Mr. Kidan reveals.

He quips: Dial-A-Mattress' slogan "has always been 'Leave off the last S, that's for savings,' but maybe it should be changed to 'Leave off the last S, that's for solicitations.'"

There was no Dial-A-Mattress franchise in Washington when the Clintons moved into the White House in 1993.

What may seem like a small error or a little white lie is in fact indicative of a broader truth: Kidan's public demeanor was increasingly at odds with private reality. Behind the press mentions and charity drives, behind the appointments to the Greater Washington Urban League and the D.C. Chamber of Commerce Political Action Committee, behind the radio commercials and the speeches to undergraduates at George Washington and the rose-tinted business projections, by the end of the nineties Kidan was mired in litigation and his business was at risk.

In 1995, Kidan had filed a twenty-nine-count lawsuit against the Dial-A-Mattress franchiser in New York. He lost. In 1995, he declared personal bankruptcy. In 1999, he was forced to sell his Dial-A-Mattress franchise, and his online mattress company, eMattress.com, collapsed. The same year, Sami Shemtov sued Kidan for stealing $250,000 from a business deal as well as the $15,000 Shemtov had put up as reward money after Judy Shemtov was murdered. Kidan was forced to repay him. In 2000, New York State had Kidan disbarred.

Kidan told people that he had founded Dial-A-Mattress. He had not. Kidan said that he had been a "principal" in, and "general counsel" to, the St. Maarten Hotel Beach Club and Casino. No such establishment exists. Kidan boasted that he was a "former partner" at the law firm "Duncan, Fish, Bergen & Kidan." I have found no evidence that there was ever such a firm. Kidan claimed that his friend Anthony Moscatiello was a graduate of the Culinary Institute of America. Moscatiello was not. Adam Kidan is a bold and unapologetic liar.

This is the man whom Rep. Bob Ney described as having a "renowned reputation for honesty and integrity."

It is unclear why Foothill Capital and Citadel Equity lent more than $60 million to, as the *Washington Post* put it, "someone such as Kidan." It has been reported that Foothill Capital performed a background check on Kidan that confirmed his many failed businesses, lawsuits, and bankruptcies. Why take such a chance? Perhaps Foothill Capital chose instead to focus on Kidan's partners, Abramoff and Waldman. In September 2000, Abramoff was at the height of his power in Washington. Earlier that year, he had been the subject of a celebratory front-page profile in the *Wall Street Journal*. Tom DeLay had described him as one of his "dearest friends." His lobbying clients brought his firm millions of dollars in revenue.

Waldman also must have seemed a sure bet. Like Kidan, he had met Abramoff through College Republicans, but unlike Kidan he went into government. He worked in the Reagan administration at the Department of Housing and Urban Development and in the West Wing as the head of the Office of Public Liaison. In the mid-eighties he ran some outside nonprofits—the Foundation for the Private Sector, the Reagan-Bush Jewish Coalition—and in the 1988 Republican presidential primaries he flacked for Pat Robertson. After Robertson's candidacy failed, Waldman moved to West Virginia. He ran twice—in 1992 and 1994—as the Republican candidate in that state's Third Congressional District. He lost both times, then went into the computer business. He had never worked in a casino. (One should pause here to note that as of early 2006, Waldman had not been implicated in any wrongdoing.)

In May 2005, Susan Schmidt and James Grimaldi of the *Washington Post* asked Greg Walker, the vice president of Foothill Capital, why he extended the loan to Abramoff, Kidan, and Waldman.

Walker replied, "You'd have to be there at the time."[24]

The SunCruz deal collapsed in the space of a few months. The company was fraught with infighting. By December 2000, Kidan and Boulis were no longer speaking. On December 5, Joan Wagner, Boulis's lieutenant, called a meeting. All the principals attended except Abramoff, who was traveling.

The meeting was a disaster. Witnesses later told police that Kidan began to scream, threatening and insulting Boulis and Wagner. Furious, Boulis assaulted Kidan. Someone called 911. Kidan filed a police report in which he accused Boulis of stabbing him in the neck with a pen.

That night, Wagner sent Abramoff an e-mail:

The crisis at suncruz took on new meaning today with gb [Gus Boulis] and ak [Adam Kidan] getting physical. Money is being wasted and lost and it shouldn't continue. . . . I'm telling you that you must address the issue asap. Your delay is only emboldening Adam and he is really on the edge.

At the end of her e-mail, Wagner suggested that Abramoff join Boulis and Ben Waldman to vote Kidan out of SunCruz.

Abramoff forwarded Wagner's e-mail to Kidan.

"We need to shut her down," Kidan replied. To which he added: "Jack, you need to act above all of this."[25]

Here we reach something of an impasse. While the Washington investigation into Abramoff and his dealings with Indian tribes has opened a gusher of material to the public—e-mails, documents, testimony, and so forth—the Florida criminal investigation has not. A few e-mails have been published here and there. Documents are hard to come by. Testimony so far is nonexistent. It is difficult to reconstruct events.

Here is what we know. After the December 5, 2000, meeting, Kidan and Abramoff exchanged a flurry of e-mails. Kidan suggested a "concerted press effort" targeted at Boulis. "I was the victim of family violence before," Kidan wrote. "Let's use that in our favor (my mother wouldn't mind) to show how we can't tolerate violence and the likes of criminals. Let's get the protective order. By painting the picture we box him. The negative is that his profile shows that he will retaliate against me."

Abramoff replied: "I agree with this completely."

Then Abramoff sent an e-mail to Boulis's attorney, Anthony Damianakis: "It is my belief that Gus and Adam need to resolve the issue of what Gus is owed and Gus needs to move on out of the company."

Kidan began to behave as though his life were in danger. He obtained the restraining order against Boulis that he had mentioned to Abramoff. He hired bodyguards. He purchased a $180,000 lease on an armor-plated Mercedes. And in his e-mails to Abramoff, Kidan began to refer to a "friend in NY," who he said was "acting out of concern for my safety." "By sending security I am afraid it will make things worse," Kidan wrote Abramoff, somewhat cryptically. "And I will ask him today to remove them. I appreciate his efforts, but the situation is at a critical point."

Meanwhile, Kidan's media strategy took shape. When he obtained the restraining order against Boulis in January 2001, Kidan made sure to contact Jeff Shields, a reporter at the *Sun-Sentinel* covering SunCruz. "This guy is violent—he's sleazy," Kidan said. Later, describing his December 5 fight with Boulis, Kidan would tell Shields, "If someone's going to jump across at me in a business meeting, that's when someone shows they're violent—they don't care. That's when what happened with my mother hits home with me."

Around this time, Kidan put Anthony Moscatiello—presumably his "friend in NY"—on the SunCruz payroll. In December 2000, he sent $20,000 in checks to Jennifer Moscatiello, Big Tony's daughter. Between December 13, 2000, and June 8, 2001, Kidan authorized $145,000 in checks to Anthony Moscatiello's daughter and his company, Gran-Sons Inc. Also in December 2000, Kidan sent $40,000 in checks to Moon Over Miami Beach, a mysterious company incorporated by one Anthony "Little Tony" Ferrari, who was known around town for bragging that he was John Gotti's "cousin." Ferrari had been arrested several times, pleaded guilty several times, and been put on probation. The most recent arrest was in 1999, when Ferrari was accused of attacking a lawyer who had brought suit against his business partners, Frank J. and Thomas L. Pepper. Ferrari and his associates had been forced to pay $20,000 in damages. Between December 7, 2000, and March 29, 2001, Kidan authorized $95,000 in checks to Moon Over Miami Beach, not including the $10,000 in free poker chips Kidan provided Thomas Pepper and three associates on July 5, 2001.[26]

In 2001, asked about the checks to Moscatiello, Kidan said they were for catering and "food and beverage" services that Moscatiello had provided. There is no evidence any such services were provided. Asked about the checks to Anthony Ferrari in 2001, Kidan said they were for security operations. There is no evidence that Kidan's life was ever in danger.[27]

Why did Adam Kidan pay more than $200,000 to known mobsters?

In February 2001, when Boulis was murdered, a small brigade of government agents and outside litigators were already peeking inside SunCruz's complicated financial structure. About two weeks before the murder, on January 19, a Florida judge had held Boulis in contempt of court for not extricating himself fully from Sun-Cruz Casinos. Also, Boulis was scheduled to testify about his finances in divorce court two days after he died—which testimony would almost certainly have involved detailed answers to questions about Boulis's stake in SunCruz and about the circumstances surrounding the sale to Abramoff and Kidan. The day Boulis was killed, several lawsuits were filed in Florida courts involving him and Adam Kidan: In one, Kidan accused Boulis of stealing slot machines; in another, one of Boulis's former business partners accused him of dissembling; in another, Boulis accused Kidan of stealing his money and driving SunCruz toward bankruptcy; and in another, Kidan accused Boulis of conspiring to kill him.

Boulis's death did nothing to slow SunCruz's unraveling. Lawsuits continued to multiply, with the Boulis estate first suing Kidan for ownership of SunCruz, then suing him for conspiring to kill Boulis. On June 22, 2001, SunCruz filed for bankruptcy. Abramoff and Waldman signed over their stake to the Boulis estate, making Boulis's heirs the majority shareholders. Kidan was left with 20 percent. But not for long. On July 9, Kidan cut a deal in which he would give up his stake in exchange for $200,000 and an end to the civil suit against him. Almost as quickly as they had entered the casino industry, Abramoff and Kidan made their exit.[28]

By 2002, the investigation into the murder of Gus Boulis had stalled. "Boulis Slaying Investigation Loses Impetus," read the front-page headline in the *Sun-Sentinel*. The problem was that police had not been able to secure the cooperation of key witnesses. Moscatiello and Ferrari refused to talk to the authorities. Kidan answered questions, but Fort Lauderdale police told the *Sun-Sentinel* that they felt he had not been "totally candid with us." The police had also scheduled several appointments to talk to Jack Abramoff. He broke each one.[29]

CHAPTER SIX

THE TRIBES

THE TRIUMPH OF
K STREET CONSERVATISM

I want all their MONEY!!!
—MICHAEL SCANLON

Do views flow to money? Or does money flow to views? That depends on whom you ask. With Jack Abramoff and other K Street Conservatives, it is always hard to tell.

In 1988, the Democratic Congress passed, and the Republican president signed, the Indian Gaming Regulatory Act, a little-noticed bill that said tribes could build casinos on tribal land if they received prior approval from their state. Few people noticed. According to the Lexis-Nexis research database, there were only four news mentions of the bill in the year it was passed. The next year, there were only eighteen.

The Indian Gaming Regulatory Act was a back door into legalized gambling across the United States. Recall that the tribes are sovereign entities; whatever vice happens on an Indian reservation is happening in what is more or less a foreign country. Tribal casinos began to spring up across the country.

This had two consequences. One was that tribal governments suddenly were awash in cash—your average Indian casino brings in up to $30 million a month. The other was that the tribes were now even more dependent on lawmakers and regulators in Washington to keep the floodgates open. For years, tribal governments had been the caretakers of small, poor, out-of-the-way communities of American Indians. Now they were the caretakers of hundreds of millions of dollars in profits. They were important actors in Washington. And like all important actors, they needed representation. They needed lobbyists. They needed someone to navigate the corridors of power and secure deals to the tribe's advantage. They got Jack Abramoff.

In 1995, when Abramoff returned to Washington after his adventures in Hollywood, one of his first clients was the Mississippi Band of Choctaw Indians, a small tribe (about 8,000 people) scattered in reservations throughout the state. The tribe's chief, Philip Martin, who had first been elected in the 1960s, had worked for decades to enrich his people. Casino gambling was his latest method, and it was a cure-all. Unemployment vanished; personal income soared. This is unsurprising. Casinos are an extremely easy way to make gobs of money.

The Choctaw opened their Silver Star Hotel and Casino in 1994. The following year, eyeing the profits of casinos like the Silver Star, Republicans on the House Ways and Means Committee floated a plan to tax tribal incomes. The Choctaw's "legislative liaison," Nell Rogers, negotiated a lucrative contract with Abramoff, who was able to quash the plan. "What followed was a very positive relationship with Preston Gates," Rogers told the Senate Indian Affairs Committee in June 2005. "They did very effective work for the tribe, both at the federal level and through various grassroots projects."[1]

Rogers and the Choctaw had reason to be happy with Abramoff's work. He applied the teachings of K Street Conservatism to casino gambling. The tribes, Abramoff would tell the *Washington Post*, "are engaged in the same ideological and philosophical efforts that conservatives are—basically saying, 'Look, we want to be left alone.'" This, of course, was an echo of Grover Norquist's "leave us alone" version of conservatism, and reminiscent of the arguments put forth on behalf of the Commonwealth of the Northern Mariana Islands. Norquist, one should further note, was an early and eager champion of the Choctaw's cause.[2]

The first tenet of K Street Conservatism is that a client's financial interests are actually ideological interests. So an effort to tax tribal casino income—just as casino income in Vegas is taxed—is really an effort to squelch entrepreneurship and constrain the dynamism of a free-market economy. Just as he had done with the Mariana Islands and other clients, Abramoff enlisted conservative writers and ideologues in his clients' various causes. Within a year of the Choctaw's hiring of Abramoff, op-eds championing "tribal sovereignty" began to appear in the pages of conservative journals and newspapers. "American Indians are beginning to throw off the shackles of government dependency and revive economically," Peter Ferrara wrote in the *Washington Times* on August 1, 1996.

Territories controlled by the Mississippi Choctaw, Ferrara went on, amounted to vast, unregulated "free-enterprise zones"—a phrase that acts like catnip on conservatives, who use it to describe an Elysian paradise of busy workers, untrammeled CEOs, and incredibly high profit margins. Ferrara's essay took issue with a provision in a House bill that would have limited a tribe's ability to buy new land. "Cutting back on the effective enterprise-zone policy for Indians rather than correcting mistakes through established Interior Department authority would be incredibly shortsighted," Ferrara concluded. What Ferrara left out was that the Choctaw were, at Abramoff's behest, regular contributors to his employer, Americans for Tax Reform.[3]

Ferrara was the most vocal of the conservative gaming advocates—he testified before Congress on the Choctaw's behalf ("the Choctaw reservation, like other Indian reservations, is effectively an enterprise zone"), and eventually wrote an entire book, titled *The Choctaw Revolution*, arguing that Indian casinos had allowed the Mississippi tribe to establish a libertarian utopia.[4] But the tribe had other advocates as well. There was, for example, the libertarian writer Doug Bandow, who had also written articles supporting Abramoff's clients in the Marianas. Here is Bandow in—no surprises here—the *Washington Times:*

> For a century American Indians have been victimized by the welfare strategy of development. Dependent on federal largesse, they have languished in poverty. Given the druthers of the Bureau of Indian Affairs, which makes the same request as always—"more money"—this would never change.
>
> But tribes like the Mississippi Choctaws . . . are taking the entrepreneurial path of development. Gaming is an important part of this strategy.
>
> Thus, after a century of mistreating Native Americans, Uncle Sam should apply the overriding rule of government: First do no harm. Whether through new taxes or measures growing out of the National Gambling Impact Study Commission, Washington should keep its hands off what has proven to be a good thing.[5]

Nowhere in this column, which carried the dateline "Philadelphia, Mississippi"—the town where the Choctaw had their casino— did Bandow mention that he had gained his firsthand knowledge of the Choctaw on a junket sponsored by Jack Abramoff. Nowhere did he mention that Abramoff had paid him directly to write his article. Abramoff had also paid Ferrara a couple thousand dollars for each article favorable to his client.[6]

On September 16, 1998, Americans for Tax Reform presented Chief Martin with its "Hero of the Taxpayer Award." In a column published in that day's *Washington Times,* Norquist explained why Martin deserved the prize:

> He has shown the way for American Indians and tribes across this nation to climb out of government dependency and join in the mainstream American economy.
>
> He has shown that the Enterprise Zone model of economic

development, with greatly reduced tax and regulatory burdens and local control, can work incredibly well in the most difficult of circumstances.

He has been a leader and innovator in contracting out services and programs from the Bureau of Indian Affairs and Indian Health Service, so that now virtually all Federal Indian programs and services for the Mississippi Choctaw are run by the tribe rather than the federal government. He has consequently shown how the federal role in Indian affairs can be greatly diminished and the role of tribes in running their own affairs greatly increased.

Most important:

Even though the tribe is effectively the state and local government for the Mississippi Choctaws and provides all state and local services, Chief Martin runs it and has accomplished all of the above to boot with virtually no tribal taxes.

It should be mentioned that, between 1995 and 2002, the Mississippi Choctaw donated about $1.5 million to Americans for Tax Reform.[7]

The second tenet of K Street Conservatism is that politics is not a battle of ideas and interests but an abstruse science involving the manipulation of "grassroots" voters to achieve one's desired ends.

Enter Ralph Reed.

In 1997, Reed had resigned from the Christian Coalition and opened a consulting firm, Century Strategies. But Reed needed clients. On November 12, 1998, shortly after the Republicans lost five House seats and failed to make any gains in the Senate, Reed sent Abramoff an e-mail. "Hey," he began, "now that I'm done with electoral politics, I need to start humping corporate accounts! I'm counting on you to help me with some contacts." Reed was in luck. Abramoff had assembled a vast Rolodex of clients and contacts that he could pass on to his former comrade.[8]

According to its Web site, www.censtrat.com, Century Strategies is "a full-service firm providing Strategic Business Development Assistance, Organizational Development, Direct Mail and Voter Contact Services, Fundraising Management, Research and Analysis, Creative Media Planning, Public and Media Relations, and List Management and Procurement." The firm has two offices—one in Atlanta and another in Washington; as of mid-2005 it had ten employees, and, according to a spokeswoman, it has "around" two dozen clients. As "one of the nation's leading public affairs and public relations firms"—that is, not a lobbying firm—Century Strategies does not have to disclose its clients or its fees. But the names of some of those clients have surfaced over the years.

Enron, for example. The energy trading company was one of Century Strategies' first clients, in fact—it signed its first contract with Reed, for $114,000 plus expenses over twelve months, in September 1997. Century Strategies helped Enron push an energy deregulation plan through the Pennsylvania state legislature. Enron chose not to renew the contract in 1998. A few years later, on October 6, 2000, Enron signed another contract with Reed, this one for $75,000 plus expenses for six months.[9]

In October 2000, Reed wrote a memo to Enron executives that gives us some clues to what a firm like his does. The memo first surfaced in the *Washington Post* in 2002. "In public policy it matters less who has the best arguments and more who gets heard—and by whom," Reed wrote. He promised his firm would make calls, collect voter lists, and place op-eds in influential newspapers—the sort of work any top-shelf lobbying firm performs on a daily basis. "I will assume personal responsibility for the overall vision and strategy of the project. I have long-term friendships with many members of Congress." Enron must have been pleased with Reed's work, because when the October 2000 contract expired, it signed Century Strategies to another, indefinite contract for $30,000 plus expenses per month. This arrangement lasted just a few months, however. Then Enron went bankrupt.[10]

Enron wasn't Reed's only client, and Reed wasn't Enron's only "public affairs specialist." One of the unwritten rules of K Street is that hiring only one firm isn't enough to pass your agenda. You have to employ several firms, donate to as many pols as possible, spread your money around to as many people as you can—provided they are the right people. And since 1994, the right people have been the Right people: Republicans. So Enron employed registered lobbyists, it donated to nonprofits allied with politicians and political causes, it gave money to political action committees, and it contracted firms such as Century Strategies to gin up "grassroots support" for utility deregulation. In its brief but dizzying existence, Enron was an exemplar of the ways in which corporations pay lobbyists and legislators to manipulate public life for private gain.

The private gain in question does not have to be financial. And it doesn't even have to be a corporation doing the paying. A few months after he started to work with Enron, Reed visited San Juan, Puerto Rico, where he gave a speech on Puerto Rican statehood. Reed was for it. "Let's let Puerto Ricans freely express their status preference," Reed told the audience at the local Chamber of Commerce on February 9, 1998, "and if they choose, let's welcome them as the fifty-first state." Puerto Rican statehood would benefit Republicans: "We must demonstrate that our party is the natural home for millions of Americans of Hispanic heritage and the true representative of their ideals and values." A referendum would be to the benefit of self-government: "I think it is right to allow the people of Puerto Rico a voice and a vote on their future."[11]

Reed's timing was auspicious. On March 5, 1998, a few weeks after he became an advocate of Puerto Rican statehood, the House passed—by a single vote—HR 856, the Puerto Rico Self-Determination Act, which established a timetable and referendum process by which Puerto Rico could become a state. According to the Associated Press, two days before the vote, Reed issued a "report" that said "winning the Hispanic vote would be critical to maintaining congressional majorities," and that supporting Puerto Rican statehood was the key to winning the Hispanic vote.[12]

At first blush, the Puerto Rico bill, cosponsored by then-Speaker of the House Newt Gingrich and then-Majority Whip Tom DeLay, came out of nowhere. In fact, it was the result of months of intense lobbying, of which Reed's advocacy was only a part. According to *Roll Call*, lobbying firms employed by pro-statehood interests had been paid over $2.3 million in the first half of 1997. One such firm was Preston Gates, where Jack Abramoff registered as a representative for the Future of Puerto Rico Inc., in November 1997.[13]

Because of the loophole in disclosure law, one can only infer that Century Strategies had taken on a pro-statehood interest as a client. It would make sense, given Reed's outspoken support for HR 856. And it would make sense, further, given that Reed's old friends Jack Abramoff and Grover Norquist shared his outspoken support. On March 2, 1998, Peter Ferrara published an op-ed in the *Washington Times* in support of HR 856, which, he wrote, "simply requires us to face the Puerto Rico commonwealth anomaly and resolve it." Also, "it would free U.S. taxpayers from a growing $12 billion per year subsidy bill." (It's worth noting here that support for Puerto Rican statehood has been a long-standing GOP position.)

The Puerto Rico bill passed the House, but it ended up dying in the Senate—besides which, Puerto Rican voters rejected statehood in a December 1998 referendum, making the whole exercise moot. But a host of flacks grew fat off the bill nonetheless.

More significant, however, HR 856 exposed a growing rift between Reed and other social conservatives, who were often at odds with Century Strategies' corporate clients. Phyllis Schlafly, for example, opposed Puerto Rican statehood and cheered the bill's death in the Senate: "It looks as if it's a lot easier for big political money to buy Congress than it is to win the hearts of grassroots voters," she wrote in a January 1999 column.[14]

The rift grew wider in 1999, when Reed took the Channel One television network as a client. Located in Los Angeles, Channel One is a for-profit television station that supplies schools with free audiovisual equipment, provided those schools broadcast the network's twelve-minute news broadcast, which includes two minutes of commercials. Each day, about 8 million students in 12,000 secondary schools watch the broadcast. And it's a captive audience. Channel One allegedly promises its advertisers, who typically pay $200,000 for a thirty-second spot, that students are not allowed to leave their seats—even to go to the bathroom—when the ads are on-screen.[15]

Over the years, Channel One drew criticism from lefty anticorporate types who thought the network was a scam by profit-hungry advertisers to reach gullible, splurge-happy kids. But it also drew criticism from social conservatives, who complained that the network exposed impressionable young people to sex, drugs, and rock 'n' roll. Kids are forced to watch advertising for junk food and Nike sneakers, went the thinking on the left. And kids are forced to watch interviews with Joycelyn Elders and listen to music clips from Marilyn Manson, went the thinking on the right. Eyeing an opportunity for political triangulation, in April 1998, Alabama's Richard Shelby, who sat on the Senate Health, Education, Labor, and Pensions Committee, called for hearings into the network.

But the hearings were delayed, primarily because Channel One launched an expansive and expensive lobbying campaign to protect its interests. The progressive journalist Ruth Conniff estimates that by the time the actual hearings occurred on May 20, 1999, the network had spent more than $1 million in lobbying fees.[16] In 1998, for example, Channel One paid its lobbying firm, Preston Gates—Jack Abramoff handled the account—$120,000, according to Senate disclosure reports. In the first half of 1999, Channel One paid Preston Gates $820,000. In 2000, Channel One paid Preston Gates $380,000. Grover Norquist got into the mix, too, writing a *Washington Times* op-ed on January 30, 1999: "An independent news media outlet not controlled by liberals has seeped into the public schools," he wrote. "The liberals are trying to stop it."

But liberals were not the only people concerned about Channel One. So were social conservatives like Phyllis Schlafly and James Dobson. Schlafly even appeared before Shelby's committee alongside Ralph Nader. In the end, however, the Senate hearings never amounted to much. Channel One still broadcasts. It still shows advertisements for junk food, and it still plays clips of Britney Spears. And all indications are that it still pays Century Strategies consulting fees. As recently as September 2002, Reed was making calls on behalf of Channel One to members of the Texas State Board of Education.[17] How much those calls cost Channel One isn't known. Reed won't disclose it.

There were further rifts between Reed and the Religious Right. Social conservatives have a long and noble history of opposing Communist China's persecution of religious minorities. And Ralph Reed is a part of that history. Back in 1997, Reed went on the record with several reporters to share with them his concerns about granting China most-favored-nation trading status. "This can't just be about profits and losses and dollars and cents," he said. "It has to be about matters of the heart and matters of the soul and America being a moral leader in the world."[18] According to a Knight Ridder dispatch from May 15, 1997, Reed was "particularly concerned" about China's one-child, forced-abortion policy and its "intolerance of Christianity."

Today, it is difficult to get Reed to go on the record, which is unfortunate. Because it would be nice to have the opportunity to ask him about reporting done by *National Journal*'s Peter Stone. Stone has reported in *Mother Jones* that, in 2000, Boeing and the Business Roundtable hired Reed and Century Strategies to press for normalizing trade relations with China. According to Stone, Reed "helped write ads aimed at conservatives arguing that a closer economic relationship with China could improve human rights." In fact, a public relations executive, Brian Lunde, told Stone that Reed was "instrumental" in pushing through "permanent normal trade relations" with China in the spring of 2000.[19] "Reed was horrible on China," one Republican foreign policy analyst told me in June 2005.

Ralph Reed's principles appear to be no match for his profit margins.

Reed and his employees at Century Strategies are experts at fomenting anger among Christian conservatives, deploying direct-mail campaigns, phone calls, and television and radio advertising—including voice-overs from such prominent social conservatives as Pat Robertson and James Dobson—to further their clients' goals. Here, for example, is a typical "robocall":

Hello, My name is John and I am calling from Citizens Against Gambling. We urgently need your help to stop the spread of gambling in Michigan. Right now, some politicians in Lansing are trying to pass a law that would allow slot machines at horse tracks. This is an outrage! Would you be willing to call [Name] office to tell him/her to stop the gambling? If no, disconnect. If yes, we can connect you at no charge. When they pick up, tell them that ENOUGH IS ENOUGH; vote no on slots at horse tracks.[20]

The client in this case was the Chippewa tribe of Saginaw, Michigan. The "SagChip," as they are often called in e-mails between Abramoff and others, were afraid that legalized slot machines would cut into their profits. They paid Abramoff, who paid Reed's firm, who used the money to help block the legislation. It's easy to see that the cash going to Reed ultimately originated from the Chippewa. But Reed, above all things, is extremely careful with his reputation, and to this day he says he never took money from Indian casinos. In 2005, a Century Strategies spokesman sent the following statement to me about her company's involvement with Abramoff:

Ralph Reed and Century Strategies have long been opposed to the expansion of casino gambling. Century Strategies was approached about assisting with a broad-based coalition opposed to casino gambling expansion, and we were happy to do so. Our firm recruited coalition partners, raised funds, and mobilized grassroots citizens. Our work was legitimate, lawful, and effective. We helped to close illegal casinos that violated federal and state law. Greenberg Traurig also raised funds and recruited coalition members. Although we were aware that Greenberg had tribal clients, we had no direct knowledge of their clients or interests. At no time were we retained by nor did we represent any casino company.

All of the above is true—technically, and up to a point. Yes, Century Strategies was never "retained by," never "represented" a "casino company." Century Strategies was retained by people who were retained by a "casino company." But that is only the beginning. As we shall see, the statement is woefully incomplete.

E-mails released as part of a Senate Indian Affairs Committee investigation into lobbying practices show that Reed knew exactly where the money was coming from. Consider an April 6, 1999, e-mail exchange between Abramoff and Reed. "It would be really helpful if you could get me invoices as soon as possible," Abramoff wrote, "so I can get Choctaw to get us checks asap." Reed then sent the figures—more than $100,000 spent on phone banks, mailings, and radio ads.

It wasn't enough. "Jack," Reed wrote Abramoff on April 21, 1999,

I sent you an invoice yesterday for $122,000 that covers voter contact, television and radio production, the remainder of phones, the statewide fly-around, the pastors' and activist rally, the church bulletin inserts, and other items from the last phase of this project. We have already paid most of this to vendors out of our own pocket to keep our credit good and insure prompt service, so we need that check ASAP.

You will be receiving an invoice tonight for $250,000 to $300,000 that includes the second phase of the project, including phones (which are already turned on), a week-long television buy that begins Friday (in the first phase we were only on TV for 2 days), and a saturation statewide radio buy with a new ad by Jim Dobson that he will record tomorrow.

Abramoff said the money was on its way.

And soon enough it arrived. "All systems are go on our end," Reed wrote once he had the checks, "and nothing is being held back."

"Yeaaaa baaabbyy!!!" Abramoff replied.

In 2000, Abramoff had another gambling client, an Internet start-up called eLottery.com. This company was concerned about the Internet Gaming Prohibition Act, which, as its name suggests, would have outlawed online gambling—thus putting eLottery out of business. Once more, Abramoff enlisted Reed to gin up opposition to the bill—basically by misrepresenting the impact of the legislation—among Christian conservatives. On August 18 of that year, Abramoff faxed an eLottery executive. "I have chatted with Ralph," he wrote, "and we need to get the funding moving on the effort in the 10 congressional districts" supporting prohibition. "Please get me a check as soon as possible for $150,000 made payable to American Marketing Inc. This is the company Ralph is using." The check was issued August 24.[21]

On August 29, Abramoff sent Reed an e-mail with the subject line "Internet Gambling: And so it continues."

"Where are we?" Abramoff asked his old friend. "You got the check, no? Are things moving?"

Reed replied: "1. Yes, they got it. 2. Yes, all systems go."

Throughout it all, Reed took great pains to make sure that he never *directly* received money from gambling interests. If that were to happen, it would pose a problem to his future political ambitions, as he is on record saying that gambling is a "cancer" on the body politic and that he has been "opposed to gambling throughout my entire career." So he and Abramoff found ways around direct payments. In early 2000, for example, Reed was helping Abramoff with some work for the Mississippi Choctaw. On January 27 that year, he sent Abramoff a "program" including mailings, radio and television buys, renting of voter lists (names and addresses of potential supporters), phone lists, and "legislative counsel." The total: $867,511.

Once he read over the program, Abramoff sent Reed an e-mail of his own. "OK, thanks," he wrote. "Please get me the groups we are using, since I want to give this to her"—Choctaw contact Nell Rogers—"all at once."

Reed will not speak on the record about the e-mails released by the Senate Indian Affairs Committee, except to say that he committed no wrongdoing. But one can easily see that "the groups we are using" were the tax-deductible nonprofits that would take money from Abramoff's clients, then pass that money on to Reed. In this case, the "groups we are using" were, as Reed wrote to Abramoff, "Amy, Grover, Lapin, and one other I will get to you"—Amy Ridenour's National Center for Public Policy Research, Grover Norquist's Americans for Tax Reform, and Daniel Lapin's Toward Tradition. But it was soon clear that there was a problem. The tax code made it difficult for the money to travel through Ridenour and Lapin's groups. "Let me know if it will work just to do this through ATR until we can find another group," Abramoff wrote Reed on February 2, 2000. "Yes, it will," Reed replied.

In exchange for behaving as vessels, often the nonprofits would take a small portion of the funds being transferred. On February 22, 2000, Abramoff wrote, in astonishment: "Grover kept another $25K!" This bothered him to no end. When one of Abramoff's associates asked him, on March 3, 2000, "Once ATR gets their check, should the entire $300K be sent to the Alabama Christian Coalition again?" Abramoff replied, "Yes, but last time they sent $275K, so I want to make sure that, before we send it to ATR I speak with Grover to confirm." (Norquist has told reporters that the documents released by the McCain committee are flawed, unreliable, and inaccurate.)

Reed was often impatient. He wanted his money, and he wanted it now. Here's an e-mail he sent Abramoff on March 15, 2001: "We don't have the wire yet and we're spending $ at a pretty high burn rate." (Abramoff: "We'll have it tomorrow.") And here's another, which he sent Abramoff on February 6, 2002: "Wanted to just let you know," he wrote, that "we've not received the payment for [redacted] yet. We've burned through more than half of that already in out-sourced vending with phones, mail, radio, so we appreciate if you could expedite."

The money was going to combat a bill that would have taken

business from the Choctaw. Abramoff forwarded the e-mail to his partner, Michael Scanlon, with the message "Can you get him the $50K for MS now?"

"We still haven't been paid for ms," Scanlon wrote back. "I can cover both out of louisiana money if you want"—this was a reference to another Indian client, the Louisiana Coushatta tribe—"[but] the ms money won't be here till next week."

"Shoot!" Abramoff replied. "Should I call Nell on this? We need to get some $ from those monkeys!! As to Ralph, go ahead and pay him so I can get him off my back. We'll get the Choctaw money soon enough."

It wasn't the first, or the last, time Abramoff called his clients "monkeys." And it wasn't the first, or the last, time he moved money around to pay Reed. Abramoff often groused about his longtime friend, but there was little question that Century Strategies did its job. Reed's connections with the social conservative elite ran so deep that he could easily rally powerful forces to Abramoff's side. Consider this March 21, 2001, fax from Reed to Pat Robertson: "Pat, attached is a memo and a phone script on a riverboat casino bill we are helping the pro-family forces fight in Louisiana. Jerry Falwell has done a message to 55,000 households, and we would love to have a message from you. You may recall we did this in VA and defeated the riverboats. Thanks, friend. I appreciate your leadership for our values so very much."

Robertson, almost certainly unaware of where the funding for the antigambling crusade had originated from, complied. And the riverboat casino bill—which would have cut into the profits of the Louisiana Coushatta—sank. "We have won," Reed wrote to Abramoff on March 22. "The barges are dead and the N. Louisiana boats have their taxes increased."

Abramoff replied: "You are the greatest!!" (Tax hikes, it would seem, are not, you know, *always* bad.)

Scanning the Reed-Abramoff correspondence, one notices that the two men continued to exhibit the same flair for the dramatic that they had honed in the early eighties. In his e-mails to Abramoff,

Reed would often use the word "operative" and give the impression that his "operatives" were spread throughout the South, meeting with lawmakers and gathering intelligence that could be deployed to further the cause—whatever cause happened to be paying five to six figures. "One of our operatives attends the same church with the Vice-Chair of the [Texas legislature] Calendars committee, state Representative Barry Telford," Reed wrote on April 6, 2001.

> He called the pastor's wife yesterday and she said that her husband happened to be in Austin that day on other business, and she gave him his cell phone number. Our operative then called the pastor yesterday and got him on his cell phone and got him to drop by the Vice-Chair's office at the state capitol and urge him to vote against the casino bill. This happened just hours before the Calendar Committee met to consider the casino bill.

Abramoff forwarded the e-mail to his Coushatta contact, Kathryn Van Hoof. At the top of the message, he wrote: "Don't you love this guy!"

It was a rhetorical question. Flush with cash, Abramoff generously rewarded his friends, Reed most prominent among them. There was the $4.2 million that Abramoff directed to Century Strategies between 1999 and 2002. But there were also the political contributions Abramoff sent to Reed, who in early 2001 ran for chairman of the Georgia State GOP. (Reed won.) The exchange between the two on this topic is revealing. On April 11, 2001, Reed wrote, "Jack, would you be willing to contribute personally to my state chair campaign? This race is costing me $50–100K, and I'm asking my friends to help."

"Sure," Abramoff wrote. "Give me the name of the entity."

"The actual committee is 'The Reed Family Retirement and Educational Foundation,'" Reed wrote.

"Ha ha ha," Abramoff replied.

The next day, Abramoff sent an e-mail to one of his lieutenants. "When you give Scanlon the $150K from Choctaw," he wrote, "tell him that part of the '$30k' is to be a $10K check to this committee, which should then be federal expressed by you." "This committee" was Ralph Reed's. Anything for a friend.

And Jack Abramoff had many friends, including Grover Norquist. "What is the status of the Choctaw stuff," Norquist wrote Abramoff on May 20, 1999. "I have a $75K hole in my budget from last year. Ouch." Abramoff saw that the hole was plugged. He instructed clients to donate regularly to Americans for Tax Reform. "Thank you for your generous support of our work at Americans for Tax Reform," Norquist's deputy, Jennifer Kuhn, wrote to Louisiana Coushatta chief Lovelin Poncho on May 1, 2001. "I have received your contribution of $25,000." He had Norquist raise the tribal taxation issue at White House meetings. "Get to Grover asap with a cover note," Abramoff instructed his assistant on April 5, 2001, "Grover, Here is the first of the checks for the tax event at the White House. I'll have another $25K shortly. Regards, Jack."

Because Americans for Tax Reform refuses to disclose its donor list, we do not know for certain how much money Abramoff and his clients have given to Norquist since 1995. We do know that the total is at least several million dollars. Throughout the past decade, Abramoff worked hand in hand with Norquist's group: When Abramoff needed money to go to Reed, he went to Norquist. And when Norquist needed a donation, he went to Abramoff. "Hi Jack," Jennifer Kuhn wrote in a May 6, 2002, e-mail. "ATR is again doing the state resolution project (support SDI, make the Death Tax [abolition] permanent, make the tax cut permanent and commending the Prez on the war on terrorism)." The "state resolution project" sponsored a variety of initiatives in state legislatures. "Last year your support made it possible," Kuhn went on. "Do you think the nations"—Abramoff's tribal clients—"and [redacted] would again a) pass resolutions and come to Washington for the meeting and b) be interested in underwriting our campaign to bring everyone in, put them up at a nice hotel, nice dinner, etc.?" Abramoff said he would see what he could do.

"Nice" hotels. "Nice" dinners. With Abramoff, everything was lavish and exaggerated. Such was the case with his donations to politicians. He raised hundreds of thousands of dollars for George W. Bush, becoming a "Pioneer," the highest rank of presidential donor. "So far I've raised about $120,000, and I haven't even really started making calls," he told reporters in the summer of 2003.[22] He raised money for DeLay, for Speaker of the House Dennis Hastert ($118,500), for then-Majority Whip Roy Blunt ($41,000), for Rep. Bob Ney ($50,000). Between 2000 and 2003, Abramoff instructed four tribes to donate to Republican senator Conrad Burns of Montana. The donations totaled $137,000. In all, Abramoff directed his tribal clients to make $2.9 million in federal contributions.[23] Other clients donated millions more.

In 2004, Burns pressured the administration to award a $3 million school-building program to the Saginaw Chippewa tribe in Michigan, Abramoff's client and Burns's donor. The Saginaw Chippewa are one of the richest tribes in America. But they did not want, in this case, for the federal government to "leave us alone." They got the school, Burns got the money, and Abramoff got the credit.

Contributions, meals, junkets, sporting events, fund-raisers—these were the means by which Jack Abramoff insinuated himself into the Republican Congress. His generosity was so great it encompassed congressional staff members as well. "There are a few senate staffers I would like to help reward," one of Abramoff's lobbyists, Tony Rudy, formerly of DeLay Inc., wrote to his boss on September 21, 2001. "Would the Choctaws or Coushatta donate like 10K to pay for a trip?"

"A trip where?" Abramoff replied.

"There is a hunting and fishing resort 3 hours south of Texas that [retired New Hampshire Republican senator Bob] Smith's people expressed an interest in," Rudy wrote.

This was too much even for Abramoff. "I don't see how we can sell them on funding that."

Rudy knew. "Thank you trip," he explained, "for the approps we got." By which he meant: quid pro quo for an appropriations bill that helped the tribes.

"Smith's people didn't get us the approps for Choctaw," Abramoff wrote. "But good try! :)"

Rudy was undeterred: "But how would Coushatta know? :)"

There is a deviousness to this exchange that is surprisingly earnest, a happy-go-lucky approach to exploitation that would come to characterize Team Abramoff's lobbying endeavors as a whole. The logic seems to have been: *As long as these poor saps are paying millions, why shouldn't they fund an expensive junket for me and my friends in Bob Smith's office?* In fact, Abramoff treated his clients with the same patronizing attitude to which they were supposedly subjected by the federal government. Donate here, pay for this, cover that expense, pick up that tab. Yes, Abramoff was generous—but only because the tribes followed his orders so thoroughly.

The largest recipient of this generosity, needless to say, was Abramoff himself. The tribes paid millions of dollars to him and his firm, but they also picked up his skyboxes at FedEx Field and the MCI Center, and paid for his restaurant, among a great many other things. "It would be wise for the tribe to join Choctaw and Chitimacha in hosting a wealth of fund-raising events, by cosponsoring the sports suites at the baseball (Orioles), hockey (Caps), basketball (Wizards) and football (R-dskins) venues in the DC Area," he wrote to Kathryn Van Hoof, his contact with the Louisiana Coushatta, on May 4, 2001. "The events which are not used as fund raisers are utilized by Congressional staff and Members, so every game results in tremendous benefits politically."

Don't get me wrong, Abramoff then cautioned: All of this is going to cost quite a bit of money. "By the way, the suites are leased by me and your participation check should be written to 'Jack Abramoff—Sports Suites Account.'" On May 25, the Coushatta sent a check for $185,000 to that account.[24]

The tribes paid the money that helped cover Abramoff's lunches at Sushi Taro, the Japanese restaurant near Dupont Circle in Washington where, according to his expense reports, Abramoff loved to dine. And the tribes paid the money that in the summer of 2001 helped him open a restaurant of his own: Signatures, a chichi bar and grill down Pennsylvania Avenue from the Capitol. "The restaurant will be owned by Livsar Enterprises," Abramoff instructed his accountant on August 28, 2001, "which will be owned primarily by Pam"—Mrs. Jack Abramoff. "It is an LLC." Additional funds, Abramoff continued, would come from a business called Capitol Campaign Strategies, but "they are not going to be getting a share." Why wouldn't Capitol Campaign Strategies "be getting a share"? Good question.

Like Ralph Reed's Century Strategies, Capitol Campaign Strategies, also known as Scanlon-Gould Public Affairs, was a "public relations firm" specializing in "media strategy" and "political consulting" and "grassroots outreach." What such terms mean is open to debate. The answer is next to nothing. However, what they meant for Michael Scanlon was money.

Scanlon opened Capitol Campaign Strategies early in 2001. It seemed to have been a way for Scanlon to do public relations work on the side. Since this type of "grassroots" activity was unregulated, that work would prove lucrative. On June 5, 2001, Scanlon wrote a letter, on his new company's stationery, to his accountant. "I am officially a resident of the state of Delaware as of May 25, 2001," he began. "Can you please determine if it makes sense to establish my business in DE as well?" Before his career in politics, Scanlon had spent years as a lifeguard in Delaware. His "move" to Delaware—he still lived and worked around Washington, D.C.—was propitious. Shortly afterward, on June 18, 2001, he wrote an e-mail to Abramoff:

A few weeks ago you mentioned something to me—I took the concept and have put together a plan that will make serious money. We also talked briefly about it in the beginning of the year but I think we can really move it now. Here are the broad strokes;

I have been making contacts with some larger Public Affairs companies in town for a few months. I have two solid relationships that will seriously consider acquiring Capitol Campaign Strategies. The problem is that there is not much in CCS right now. However, if we build up Capitol Campaign Strategies enough I can get it acquired by a large firm by the end of next year at 3X the firm revenue. Bottom line: If you help me get CCS a client base of $3 million a year, I will get the clients served, and the firm acquired at $9 million. We can then split up the profits. What do you think?

"Sounds like a plan," Abramoff replied.

The plan came to be called "Gimme Five." It worked like this: Abramoff would approach his clients and tell them that the only way they could accomplish their objectives in Washington was to hire Michael Scanlon, whose Capitol Campaign Strategies was the best in the business. The sort of business Scanlon was best at, he would go on, was stuff Abramoff didn't know how to do himself: political consulting, organizing petitions, creating "databases" of potential supporters, and so on. Abramoff would argue that that sort of business was *absolutely necessary* if the tribe wanted to protect its profits and its influence.

When the tribes contacted Scanlon, he would bill them, according to the Justice Department, "prices that incorporated huge profit margins." Say it cost $500 to produce a radio advertisement telling Washington to mind its own business. Scanlon would charge $1,500. He would usually find a subcontractor to produce the ad, then would split the remaining $1,000 between himself and Abramoff. Since he couldn't pay Abramoff directly, he would send the money through a variety of tax-exempt foundations and non-profits and front companies. The clients would have no idea what happened to their money. Here is an e-mail that Scanlon wrote to Abramoff on May 31, 2001, which provides, in outline, a good example of the scheme: "Here is the overall plan," Scanlon wrote.

We need about 200K to run the operation—leaving 1.3 [million] to split—or 650 [thousand] a piece. So to make you whole idea was to get the 500 to CAF [the Capital Athletic Foundation]—then have AIC [the American International Center] cut Kay Gold [Abramoff's front company] a check for the remaining 150 [thousand].

Here's another good example, from a 2003 e-mail from Abramoff to his accountant:

"I think I understand what he [Scanlon] did. We received $5 million into CCS [Capitol Campaign Strategies] . . . he divided the $5 million into three piles: $1M for actual expenses, and $2M for each of us."

It was, in short, an ingenious system: an elaborate Rube Goldberg machine, a shell game of such unheralded complexity that it would take years for anyone to catch on. In the meantime, though, Scanlon and Abramoff would be rolling in dough.

The sums involved were enormous. Between June 2001 and April 2004, the Mississippi Choctaw paid Scanlon $14,765,000, of which about $6,365,000 went to Abramoff. Between March 2001 and May 2003, the Louisiana Coushatta paid Scanlon $30,510,000, of which about $10,944,000 went to Abramoff. Between June 2002 and October 2003, the Saginaw Chippewa paid Scanlon $3,500,000, of which about $540,000 went to Abramoff. In March 2002, the Tigua of El Paso, Texas, paid Scanlon $4,200,000, of which about $1,850,000 went to Abramoff.

Total amount in money the six tribes—the four mentioned above plus the Agua Caliente Band of Cahuilla and the Pueblo Sandia of California—paid to Capitol Campaign Strategies between 2001 and 2004: $66,369,500.[25]

This is why Abramoff needed to keep business ventures like his restaurant separate from Capitol Campaign Strategies—he could not risk being tied to all these kickbacks. Because none of this money was reported to the government. Little of it was taxed as personal income. None of it was regulated. All of it was in addition to the approximately $20,000,000 the tribes paid over-the-counter, so to speak, to Abramoff while he was at Preston Gates and Greenberg Traurig. All told, it is a scandal involving upward of $90,000,000—involving, as of December 2005, at least half a dozen members of Congress.

How did they do it?

CHAPTER SEVEN

THE SHAKEDOWN

GREED GONE WILD

On October 4, 2001, Jack Abramoff sent Michael Scanlon an e-mail:

> I had dinner tonight with Chris Petras of Sag Chip. He was salivating at the $4-5 million program I described to him (is that enough? Probably not). They have their primary for tribal council on Tuesday, which should determine if they are going to take over (general elections in November). I told him that you are the greatest campaign expert since . . . (actually, I told him that there was no one like you in history!). He is going to come in after the primary with the guy who will be chief if they win (a big fan of ours already) and we are going to help him win. If he wins, they take over in January, and we have millions. I told him that you are

already in national demand and we need to secure you for them. He is very excited. GIMME FIVE lives.[1]

Petras got in touch with Scanlon, who sent an employee to the Saginaw reservation to run the campaigns of the candidates for council who would be most inclined to enter into contract with Capitol Campaign Strategies. The election was held on November 6. The day after, Scanlon sent an e-mail to his team. "Just to recap," he wrote, "we elected 7 out of our slate of 8—and the last guy— Ray Davis missed it by ONE vote."

Davis's loss was trivial. Within a month of the election, the new tribal council was preparing to vote to give Scanlon a contract. "I chatted with Petras," Abramoff told Scanlon on December 4. "They are jazzed about our coming. We're rock stars up there. Now it's time to pay for the concert!"

On December 17, Abramoff wrote to Scanlon again: "Chris said they are voting on the project today!! Can you smell the money?!?!?!"

Then the two had the following exchange:

SCANLON: Did we win it?
ABRAMOFF: The f'ing troglodytes didn't vote on you today.
    Dammit.
SCANLON: What's a troglodyte?
ABRAMOFF: What am I dictionary? :) It's a lower form of exis-
    tence basically.

It took time for the Chippewa to hire Scanlon. By January 2002, he was getting frustrated. "I can't believe that I spilled blood getting those guys elected," he wrote Abramoff on January 14, "and I got stiffed. How incredibly ungrateful. Can they at the very least sign me up to some kind of deal? I can't believe they laid a goose-egg." The subject line of one April 15, 2002, e-mail is "SagChip idiots."

Abramoff tried to reassure him. "We'll get it!" he wrote. He sent countless e-mails providing advice to Scanlon on how he could secure

the Chippewa's business. "I think it's essential that you take Otto"—
a Chippewa official—"to dinner tomorrow night," he wrote on January 29. "Can you do it? I have to meet with the monkeys from the
Choctaw tribal council." The Choctaw were already participating,
unwittingly, in Gimme Five. "You need to close the deal with him. I
set it up tonight." Scanlon had the dinner. It took another six months
for the Saginaw Chippewa to agree to the deal. That's nine months
total to secure one client. In the end, Scanlon got his money.

The same rule applied to all the tribes. Abramoff and Scanlon
would wine and dine prospective clients, who would hire Scanlon to
run tribal council campaigns. The newly elected tribal council
would once again hire Scanlon to perform "grassroots" work. On
February 27, 2002, Abramoff sent Scanlon an e-mail with the subject line "Agua Caliente." "I saw them tonight," Abramoff wrote.
"They really can't wait for you to lead them to the promised land!
Tomorrow night, after the reception at Sigs"—a fund-raiser at Signatures—"let's take them to dinner and lock up the deal."

This is how Abramoff outlined what he and Scanlon could provide the Agua Caliente in an April 1, 2002, e-mail: "I think what we
have in mind is helping the tribe set up the kind of political strength
we have done for others, but doing it very carefully . . . Mike and I
see the mission here as getting in, getting you guys organized so we
can get the slot cap off and other things the tribe needs." The tribe
remained unconvinced. As Chief Richard Milanovich put it in his
statement to the Senate Indian Affairs Committee, "I had opposed
the efforts of Mr. Abramoff and Mr. Scanlon to obtain contracts
with our Tribe, distrusting their claims, methods, and, quite
frankly, mostly their cost."[2]

During these negotiations, two candidates for tribal council of
the Agua Caliente band of Cahuilla Indians hired Capitol Campaign Strategies. And the company did, for the most part, what it
said it was going to do. It wrote phone scripts. It organized town
hall meetings. It provided its candidates with an agenda and a
"message." Here, for example, are the "talking points" drawn up

for the Agua Caliente candidate Virginia Siva, to be delivered at a March 10, 2002, town hall meeting:

- I would like to thank everyone for coming out tonight for this community meeting.
- I am Virginia Siva and I am running for Tribal Chairman.
- I have visited many of you over the past few days. And, I believe that meeting face-to-face is very important between council leadership and tribal members.

It might be hard to believe, but yes: There are people willing to pay for someone to come up with statements like "I am Virginia Siva and I am running for Tribal Chairman."

Virginia Siva lost, incidentally, but another Scanlon candidate won. And then, against Chief Milanovich's objections, the Agua Caliente band entered into contract with Greenberg Traurig on July 9 and Scanlon-Gould Public Affairs (aka Capitol Campaign Strategies) on July 24.

Once Abramoff and Scanlon obtained clients, the only question left was what to do with the swag. Typically, their first reaction was a loud, sustained round of chest-thumping. "You have a hell of a lot coming your way tomorrow," Scanlon wrote Abramoff on March 18, 2002.

"Da man!" Abramoff replied. "You iz da man! Do you hear me?! You da man!! How much $$ coming tomorrow? Did we get some more $$ in?"

Next came disappointment that the amount was not what one of them had expected. On July 9, 2002, Abramoff forwarded Scanlon an e-mail with the subject line "did we get a CCS check for Kay Gold today?" referring to one of Abramoff's many front companies. Scanlon told Abramoff that he had a check coming to Kay Gold for $800,000. "$800k?" Abramoff asked. "I thought we got $1.9M?"

Scanlon explained the situation. "We did 800 for you 800 for me 250 for the effort the other 50 went to the plan and misc expenses," he wrote. "We both have an additional 500 coming when they pay the next phase."

What Abramoff wrote next illustrates the third step in the process: discussion of tax evasion. "Sounds good to me," Abramoff told Scanlon. "As for the $64K, I want to use it to buy a car I decided. Can we do it so neither of us pays taxes on it?"

"I can think something up," Scanlon wrote. "Let's chat."

Abramoff: "You IZ da man."

Over time the avoidance of taxes and scrutiny became the focus of much of Abramoff's correspondence. On March 15, 2002, for example, he sent a personal financial statement to an assistant. Abramoff asked him to "remove the SunCruz item from it" (by this time, Abramoff had severed all ties with the accursed casino company), but to also "put in $5M revenue/yr from CCS" or Capitol Campaign Strategies—money that would be "valued at $30M (multiple of 6)." And then Abramoff offered a telling footnote:

> Check with Gail [Halpern] before we send over to anyone, since I want to make sure it's consistent with the rest of the stuff I am sending them. We should not reveal this to anyone but Gail, though, since no one knows the CCS stuff.

Halpern has refused to address the content of this e-mail in public, telling the Senate Indian Affairs Committee only that "to the best of my knowledge all information that Mr. Abramoff gave me was reported on his income tax return."

No one knew about the kickbacks Abramoff was receiving from Scanlon, because the money had been passed through a variety of shells. These shells would send checks to Kay Gold, a front company Abramoff could draw from at will. Sometimes Kay Gold received money directly from Scanlon. In 2002, for example, Kay Gold earned $13.5 million in "referral fees" from Capitol Campaign Strategies. Kay Gold operated out of Abramoff's house.[3]

The most infamous shell was the American International Center, a think tank in Delaware established in 2001. The founder of the

American International Center was Michael Scanlon. According to its "Who We Are" statement, Scanlon's think tank was

> a public policy research foundation founded in 2001 under the high-powered directorship of David A. Grosh and Brian J. Mann. While only recently incorporated, the AIC has been striving to advance the cause of greater international empowerment for many years. Based in sunny Rehoboth Beach, Delaware, the AIC staff is using 21st century technology and decades of experience to make the world a smaller place.[4]

The American International Center's Web site no longer exists, but an intrepid reporter from *National Journal* paid it a visit before it was destroyed. The Web site said that the think tank worked to "expand the parameters of international discourse in an effort to leverage the combined power of world intellect," which sounds like a pretty tall, not to mention unintelligible, order. The center also had the "global minded purpose of enhancing the methods of empowerment for territories, commonwealths, and sovereign nations in possession of and within the United States"—a helpful description of Abramoff's clients, including both the tribes and the Commonwealth of the Northern Mariana Islands.[5]

The American International Center's headquarters was a large, $4.2-million house in Rehoboth Beach, Delaware, two blocks from the ocean. The center's "high-powered" directors, David Grosh and Brian Mann, both lived in the house. They do not exactly seem like the sort of people who work at a think tank. In 1995, Grosh had been named Rehoboth Beach's "Lifeguard of the Year." Mann used to be a yoga instructor.

"I was only involved maybe five months—four or five months," Grosh told the Senate Indian Affairs Committee in June 2005. "The whole time I was involved, we rented the first floor of a house and installed some computers." Grosh is no longer a lifeguard. He describes himself as an "excavator-machine operator, construction worker, mentor in pre-schools, bartender" and laborer in "typical beach employment." Grosh has known Michael Scanlon since he was fourteen years old. One day in January 2001, Scanlon reached him at his Rehoboth Beach home and asked if he wanted to run an international corporation. "A hard one to turn down," Grosh told the Senate. According to Grosh, the American International Center, in all its time Rehoboth Beach's only think tank, held one staff meeting. It lasted fifteen minutes. Senator John McCain asked Grosh if he received any compensation for his "work" as director of the center. "No more than $2,000, $2,500," Grosh said.

"A month?" McCain asked.

"No, total."

"Did Mr. Scanlon promise you any fringe benefits?"

"We went to a Washington Capitals/Pittsburgh Penguins hockey game," Grosh said.[6]

Mann, the center's codirector, declined to answer the committee's questions. He declined to comment on a letter that the committee staff had obtained in which Grosh thanked a tribal donor for "your donation of $200,000." Grosh said he never saw the letter.

He also never saw the May 2, 2001, e-mail from Abramoff to Scanlon with the subject line "Choctaw money coming to AIC." In the e-mail, Abramoff said the Choctaw would probably donate $175,000 to the center. "$100K to Ralph," Abramoff instructed, "$25K to contributions ($5K immediately to Conservative Caucus); rest gimme five." And Grosh never saw the January 30, 2002, invoice that the center sent to the Choctaw for $1,000,000.

Another recipient of tribal money was the Capital Athletic Foundation, the charity that Abramoff set up to fund, he said, "educational programs" for "at-risk youth." Yet an audit has revealed that 80 percent of the money in the foundation went to the Eshkol Academy, a Jewish day school Abramoff had set up to educate his five children. In fact, in 2002, the foundation donated less than one percent of its revenues to actual charitable groups like the Boy Scouts of America; the Washington, D.C., YMCA; and a few others. The remaining 19 percent of the Capital Athletic Foundation's money was, as Senator McCain once put it, Abramoff's "personal piggy bank."[7]

But Abramoff's clients didn't know that. On December 19, 2001, Nell Rogers, Abramoff's Choctaw contact, received a $500,000 invoice for "professional services" from the Capital Athletic Foundation. In 2002, the Choctaw made another $1 million donation. On August 5, 2002, Chris Petras sent a memo to tribal chief Maynard Kahgegab. "This is the reminder you requested regarding the request for support of the Capital Athletic Foundation in Washington, DC, by the Saginaw Chippewa Indian Tribe of Michigan," Petras wrote. "The Foundation creates programs that teach leadership skills to disadvantaged youth in the DC-area in an effort to keep them off the streets and enhance their educational opportunities." The Chippewa sent a $25,000 donation.[8] When the Tigua tribe of El Paso, Texas, was looking for ways to pay their lobbying bill, Abramoff suggested they participate in the Capital Athletic Foundation's "elderly legacy program." The program involved the Tigua taking out high-deductible life insurance policies on elderly tribe members. The Tigua would name the Eshkol Academy (and, by extension, the Capital Athletic Foundation) as the beneficiary. The elders would die; the money would flow; the Tigua would pay off their debt to Abramoff. (The Tigua passed.)

Abramoff also used the foundation to raise money for politicians. Consider a June 6, 2002, e-mail that Abramoff sent to Tony Rudy. "Did you get the message from the guys that Tom [Delay] wants us to raise some bucks from Capital Athletic Foundation?" Abramoff asked. "I have six clients in for $25K. I recommend we hit everyone who cares about Tom's requests. I have another few to hit still. It's a tax deductible foundation doing some issues education (they do NO lobbying at all), so it's easier (though it did not matter to the tribes). I think that, if we can do $200K, that would be good."

Rudy said he thought it would work.

"Great!" Abramoff replied. "Can you e-mail Petras on the Sag Chip request (it'll look better coming from you as a former DeLay COS). We'z gonna make a bundle here."

But Rudy made a mistake. He sent an e-mail to Todd Boulanger, another Greenberg Traurig lobbyist. On June 20—subject line: "Capital Athletic Foundation"—Rudy told Boulanger to ask Petras whether the Chippewa "can make a contribution. We asked for 25K."

Boulanger was puzzled. "What is this?" he replied.

"Jack wants this," Rudy wrote.

"What is it? I've never heard of it," Boulanger asked again.

"It is something our friends are raising money for."

Probably just as confused as Boulanger was, Rudy forwarded the exchange to Abramoff.

"Shit!" Abramoff replied. "I did not want you to bring Todd into this!!!" More: "Don't you see that we have a problem now?"

The problem was that someone in his office might have been tipped off that Abramoff was using the Capital Athletic Foundation as a shell. From his response, however, it is clear that Rudy was unable to see that there was a problem. But this was because he lacked a full picture of what Abramoff and Scanlon were up to. Everyone was lacking a full picture. Abramoff had to get the Saginaw Chippewa donation himself, sending a July 31 e-mail to Petras "about getting the Capitol Athletic Foundation contribution to me asap per the delay request."

Abramoff discovered a way to direct funds from Scanlon into the Capital Athletic Foundation. He thought that this would be a way to enjoy his profits tax-free. He proposed the idea in a September 18, 2002, e-mail to his accountant, Gail Halpern. "What I have in mind is to have the CAF researchers do some research related to their mission (sportsmanship) and deliver it to CCS," Abramoff wrote. "CCS will then pay CAF. We can make this ongoing if we need to do so."

Always helpful, Halpern replied that it "sounds like you would then need to have 'researchers' on the payroll, wouldn't you? Rabbi Lapin is on the payroll. And colin as well. Can you utilize them in some way?"

"Yes," Abramoff wrote. "They will be doing the research and presenting it. I'll take care of it. CCS is all set to do this." And so it was done.

There was a third shell. We've already met Amy Ridenour and her husband, David, who had known Abramoff for decades. Since 1982, when she left College Republicans, Ridenour, as we've learned, has helmed the nonprofit National Center for Public Policy Research. Recall also that, in 1997, Abramoff joined the center's board of directors. That same year, Abramoff introduced Ridenour to Choctaw Chief Martin. The Choctaw became regular donors to the National Center. Between 1997 and 1999, the Mississippi Choctaw donated $7,500. In 2000, the tribe donated $6,500.[9]

Then, in 2001, Abramoff began to use the National Center to send money to Ralph Reed. An October 23, 2001, e-mail from Abramoff to Ridenour instructs her to "please make out an invoice for $132,500 made out to [the] Mississippi Band of Choctaw Indians." Once the Choctaw had paid up, Abramoff further instructed, "please cut a check to Century Strategies." Ridenour did as she was told.

In 2002, the relationship between Abramoff and the National Center changed again. One day in June 2002, Abramoff had lunch with David Ridenour, who served as the center's vice president. Amy Ridenour had asked her husband to mention to Abramoff that the nonprofit was having trouble finding money. David Ridenour conveyed the message. Soon, Amy Ridenour told the Senate Indian Affairs Committee in the summer of 2005, Abramoff was telling the couple about "a new kind of lobbying" that he had discovered.[10]

Ridenour told the Senate that the idea intrigued her. She thought she would be helping her longtime contributors, the Choctaw, educate the American public about what independence and free markets can accomplish. But, she continued, Abramoff quickly dropped the subject.

He brought it up again in October. Was the National Center still interested in the Choctaw? Abramoff asked. Ridenour said yes. On October 1, Abramoff sent an e-mail to Scanlon: "Amy Ridenour has asked if we can run any funds through them to pump up their nonmail donations (they will give us back 100%). Let's run some of the non-CAF Choctaw money through them to the Caymans."

Abramoff told Ridenour to send the Choctaw a $1 million invoice. The Choctaw cut a check for that amount on October 10, 2002.

"When the funds arrived," Ridenour explained to the Senate, Abramoff "told me how they should be dispersed—$450,000 to the Capital Athletic Foundation, as a grant; $500,000 to Capitol Campaign Strategies; and $50,000 to a company called Nuremberger & Associates."[11] (Abramoff owed money to Nuremberger, a friend from Hollywood.)

Ridenour says that she repeatedly asked Abramoff for documentation that the money was being used for "educational purposes." She never received any. "I trusted Jack," she explained to the Senate that day in June 2005. "I believed not only that he had a fiduciary responsibility to us, but, in fact, was attempting to serve his clients, the Choctaw, as a nonprofit entity, to the best of his ability as well. So what I did do was talk to him. Not enough."

The next year, in the summer of 2003, as part of a "sports and politics" project, Abramoff's firm Greenberg Traurig sent the National Center $1.5 million. "Jack told me $250,000 had been designated to the Capital Athletic Foundation as a grant," Ridenour explained, and that "$1.25 million was to be paid to Kay Gold, a company I believed was owned by Michael Scanlon."

Sensing that she might be wrong, and frustrated that Abramoff was not providing the documentary evidence proving that the money passing through her nonprofit was actually used for "educational" purposes, Ridenour pulled out of the financial arrangement.

She was a shell. "When you have worked with someone for twenty-two years," Ridenour told the Senate,

When they have been a member of your board of directors, by October of 2002, for five years, when you've worked on projects together, when you know someone personally, when you believe—even though technically it's irrelevant—that you are close, personal friends, when you believe all of these things and you also know that it is in—and I still believe to this day that it is in a person's best interest to do a job right—your natural assumption is that the things they say to you are correct and true.

Ridenour paused. "In my future career," she said, "I will never make, pretty much, assumptions on anything again."

Such is the toxicity of Jack Abramoff's poison.

"We are in overdrive and all pistons are firing," Ralph Reed wrote Abramoff on November 9, 2001. Abramoff forwarded the e-mail to Scanlon with the message "Now we're talking!"

The Louisiana Coushatta tribe had hired Abramoff—who told them to hire Scanlon, who was sending money to Reed—to combat a casino that three rival tribes had opened in East Texas. Texas attorney general John Cornyn, who in 2002 was elected to the U.S. Senate, had opposed the casinos for some time and had waged a court battle against them. Abramoff's strategy was to win in the courts, but if that failed, move to the legislature. "Cornyn needs to get the Indians to lead the way," he wrote Reed on November 12, 2001. "Let us help with that."

Reed replied: "Get me details so I can alert Cornyn and let him know what we are doing to help him."

Abramoff mentioned that there was a full-page ad in that day's *Washington Post* attacking Cornyn.

"Wow," Reed replied. "These guys are really playing hard ball. They also did a full page ad in the Austin-American today. Do you know who their consultant(s) are?"

"Some stupid lobbyists up here who do Indian issues," Abramoff wrote. "We'll find out who and make sure all our friends crush them like bugs."

The Louisiana Coushatta deal had all the characteristics of an Abramoff/Scanlon/Reed effort. There was the religious posturing: When opponents attacked Cornyn's crusade against the Alabama Coushatta and El Paso Tigua, saying it was politically motivated, Reed wrote Abramoff: "We are sending 50 pastors to give him moral support." There was the with-us-or-against-us team mentality: When Texas governor Rick Perry, a Republican, acknowledged he had accepted donations from the Tigua and suggested that he would send tax dollars to aid the tribe if their casino was closed, Abramoff was mystified. "What is he thinking?" he wrote Reed. There was the shameless boosterism: When Cornyn filed a lawsuit shutting down the Alabama Coushatta casino in early 2002, Scanlon sent this memo to his employees:

> This means that the threat of a class III facility near Houston has been completely eliminated AND the smaller facility will be shut down as well. To put this in perspective, the Tigua's facility has been open an[d] operating illegally in Texas for 6 years. We shut down the Alabama Coushatta facility in roughly ninety days.

Scanlon did not shut down the Alabama Coushatta casino. The courts did that. But he was willing to take all the credit.

Another victory arrived on January 18, 2002, when the Fifth Circuit Court of Appeals upheld a Texas District Court ruling that the Tigua casino was illegal and should be closed. For some lobbyists, the job would be done once they had shut down their clients' rivals. Not for Abramoff. To him, the ruling against the Tigua was a new opportunity. Abramoff understood that the ruling would wreak economic, political, and social devastation on the tribe. So he approached their political contact, Marc Schwartz . . . and offered to help get Congress to reopen the casino.

On February 6, 2002, Abramoff sent Scanlon an e-mail. The subject line: "I'm on the phone with Tigua!"

"Fire up the jet baby," Abramoff wrote, "we're going to El Paso!"

Scanlon replied: "I want all their MONEY!!!"

Later that week, Abramoff contacted the Tigua representative again. "We are Republicans," he wrote, "and normally want all Republicans to prevail in electoral challenges." But "this ill-advised decision on the part of the Republican leadership in Texas must not stand. And we intend to right this using, in part, Republican leaders in Washington."

Abramoff told the Tigua he would handle this effort for free. There were, however, some conditions. "If we succeed," he wrote, "we can expect to have a long-term relationship with the tribe by representing their interests on the federal level." More, the Tigua should hire—no, *had* to hire—Michael Scanlon to do their grassroots work. "He's the best there is in the business."

On February 18, Abramoff sent Tigua rep Marc Schwartz a copy of "Operation Open Doors," a ten-page report Scanlon had prepared outlining his proposed lobbying strategy. "The proposal Mike Scanlon has prepared," Abramoff began,

> is, in our view, the best chance the tribe has to overcome the gross indignity perpetuated by the Texas State authorities. Indeed, as I mentioned on the phone, the several day delay getting this to you was the consequence of our wanting to insure that we have a path to get this done, and a couple of Senators willing to ram this through initially. I am pleased to note that both are in place.

And he added:

> Coupled with this plan, we anticipate that the tribe will have to make approximately $300,000 in federal political contributions. We are currently preparing a target list of those contributions and hope to have that to you shortly.

What was "Operation Open Doors"? It was, Scanlon wrote in his proposal, a

> political operation [that] will result in a Majority of both federal chambers either becoming close friends of the tribe or fearing the tribe in a very short period of time. Simply put you need 218

friends in the U.S. House and 51 Senators on your side very quickly, and we will do that through both love and fear.

If love and fear didn't work, Scanlon went on, they always had two "fully customized databases"—one dealing with "Grassroots," the other with "Qualitative Research"—which would contain "every piece of information fathomable."[12]

In other words: Operation Open Doors was a bunch of baloney.

More important to Abramoff and Scanlon, though, it was also an extremely expensive bunch of baloney. Total cost: $5,400,000. Gimme five.

On February 19, Scanlon forwarded his partner an article from that day's *El Paso Times* about layoffs at the now-illegal Tigua casino. "This is on the front page of today's paper while they will be voting on our plan!" Scanlon wrote.

Abramoff replied: "Is life great or what!!!"

On March 5, the Tigua agreed to the deal and sent a $2.1 million check to Capitol Campaign Strategies.

Now the only question was how to reopen the casino. A couple days after Scanlon received the Tigua's money, Abramoff wrote to one of his subordinates, subject line: "Moving Legislation." "I need to know asap which pieces of legislation are likely to be passed through both House and Senate in the next three months," Abramoff wrote. "Please work with the guys to get a complete list. They need to discuss with leadership in house and Senate (r and d). thanks."

"For whom?" Abramoff's interlocutor replied. "Or does the focus of the bills not matter?"

"It would be where we put the Tigua provision," Abramoff wrote. "It will start in the Senate and we'll protect it in the house. Nothing to do yet but find possible vehicles."

His answer came quickly. "Vehicle 1: unemployment insurance stimulus bill," wrote the subordinate. "That will go to conference shortly. 2. Terrorism insurance bill. Passed house starting to move in senate [redacted]."

Abramoff: "Ya da man."

The interlocutor continued: "3. Energy bill. More problematic. Might not become law but possible [redacted]."

"Thanks," Abramoff wrote, before asking: "How do we find little silly things which are moving which can have some technical correction language attached?"

Eventually, one such "little silly thing" bubbled up to the surface— an election reform bill sponsored by Abramoff's friend Rep. Bob Ney. In February, Ney's chief of staff had joined Abramoff at Greenberg Traurig. On March 20, Abramoff wrote to Scanlon: "Just met with Ney!!! We're f'ing gold!!! He's going to do Tigua." About a week later, he wrote to Marc Schwartz. The subject: "Cong. Ney."

"He is the chairman of the committee doing election reform," Abramoff wrote. "Please get us the following checks for him asap." Attached was a list:

Bob Ney for Congress—$2,000
American Liberty PAC—Federal - $5,000
American Liberty PAC—non-Federal - $25,000

"Things are moving even faster than we thought when we last chatted," Abramoff concluded.

On April 8, Capitol Campaign Strategies cut a check to Kay Gold for $2,138,025, Abramoff's share of the Tigua lucre.

On April 16, Schwartz wrote Scanlon. "Anything to report?"

The answer: No. But Scanlon shot him a mealymouthed response:

Next Tuesday—till vote on conference report: Gramm shits his pants and threatens to bring down whole bill over this—we have phones and mail turned on beating him back. We have enough votes for cloture and to beat a filibuster right now so we are golden, we just need to keep the calls letters and political support coming as Gramm pounds his chest.

Truth was, everything was riding on Ney's ability to shepherd the Tigua provision through a House-Senate conference. Abramoff had assured Ney that the election reform bill's Democratic sponsor, Connecticut senator Christopher Dodd, would support the casino provision. It was only a matter of timing. Democrats controlled the Senate, which meant that Scanlon's work had to be bipartisan. "Senator Christopher Dodd (D-CT)," he later wrote, "managed the Senate."[13]

Schwartz told Sen. John McCain in November 2004 that he recalled "an agreement between Mr. Abramoff and Senator Dodd early in the process. And Representative Ney came on the scene somewhat later."[14] Schwartz's testimony jibes with the contents of an April 12, 2002, memo Scanlon sent to his tribal contacts, in which he wrote that "we have Senate support" but that "they are looking for political cover."[15]

The route by which Scanlon had supposedly secured Dodd's cooperation was circuitous. His firm paid another firm, Lunde & Burger, $50,000 to lobby the Connecticut Democrat. "He called me about the Tiguas' wanting to reopen their casino," Brian Lunde, a former Democratic National Committee executive director who in 2004 was the national chair of Democrats for Bush, later told the *New York Times*. "I checked around, and it was the formal position of the DNC to have that reopened." Lunde & Burger entered into a $10,000 subcontract with yet another "public relations strategist" to lobby Dodd directly.[16]

Enter Lottie Shackelford.

Like many Washingtonians, Lottie Shackelford came to the capital to do good and stayed to do well. She has been a vice chairman of the Democratic National Committee since 1989. She is also a lobbyist. She was the first woman to be elected mayor of Little Rock, Arkansas, and her career has followed the arc of that state's former governor, Bill Clinton. In 1993, Clinton appointed Shackelford, who had served on his presidential transition team, to the Overseas Private Investment Corporation, an obscure government agency that oversees subsidies for U.S. businesses investing abroad. Also that year, she was named executive vice president of U.S. Strategies Inc., a lobbying firm. Later she became executive vice president of another lobbying firm, Global USA Inc. (Much of her bio can be read on the Web site of the pharmaceutical company Medicis, on whose board Shackelford sits.)

Among Shackelford's clients in 2005: FM Policy Focus, which paid Global USA Inc. $45,000 for six months' work to lobby the House and Senate on "regulatory reform issues" and the "Federal Housing Finance Reform Act of 2005"; the "Metro-Miami Action Plan Trust," which hired her to "assist with procurement of appropriated funds"; and Hyundai Motor Company, which paid her to work on "issues related to hydrogen fleet and infrastructure demonstration and validation project," specifically "HR 2419, Energy and Water Development Appropriations Act, 2006, provisions relating to Department of Energy hydrogen program," according to Senate disclosure reports.

In 2002, when she contacted Dodd about the Tigua provision, Shackelford was also a registered lobbyist on behalf of Quest Software, as well as United to Secure America, which paid Global USA Inc. $10,000 to influence immigration reform legislation. She was not a registered lobbyist on behalf of the Tigua. She was, however, a member of Dodd's fund-raising committee. "We directed her to make personal contact with the Senator throughout the campaign starting in April and lasting through the passage of the legislation in October," Scanlon wrote in his 2003 memo. Shackelford, he continued, was "critical."

In 2004, Dodd delivered a statement to the Senate Indian Affairs Committee. Shackelford "did approach my office," he wrote, "during the waning hours of negotiations over the HAVA legislation." And Shackelford did "inquire whether recognition provisions for the Tigua tribe could be included in the bill." However, according to Dodd, "the suggestion was summarily rejected."[17]

No one told Ney that.

Meanwhile, Abramoff had his annual trip to St. Andrews golf course in Scotland. On June 7, he wrote Marc Schwartz. The subject: "Our Friend." Here is what Abramoff wrote:

Asked if we could help (as in cover) a Scotland golf trip for him and some staff (his committee chief of staff) and members for

August. The trip will be quite expensive (we did this for another member—you know who) 2 years ago. I anticipate that the total cost—if he brings 3-4 members and wives—would be around $100,000 or more. I can probably get another one of my tribes to cover some of it. Let me know if you guys could do $50K and I'll get them to do the other $50K, though I'll have to get him to bring someone who has relevance to their matters—our friend does not as you can imagine. They would probably do the trip through the Capital Athletic Foundation as an educational mission. I have to start planning this now to make sure they can get tee times. Can you let me know if this would be OK, and possibly start to process it as a donation to Capital Athletic Foundation?

"Our friend" was Ney. Schwartz said he would see what he could do. In the end, the Tigua, strapped for cash, never made the donation.

But there was a larger problem. On July 25, 2002, Abramoff e-mailed Scanlon: "I just spoke with Ney who met today with Dodd on the bill and raised our provision. Dodd looked at him like a 'deer in headlights' and said he has never made such a commitment and that, with the problems of new casinos in Connecticut, it is a problem!! . . . Ney feels like we let him out to dry. Please call me!!!!" Yet there was nothing they could do. Dodd had, in his own words, "summarily rejected" the inclusion of language reopening the Tigua casino.

"I had been misled by Jack Abramoff," Ney has said in a statement. "The matter was then closed from my perspective."

Not quite. In August, Ney—along with Ralph Reed and White House official David Safavian—went to Scotland with Abramoff, who paid for the trip with money from the Capital Athletic Foundation. The trip cost $150,000. In his disclosure reports, Ney wrote that he had traveled to Scotland to deliver a "speech to Scottish Parliamentarians." There is no record of such a speech taking place. A spokeswoman for the Scottish parliament has told the *Washington Post* that the parliament was in recess when Ney went on the St. Andrews junket.[18]

After the Scotland trip, members of the Tigua flew to Washington for a meeting with Ney. The tribal entourage stayed at the JW Marriott on Pennsylvania Avenue and Fourteenth Street, near the White House. "BN had a great time" in Scotland, Abramoff wrote Marc Schwartz on August 10. And BN "is very grateful, but is not going to mention the trip to Scotland for obvious reasons. He said he'll show his thanks in other ways, which is what we want."

He never did. The Tigua provision was stripped from the election reform bill. The deal had gone sour. On December 29, Schwartz e-mailed Abramoff and asked how things were going.

"We're coordinating efforts to attach our legislative fix to the upcoming omnibus appropriations bill," Abramoff replied. "Our hope is that an omnibus bill is put together so we can work through our friends on the leadership staff to insert the language at the very end of the process, instead of working through the normal appropriations process—which involves too many people and could jeopardize our legislative fix."

This was Abramoff at his most evasive. The show was over. There would never be a "legislative fix."

The Tigua fiasco damaged Abramoff's relationship with Scanlon. It seems that Abramoff blew up, yelling, accusing Scanlon of not doing his job. On October 8, 2002, Scanlon wrote his partner:

> Hey—I know you are pissed about the Tigua thing but we gotta do the best we can to recover. I feel totally comfortable that we lived up to every bit of our contract, and things just went the other way—and I am very very sorry about that.
>
> But I don't want this hanging over my head anymore, we need to get past it ASAP, and get back on track. I don't like you being angry with me on this, and if it's going to be an issue going forward you need to let me know. . . . Are we cool?

"We'z cool," Abramoff replied. "I was not really pissed at you. I have been going through hell on the school in the last few days and it has really put me in a horrible mood. Sorry about that." He went on: "Hold tight, but get our money back from that motherfucker who was supposed to take care of Dodd."

It would have been difficult to tear Abramoff and Scanlon apart. The two were good friends, and they had much in common. What unified them most was their ambition. The world, as they say, was their oyster. "There are a ton of potential opportunities out there," Abramoff wrote Scanlon on December 7, 2002. "There are 27 tribes which make over $100M a year (according to a NY Times piece on Nov 24—can you have your guys do the research and find out which tribes these may be?). We need to get moving on them."

Older and wiser, Abramoff was a big brother to Scanlon, a thirtysomething huckster prodigy. Big brother often gave advice: "I think the key thing to remember with all these clients is that they are annoying," he wrote on March 5, 2003, "but that the annoying losers are the only ones which have this kind of money and part with it so quickly." And big brother often dispensed gifts: "By the way I have a couple of asks on the sports suites—but they are personal in nature," Scanlon asked in January 2002. "I promised my nephew I would get him on the floor to see Jordan for Christmas. Any chance I could get 4 on the floor anytime soon? Also any chance I could get 4 tix to the hippie band Dave Matthews Band? You da man!"

Abramoff replied: "You can have tickets to anything and everything you want, personal or business. Work with Ilisa to get a floor game for your nephew and that hippie crap."

Both men were fiercely competitive. It seems as though Scanlon was always bugging Abramoff to play racquetball. On one occasion, Abramoff put him off, writing, "I'll play rb at 10 with a real man," which resulted in this colloquy:

SCANLON: You fucking lame ass—you better start pulling some
real opponents or I am going to beat your ass to a pulp next
time we get out there!
ABRAMOFF: Hey bitch, I am ready fo yo ass, but yu get a big time
faggot and afraid of a real man!

SCANLON: We will see about that fucko.

ABRAMOFF: I love this bitch talk you punk ass bitch. As soon as I get yo ass on the court, you be crying like a baby! :)

It would take several years for a room full of French semioticians working hand in hand with several dozen Freudians to unpack all the innuendo, euphemism, posturing, and playground antics contained in this exchange. Clearly, though, the two were dear friends and looked upon each other with compassion and, indeed, love.

Not so Ralph Reed. As Abramoff and Scanlon worked with Reed, the two constantly spoke ill about their partner. December 4, 2001, Abramoff to Scanlon: "Ralph is toast from now on, or we'll only give him a slight scrap. Pathetic." January 7, 2002, Scanlon to Abramoff: Reed "is out of his fucking mind!" (To which Abramoff replied: "Damn right.") February 5, 2002, Abramoff to Scanlon: Reed is a "whining idiot." February 12, 2002, Abramoff to Scanlon: Reed is "pathetic." "I know you (we!) hate him," Abramoff wrote to Scanlon about Reed on Valentine's Day 2002, "but it does give us good cover and patter to have him doing stuff. Let's give him a list of things we want, especially on Jena, and give him some chump change to get it done." February 19, 2002, Scanlon to Abramoff: "Please tell Ralph, that if I or anyone in my office gets another call from Sandra like the one we received yesterday, two weeks turn around will start turning into two years. We are not their bank." (To which Abramoff replied: "Tell me about this one. I'd love to ream him.")

Perhaps the worst insult arrived in a January 4, 2002, exchange. "Did Ralph spend all the money he was given to fight this—or does he have some left?" Scanlon asked Abramoff.

"That's a silly question!" Abramoff answered. "He spent it all the moment it arrived in his account. He would NEVER admit he has money left over. Would we?"

"No," Scanlon acknowledged, "but I'd like to know what the hell he spent it on—he didn't even know the damn thing was there— and didn't do shit to shut it down!"

"I agree," Abramoff said. "He is a bad version of us! No more money for him."

"You are a great partner," Abramoff wrote Scanlon in June 2002. "What I love about our partnership is that, when one of us is down, the other is there. We're gonna make $ for years together!"

Scanlon responded: "Amen! You got it boss—we have many years ahead!"

Looking back, it all seems like a grim fantasy: untamed ambition coupled with unrestrained greed. That the charade lasted as long as it did was a testament to the power of fantasy. Abramoff had always been drawn to the fantastic, from his days aiding anti-Communist insurgencies to his days producing movies to his days fashioning "a new kind of lobbying." But fantasies are fictions, and fictions are lies. With Abramoff the small lies expanded into big lies, and the big lies, over time, collapsed under their own weight.

Sometimes the sum of a man is written in a single e-mail. Consider the message Abramoff sent to Rabbi Daniel Lapin on September 15, 2000:

I hate to ask your help with something so silly, but I have been nominated for membership in the Cosmos Club, which is a very distinguished club in Washington, DC, comprised of Nobel Prize winners, etc. Problem for me is that most prospective members have received awards and I have received none. I was wondering if you thought it possible that I could put that I have received an award from Toward Tradition with a sufficiently academic title, perhaps something like Scholar of Talmudic Studies? I wish you were still heading PJC (for this reason only!) so I could get one from them too, perhaps something like Distinguished Biblical Scholar Award. . . . Do you think this is possible? It would only be used for this situation, but there is a chance that they would have to call someone to verify.

"Mazel tov," Rabbi Lapin wrote back. "The Cosmos Club is a big deal." Then he suggested they have a meeting where, as Lapin put it, they could "organize your many prestigious awards so they're ready to 'hang on the wall.'" "I just need to know what needs to be produced," Lapin wrote Abramoff. "Letters? Plaques? Neither?"

"Probably just a few clever titles of awards, dates, and that's it," Abramoff answered. "Do you have any creative titles, or should I dip into my bag of tricks?"

Another exchange suggests that beneath all the layers of fraud, the many coats of deceit, Abramoff knew something was terribly, terribly wrong. "Preston Gates sent around their 'Alumni Directory' today," a former colleague, William Jarrell, wrote on June 26, 2001. "Don't know what's funnier, the fact that half the book has people listed as GT [Greenberg Traurig] or the fact that Mike Scanlon is listed as 'Lost Alumni.'"

"I'm just surprised I am not under 'dead, disgraced, or in jail,'" Abramoff said.

He would not have to wait very long.

CHAPTER EIGHT

THE SORCERER'S APPRENTICE

HOW ONE LOBBYIST BECAME ENTANGLED IN JACK ABRAMOFF'S WEB

You've got to have ethics and integrity in everything you do.
Especially here in D.C. It's such a small town that if you gain a
reputation as someone who does not play by the rules, that
does not do things with integrity, your career is ended.
—DAVID SAFAVIAN

TOM DELAY. Ralph Reed. Grover Norquist. Bob Ney. Conrad Burns. These men are famous, at least in Washington. But Jack Abramoff spent most of his days and nights working alongside less-famous others. These were the congressional underlings who often helped him secure favors and carve out loopholes for his clients—and who were often rewarded with jobs in the lobbying industry for themselves. These were the men and women who had watched Washington Wizards basketball games from Abramoff's skybox at the MCI Center, who had dinner at Signatures, who studied the comings and goings of Casino Jack.

Some had left jobs in Congress for the executive branch. An ex-lobbyist on the Mariana Islands account worked as an assistant secretary at the Department of Labor. President Bush nominated a former Abramoff client and ex-Tyco legal counsel to be deputy attorney general (the nomination was later withdrawn). Abramoff's executive assistant at Preston Gates, who had worked previously for Ralph Reed, went on to a similar job with presidential adviser Karl Rove. None of these people has been accused of doing anything illegal.

Not so David Safavian. For almost three years, from 1995 to 1997, Safavian worked with Abramoff at Preston Gates, then went into business with Grover Norquist. His story is worth examining, because it illustrates, better than most, Jack Abramoff's appeal—and Jack Abramoff's position of power in Washington.

Safavian had been born in Pontiac, Michigan, in 1967. His family sold auto parts, and he worked in the family store. He went to school in Missouri, at St. Louis University, where he was a member of Phi Kappa Theta. According to his now-deleted biography on the White House Web site, he graduated fifth in his class at the Detroit College of Law. The year was 1993. He was drawn to politics. While in college, he interned in the office of Republican congressman Robert Davis. After graduation, he served briefly as a legislative assistant in the office of Republican congressman Bill Schuette, and worked on Schuette's failed Senate campaign in 1990. Additional internships followed: for McDonnell Douglas, for U.S. Magistrate Judge David McConnell, for the U.S. Army Aviation and Troop Support Command in St. Louis. He moved to Washington to take a job at KPMG after law school, and earned a certificate in tax law from Georgetown in 1994. He joined Preston Gates the following year. Abramoff was his boss.[1]

Majority parties attract opportunists. When a party is in power, it serves as a beacon for ambitious young people, drawing them into the party ranks, where they find internships, jobs, and mentors. No doubt Safavian's ideological convictions were sincere; most people's are. But where did those convictions come from in the first place? Which comes first: the allure of power or the identification with an idea? It is always difficult to tell. However, unlike Abramoff, Norquist, and Reed, Safavian was never an activist. He was a professional. For him, institutionalized conservatism was a career path.

For him, and for others. Over the years, Abramoff assembled a group of protégés, often former congressional aides who were attracted to his charisma and to his power. This is unsurprising. Anyone who spends his career in Washington will have his own set of acolytes. And people enjoyed being around Abramoff. Several people have told me that Abramoff was a formidable presence—quick with a joke, garrulous, smart, filled with energy and ambition. He would quote *The Godfather* to his subordinates; pump up their egos with the idea that they were the best; challenge, impress, and inspire them. It takes confidence to be a con artist.

In reality, apprentices are often little more than cogs in a great machine. A master gains influence by distributing his apprentices throughout the government; in so doing, he gains access and information. With Abramoff, the door opened both ways. He would often hire other people's apprentices, the former legislative assistants to congressmen. These were people like Edward Ayoob, who had worked for Harry Reid before joining Abramoff's team at Greenberg Traurig; Kevin A. Ring, former legislative director for California Republican representative John Doolittle; Neil Volz, former chief of staff to Ohio Republican representative Bob Ney; and Michael Scanlon and Tony Rudy, who had both worked for Tom DeLay.

Together, these career lawyers made up Team Abramoff—of which, for a while, Safavian was a charter member. Of course, it should be remembered that not everyone groomed by Abramoff turned out like him, or like Safavian. But sometimes the flaws of the teacher are present, or even magnified, in the student.

At Preston Gates, Team Abramoff's accounts included, among others, the exile government of Macedonia, the Commonwealth of the Northern Mariana Islands, the Microsoft Corporation, and Soyuzkontrakt Trade & Finance, a Russian conglomerate with business in the United States. As an associate, Safavian would have watched his boss flatter and pamper clients, arrange junkets to foreign countries for sympathetic lawmakers and journalists, and, most of all, make a gigantic pile of money. He would also have learned, like other lobbyists, how to substitute the private for the public interest with ease. In short, he was on his way to becoming an enormous success.

In 1997, when Abramoff's longtime comrade Grover Norquist opened a lobbying firm of his own, he made Safavian a partner. The new company was called the Merritt Group, later Janus-Merritt Strategies. "We represent clients who really do have an interest in a smaller federal government," Safavian told *Legal Times* in a 1997 interview. "We're all very ideologically driven, and have a bias in favor of free markets." He went on: "We're not letting people who offer us money change our principles."[2]

Scanning Janus-Merritt's lobbying registry, one might divide the firm's clients into a few types. There were businesses like BP America, the U.S. division of British Petroleum, and Microsoft. There were foreign companies like the Corporación Venezolana de Cementos and Grupo Financiero Banorte. There were Muslim activists, some of whom we met in Chapter 4. There were foreign powers; Safavian, for example, registered as a lobbyist for Pascal Lissouba of the Congo and Omar Bongo of Gabon. And there were gaming interests, including Indian tribes. Janus-Merritt flacked for the Saginaw Chippewa—a client the firm shared with Jack Abramoff—the Viejas band of Kumeyaay Indians, and the National Indian Gaming Association.

Safavian was a passionate advocate of Internet gambling. His clients included the Interactive Gaming Council, a trade association for online betting houses, and CDM Fantasy Sports, which, according to its Web site, is "one of the leading providers of fantasy sports products and services in North America." In 1997, he founded the Internet Consumer Choice Coalition, a nonprofit whose sole purpose, it would appear, was to fight a bill authored by Republican Arizona senator Jon Kyl that would have made online gambling a federal crime. Coalition members included the American Civil Liberties Union, the Association of Concerned Taxpayers, Citizens for a Sound Economy, the Competitive Enterprise Institute, the Interactive Services Association, the Small Business Survival Committee, and the United States Internet Council. As is common in the incestuous world of paid advocacy, some coalition members—the Interactive Services Association, for one—were also clients of Safavian's. Another was Americans for Tax Reform.[3]

Month after month, year after year, ten-thousand-dollar check after check, Safavian helped to defeat the Kyl bill. He was proud of his efforts. And he wasn't afraid to brag about his accomplishments. On December 15, 2000, the Fantasy Sports Trade Association posted a message titled "from Safavian" on its Web site. It was a pithy message, but it captured, in its own way, the biases and assumptions, the Manichaean worldview, that lobbyists and activists carry around in their heads. First, using capital letters for emphasis, Safavian wrote: "I am please [sic] to let you know that we were successful. There are no internet gambling provisions in the final appropriation [sic] bill."

Then he urged his clients—and, presumably, online poker addicts across the globe—to "relax a bit." At least "for now." Because "policy beat politics once again. (Maybe the American system isn't really that bad.)" In this case, he said, "the good guys won."[4]

"As a lobbyist, you always need to be thinking," Safavian told the Michigan State Law School alumni magazine in the summer of 2002. "You spend your time moving legislation. It all comes down to being an advocate." He had left Janus-Merritt in June 2001 to become Utah Republican congressman Chris Cannon's chief of staff. A reliable conservative, Cannon had hired Safavian, along with Norquist protégée Bethany Noble, for many reasons, fundraising foremost among them.

The two knew how to raise cash. Safavian started the Western Leadership Fund, a political action committee, run out of his home, devoted to Cannon's reelection. Many of the donors had been clients of Safavian's in the private sector, including Indian gaming tribes. Never mind Cannon's position on the gaming issue ("I oppose gambling. I think it's a pernicious vice. I'd like to eliminate it.")—a tide of casino money flowed into his war chest between 2001 and 2003. Meanwhile, Cannon voted repeatedly against efforts to restrict online gambling. He and his chief of staff were in sync. All indications are that Safavian liked his boss and that his boss liked him.[5]

While he was working for Cannon, Safavian took a leave of absence from Janus-Merritt. That is, he did not resign altogether. He left open the possibility that he would buy back his stock in the lobbying company, where he was a principal, once his stint in government was over.[6] This led to possible conflicts of interest, not the least of which was Cannon's reversal on gambling. A November 23, 2005, article in the *Salt Lake Tribune* mentions some further examples. For instance, on June 19, 2002, Cannon issued a press release praising Covad Communications, an Internet service provider. Covad had recently dropped the amount in service fees that it charged clients. "I am not endorsing Covad's product or its new price—I'll let consumers decide that for themselves," Cannon said in the release.[7] "But Covad's announcement, along with other recent announcements by Bell Companies, illustrate what happens when competition is allowed to work its magic in the market." The press release neglected to mention that Covad Communications was a client of Cannon's chief of staff's former lobbying firm, or that Covad Communications would donate over the following years some $5,200 to Cannon.

Some additional examples. At a February 7, 2002, meeting of the Energy Policy, Natural Resources, and Regulatory Affairs Subcommittee of the House Government Reform Committee, Cannon said that "I'm not a fan of Indian gaming," but that "I do support the idea, as you know, of tribal sovereignty." The tribal sovereignty he had in mind was that of the Viejas Band of Kumeyaay Indians, who operate a casino in Alpine, California. At the time of the hearing, the Viejas were engaged in a dispute with another tribe. Cannon sided with the Viejas. He neglected to mention that the Viejas Band were a client of his chief of staff's lobbying firm. He neglected to mention that the tribe had contributed $5,000 to his political action committees.[8]

As these examples might suggest, Safavian's tenure as Cannon's chief of staff was relatively painless. It was also quick. Less than a year had passed before he moved on to the executive branch, becoming chief of staff to Stephen Perry, the administrator of the General Services Administration. The GSA acts as custodian for all federal properties—it buys them, sells them, and takes care of them in between. It's a peripheral agency, staffed mainly with career bureaucrats. It is far from the center of power.

Safavian's first day on the job was May 16, 2002. Within a week, Jack Abramoff e-mailed him to ask for a favor.[9]

Abramoff had a problem. In 2001, he had taken millions of dollars from the coffers of the Capital Athletic Foundation to start the Eshkol Academy. Now the school needed a new location. Abramoff must have thought that, with Safavian in a key position, he could get a sweet deal on some government property. Specifically, he had in mind renting, and perhaps ultimately purchasing, a forty-acre tract of land at the White Oak government facility in Silver Spring.

While Safavian was at it, Abramoff had another favor to ask. One of the Indian tribes he represented was also looking to buy some property. Tribal leaders were eyeing the Old Post Office building in downtown D.C., a storied and majestic structure on Pennsylvania Avenue that GSA held in trust. Because American Indians are a minority group, they are eligible for special tax breaks and subsidies when leasing government space. Abramoff wanted his clients to have a heads-up on any potential sale of the Old Post Office.

According to the criminal affidavit later filed against Safavian, Abramoff first e-mailed Safavian about the White Oak property on May 24, 2002. A few weeks later, on June 14, Abramoff sent an e-mail to one of his coworkers saying that Safavian was "going to join us in Scotland." The Scotland trip—a golf junket to the famous St. Andrews course—had been planned for some time. Recall that in June 2002, Abramoff had asked the El Paso Tigua to pay for the trip. Recall as well that the Tigua had no money. They couldn't pay.

After reading Abramoff's e-mail saying Safavian would be on the golf trip, the coworker shot back: "Why dave? I like him but didn't know u did as much. Business angle?"

Abramoff replied the next day. "Total business angle," he wrote. "He is new COS of GSA."[10]

On June 19, Abramoff e-mailed Safavian to ask how his casino clients could best lease the Old Post Office from the government. And on June 30, he wrote Safavian yet again, this time returning, once more, to the subject of land for his school:

Can you find out if you guys have control of any part of a huge federal property called the White Oak Federal Research Center, off New Hampshire Ave in Silver Spring? I want to try to get 40 acres of that tract if possible for a non-profit. Is it doable?

A few days later, Safavian replied:

We have not fully allocated all of the acreage at White Oak. We are still surveying whether any other federal agencies are interested. If not, we would begin disposal (i.e., sale or donation) proceedings. As for the other project . . .

Safavian was referring to the potential lease of the Old Post Office.

. . . you should know that aside from section 8a preferences, Indian tribes also have "hub zone" status, which provides for enterprise zone-like tax benefits. You will need to ramp up on this as it is progressing. Let's discuss. Dhs.

The two continued their correspondence throughout the month of July. We're told that they mostly talked about the upcoming golf trip. Then, on July 21, Abramoff wrote to Safavian, in an e-mail with the subject line "White Oak": "The facility is secured, as I understand. Any thoughts on how we could get a tour there without giving a heads up to too many folks?" Abramoff must have thought that Safavian would work something out. Later in the day, he wrote a coworker that the chief of staff was "totally supportive."

Meanwhile, Safavian advised Abramoff on the Old Post Office deal. On July 22, 2002, Abramoff sent Safavian a draft of a letter that his allies in Congress were willing to send to Safavian's boss. According to the affidavit, the letter urged the GSA to give "special consideration" to "HUBZone businesses," such as those owned by Indian tribes. Appended to the letter was a question Abramoff had for Safavian: "Does this work, or do you want it to be longer?"

And so it went, on and on, Abramoff e-mailing questions about both the Old Post Office and the parcel of land in Silver Spring, Safavian responding with answers and suggestions. Reading these e-mails, one is struck by their banality, the drudgery of government life, the glacial speed with which the federal bureaucracy conducts business. Neither party gave any hint that he was behaving suspiciously or unusually. And perhaps neither was behaving so. Perhaps this was just business as usual.

But then something changed. On July 25, a few days before leaving for Scotland, Safavian contacted a GSA ethics official. What was the policy, he wondered, governing overseas vacations paid for by lobbyists? At issue, he wrote in an e-mail, "is airfare":

> The host of the trip is chartering a private jet to take the eight of us from BWI to Scottland [*sic*] and back. He is paying the cost for the aircraft regardless of whether I go or not. In fact, none of the other guest [*sic*] will be paying a proportional share of the aircraft costs. I need to know how to treat this activity.
>
> One other point of relevance: *the host is a lawyer and lobbyist, but one that has no business before GSA (he does all of his work on Capitol Hill).*

The emphasis here is added, just as it is in the affidavit, for what should be obvious reasons: To write that Abramoff "has no business before GSA" was a stretch, to say the very least. Unaware of all the details, however, the ethics officer took Safavian at his word. "Based upon the information you have provided," he wrote to Safavian, "you may accept the gift of free transportation from your friend." No doubt pleased with this answer, Safavian forwarded the ethics officer's e-mail to Abramoff under the message "It looks like Scotland is a go."

That wasn't the only thing he forwarded to Abramoff on July 26, 2002. He also sent along an e-mail that had been under discussion at the agency, which, according to the FBI affidavit, outlined "alternatives for transferring NSWC-White Oak to 'high school and sports academy'"—specifically, Abramoff's Eshkol school. Safavian was frustrated. "This is the type of bureaucracy I'm dealing with," he vented in another e-mail to his mentor. "I am still running the traps on the [one] year lease."

A few days later, in a reply to a message that Abramoff had sent to his home e-mail, Safavian added a few comments, in brackets, to a letter that Eshkol's lawyers planned to send to the General Services Administration:

> I would add a couple of paragraphs concerning the school's history (if there is some), its mission, its annual budget, etc. How is this unique or different than schools currently available to students from the area. If you are comfortable with it, I would also add a paragraph explaining what happened with Montgomery County in order to drive home the urgency of this issue. . . . I would NOT raise the possibility of obtaining GSA land from White Oak. That could be seen as an unofficial reason to deny your request for use of the property this year.

Meantime, Safavian wanted to hold a meeting. He talked to Abramoff, who then wrote to his wife and to two other school employees. Things were moving ahead at full speed, Abramoff explained. "They"—GSA officials—"want to meet downtown on Friday at 11:30 A.M. at the GSA building. . . . David"—Safavian—"does not think that I should be there, given my high profile politically. I agree. The three of you can go, though."

Later, Abramoff sent another e-mail to his wife:

> David does not want [the name Abramoff] used in the meeting. when you check in at the door, however, you'll need your driver's license, and it's OK for you to be [Abramoff] there, since that

won't get up to the guy in the meeting (who probably does not know me, but David and I don't want to take a chance). OK?

The meeting took place on August 2. All indications are that it went off without a hitch.

The very next day, Safavian, Abramoff, Ney, and Ralph Reed, among others, boarded a private jet to Scotland. The St. Andrews trip lasted eight days, August 3 to August 11. It included a stop in London, and like all Abramoff junkets it was a lavish affair, costing more than $100,000. Everyone had a blast.[11]

Which man was getting the better of the other? Safavian was helping Abramoff on several fronts, and perhaps, to his mind, got a golf trip out of it. And although Safavian told the ethics officers that Abramoff had "no business pending" at the agency, Abramoff certainly thought he did. A lobbyist of his caliber, no doubt, would have thought that a week on the links could only help his cause. Then again, perhaps the two were playing each other, or each was simply trying to help a friend. With Abramoff and his friends, one never truly knows.

In the end, though, Abramoff's efforts went nowhere. The Indians never leased the Old Post Office building. The Eshkol Academy never found a new home on government property. A lack of success is one of the Abramoff saga's recurring themes—a lot of people paid him a lot of money, but no one, in the end, can tell you exactly what the clients got in return. Eshkol closed in 2003. Abramoff had spent more than $4 million of the Capital Athletic Foundation's money on it.

On March 26, 2003, according to the FBI affidavit, an anonymous tipster contacted the General Services Administration's office of the inspector general. The tipster had information regarding Safavian's trip to Scotland. The information seemed substantive enough to warrant further inquiry. The GSA inspector general interviewed Safavian, who said that Abramoff had no business with GSA in August 2002; that he had taken the time for the trip from his annual leave; and that, in fact, he had reimbursed Abramoff for his plane tickets and accommodations. Then Safavian gave the inspector general a copy of a check he had written to Abramoff for $3,100, dated August 3, 2002, the day he left for St. Andrews. Safavian was cooperative. Everything seemed in order. The inspector general closed the inquiry.

On November 3, 2003, President Bush nominated Safavian to head the Office of Management and Budget's Office of Procurement Policy. Bush resubmitted the nomination on January 22, 2004. A few months later, on April 29, the Senate Committee on Governmental Affairs held a hearing on the nomination. The transcript of that hearing bears rereading. Representative Cannon appeared on the nominee's behalf. "Mr. Safavian was a remarkably helpful person in the process of bringing together my staff and that of Mr. Conyers and the minority staff on the Judiciary Committee to deal with issues of great importance to the American people," Cannon told the committee, "including telecom policy and helping to avoid the remonopolization of the Baby Bells." Safavian had experience with telecom issues both as a lobbyist and as a congressional staffer. Cannon further told the senators that his former employee "is a person of great mental capacity" who "understands the technology and the great issues of our time," and who was also a "great advocate." In his testimony, Democratic representative John Conyers of Michigan added that "this is probably a very great morning, a very great day for our country, for his family." At the conclusion of the hearing, Sen. Carl Levin, Democrat of Michigan, told Safavian, "I wonder, also, if you would tell your daughter when she is old enough to know"—she was ten months old at the time—"that we missed her being here this morning."[12]

The inquiry was not entirely over, however. Some senators had further questions for Safavian, mostly concerning his lobbying on behalf of foreign governments, such as Montenegro ("The extent of my work was to review regulations issued by the Treasury Department's Office of Foreign Assets Control") and Congo and Gabon (Safavian ignored questions on this topic).[13] But the senators were also curious about his work lobbying for Islamic radicals like Dr. al-

Barzinji (see Chapter 4). Safavian denied any involvement with al Barzinji and his associates. But it might have been prudent for the senators to return to an op-ed Safavian had written on October 25, 2000, for the *Washington Times*. In that op-ed, titled "Racial Profiling, Gore-style," Safavian took issue with the recommendations of the Gore Commission on Aviation Safety and Security, which as part of its final report had recommended, in 1997, that "passengers could be separated into a very large majority who present little or no risk, and a small minority who merit additional attention."

As a result, "While I cannot prove it, it is pretty clear that I am routinely racially profiled at the airport," Safavian wrote. "The Gore Commission itself," Safavian further argued, "was a knee-jerk response" to the "(false) assumption that TWA Flight 800 was a terrorist act." And this "knee-jerk response," Safavian wrote, led to the provision of "stops and searches for all individuals traveling to 'suspect' destinations. Unfortunately, almost all of these suspect destinations turned out to be Arab or Islamic countries."

Unfortunately?

Regardless of the implications of Safavian's ideas about American national security, the senate confirmed him to the procurement post, by unanimous consent, on November 21, 2004.

The director of federal procurement is a little-discussed but important job inside the Bush White House. As director, Safavian supervised and managed annual purchases of goods totaling upward of $300 billion. He was responsible for contracting and leasing. He formulated policies dealing with the methods of federal purchasing, and he saw that those policies were carried out.

Except for a brief college internship at the Pentagon, Safavian had little experience in federal procurement, but, as Conyers pointed out, he did have a happy family. His wife, Jennifer, was chief counsel to Republican representative Tom Davis of Virginia, head of the House Committee on Government Reform. Jennifer Safavian's purview included federal procurement. Which her husband now ran for the executive branch.

Eager to stave off any potential conflicts of interest, Mrs. Safa-vian's superiors dashed off a letter on December 9, 2003, outlining the committee's recusal policy. "Effective immediately," they wrote, "Ms. Safavian will be recused from all matters where the conduct of officials and employees of the Office of Management and Bud-get is the central issue." Furthermore, "Ms. Safavian will be recused, also effective immediately, from oversight or investigation of any specific procurement matter at an agency or department other than OMB." This recusal policy doubtless also extended to the Safavian breakfast nook and television room. And yet, if this was a conflict of interest, no one raised a fuss.

There is no evidence, as I write, that Safavian provided favors to Abramoff after he had been named federal procurement director. Rather, there is almost no evidence.

Soon after Safavian settled into his new job, reporters and fed-eral investigators began to look into the August 2002 junket. When asked about his week in Scotland, Safavian repeated what he had told the GSA inspector general in 2003. "The trip was exclusively personal," he told the *Washington Post* in January 2005. "I did no business there. . . . Jack is an old friend of mine." He would not elaborate further.[14]

He told the same thing to the Senate Indian Affairs Committee:

As you may know, I was invited by [Abramoff] to join his trip to Scotland in August, 2002. [Abramoff] and I have had a relation-ship since 1994, when I worked as a new associate at [the Wash-ington, D.C.] law firm where he was a partner. When the invitation was made, I was the chief of staff to the U.S. General Services Administration ("GSA"). [Abramoff] did not have any business before the agency at that time. . . . Counsel determined that I could accept the value of the trip gratis; it did not meet the definition of a "gift from a prohibited source" under the applica-ble regulations, nor was it considered a gift given because of my official position. Nevertheless, in the exercise of discretion, I gave

[Abramoff] a check for the value of the trip prior to departure. In addition, I took leave without pay to travel.[15]

And, according to the FBI affidavit, he told the same thing to the federal task force investigating Abramoff:

During this interview, SAFAVIAN stated in substance and in part that [Abramoff] had asked about acquiring land for Entity A and the OPO significantly well after the August 2002 Scotland trip and that, at the time of the trip, [Abramoff] had no business with GSA.

It was this series of obfuscations, of sly recastings of events, that ultimately led to Safavian's arrest on September 19, 2005.

He was arrested outside his Alexandria, Virginia, home on his way to work, and charged, according to the affidavit submitted for his arrest, with impeding "the due and proper administration of law." In other words, he had allegedly provided a final favor to his friend and mentor—he had covered for Abramoff. Prior to his arrest, we are told, Safavian was working feverishly to supply relief and reconstruction efforts along the Gulf Coast in the aftermath of Hurricane Katrina. He had resigned from the White House the previous Friday.[16]

In the larger story of Jack Abramoff's wheeling and dealing, Safavian is a minor player. Yet his career mirrors the trajectory of not only his teacher but also his teacher's other apprentices, men like Michael Scanlon and Tony Rudy. Safavian cut corners, bent the rules, twisted the facts. No one knows what causes such disregard. A possible explanation, however, is the hubris associated with power. In the service of a great cause, at the helm of the most powerful government in the world, what is to stop someone from doing himself and his friends an occasional favor?

There is a broader lesson here as well. Safavian's arrest came the week that the Republican Party typically celebrated the anniversary of its Contract with America. Yet, in 2005, few mentioned the document. The Republicans were now a "governing majority," not a reform-minded insurgency. The arrest of a former executive-branch political appointee was treated as an isolated incident, unrelated to the dominant party's aspirations and agenda.

How quickly we dismiss inconvenient facts. David Safavian was only the first. There would be others. The tapestry of K Street Conservatism was about to unravel.

CHAPTER NINE

THE UNRAVELING

HOW TO CATCH A CROOKED LOBBYIST

An ADJECTIVE AND a noun led to the arrest of Jack Abramoff, the fall of Tom DeLay, and the potential indictment of half a dozen Republican congressmen. The adjective is "contingency." The noun is "curiosity."

Consider the Louisiana Coushatta's internal audit.

The Louisiana Coushatta are a small and extremely rich American Indian tribe that live near Kinder, Louisiana, in that state's southwest. (There are slightly more than 850 members, and each member receives an annual stipend of approximately $40,000.) Since 1995, the Coushatta have operated the Grand Casino and Resort, a sprawling gambling palace that includes 100,000 square feet of games, more than 500 hotel rooms, and, according to its Web site, "a luxury RV resort." The casino employs 2,800 people. Annual payroll is around $80 million.[1]

In March 2001, the Coushatta hired Jack Abramoff to work on "IGRA," "tax," and "appropriations" issues, according to Senate disclosure reports. (In this case, IGRA stands for the Indian Gaming Regulatory Act.) It was a lucrative contract, amounting to about $125,000 per month, plus expenses. The tribe ended up paying far more, however.

In less than three years, from March 2001 to the fall of 2003, and in addition to the tribe's contract with Greenberg Traurig, the Louisiana Coushatta paid Michael Scanlon's Capitol Campaign Strategies more than $26 million, the American International Center "think tank" $3.6 million, and Abramoff's "charity," the Capital Athletic Foundation, $1 million. That's just shy of $32 million total.[2] And almost all of it ended up in either Abramoff's or Scanlon's pockets.

In May 2003, during a routine look at the books, the tribe's comptroller discovered that the Coushatta were running a $40 million deficit. The tribal council was shocked. None of those who had commissioned the audit—no one in the tribal power structure at all, apparently—knew exactly where the money had gone. The council hired an outside accountant, based in New Mexico, to conduct an internal audit. What the auditor found surprised the council even more. One member leaked the results to a local reporter.

The reporter's name was Julia Robb, a staff writer for the *Daily Town Talk,* Alexandria, Louisiana's, local Gannett newspaper. The *Town Talk* published her story on Sunday, September 21, 2003. The Coushatta audit, Robb wrote, had found that "more than $18 million" had been spent between 2001 and 2002 on lobbyists without most of the tribal council's knowledge. Even more disturbing, the millions had been transferred from "tribal health, education, and social service accounts" and funneled to Greenberg Traurig ($2.4 million), Capitol Campaign Strategies ($13.7 million), the American International Center ($566,000), and Jack Abramoff himself ($485,000).

There were stirrings of revolt. "It's not the chairman's money," councilman David Sickey told Robb. It's "not the council's money.

It's the tribe's money." But the outrage and sense of betrayal on the part of some of the Coushatta was not the most important detail that Robb included in her article. That distinction was left to a single sentence, which read, "The Coushatta tribe's problems have caught the attention of federal and state law enforcement officials, who met recently on the matter." The FBI were in Kinder.

Few people noticed the *Daily Town Talk* article when it was published. But there were people back in Washington who were curious about what Abramoff had been up to. Specifically: his rivals. Over the years, other lobbyists had looked on in envy and fear as Abramoff scooped up their Indian tribal clients—envy at the enormous fees those clients were willing to pay him, and fear that their own clients would soon go over to Abramoff's column. Shortly after Julia Robb wrote her article about the Louisiana Coushatta, one of those lobbyists—a student of Abramoff's career who was suspicious of the relationship between the Greenberg Traurig lobbyist and Michael Scanlon—placed a phone call that would prove consequential.

It happened sometime in the fall of 2003, when Susan Schmidt received a phone call at her desk.[3] Schmidt is a veteran investigative reporter at the *Washington Post,* a meticulous and unbiased journalist who follows a story wherever it leads. Back in 1998, she had become famous for breaking the story, along with *Post* colleagues Peter Baker and Tony Loci, of Monica Lewinsky. For that, and for her coverage of the Whitewater real estate scandal years earlier, Democrats had attacked Schmidt for being too friendly to Republicans. Soon Republicans would attack her for being too friendly to Democrats.

When Schmidt received the call, she was working the Justice Department beat, filing stories on the war on terrorism. The person on the phone was a prominent Washington lobbyist. Schmidt had never met him.[4] The lobbyist urged Schmidt to examine Abramoff's tribal connections, the fees he had been charging those tribes, and how Michael Scanlon's Capitol Campaign Strategies fit in. Schmidt went to Federal Election Commission records, discovering Abramoff's long and generous record of political giving. She went to congressional lobbying disclosure forms. What she found there, while surprising, also confirmed what the unidentified lobbyist had told her: Abramoff's tribes were paying Greenberg Traurig, according to *Washington Post* reporter Deborah Howell, "10 to 20 times as much" as the amount other lobbyists were charging. Yet still the tribes paid. Why?[5]

No one knew. Schmidt focused her investigation on the four tribes that had contracts with both Abramoff and Scanlon: the Louisiana Coushatta, the Saginaw Chippewa, the Agua Caliente band of Cahuilla, and the Mississippi Choctaw. She developed sources in those tribes, dissidents like David Sickey who were disturbed at what was going on. The sources handed her contracts that had been signed between tribal authorities and Abramoff and Scanlon. They told her about the various nonprofits and charities Abramoff had urged them to donate to: the American International Center, the Capital Athletic Foundation, Americans for Tax Reform, and another Norquist group, the Council of Republican Environmental Advocacy.

As Schmidt worked on her story, the Saginaw Chippewa elected a new tribal council, which canceled, in December 2003, Abramoff's contract. The FBI continued to ask questions in Louisiana. And in mid-February 2004, agents traveled to Michigan to talk to the Chippewa. Two investigations into Abramoff were taking place: one on the part of the Justice Department, the other by the *Washington Post*. There would be more investigations soon enough.[6]

Schmidt spent several months reporting before she contacted Abramoff. It would turn out to be her only interview with the man, and his next-to-last interview altogether. (He later spoke, against his lawyer's wishes, to journalist Michael Crowley for a *New York Times Magazine* profile.)[7] Schmidt asked Abramoff to list all that he had done for the tribes. He would not say. Then she asked him what services he delivers to those who place him on retainer. "I think we bring an order of magnitude in terms of our success and our approach on behalf of the tribes," he told her, employing political newspeak. "A lot of these tribes who have thrown off the relatively inexpensive lobbyists basically come to us with the comment of 'you

get what you pay for.'" Schmidt also asked Abramoff whether he
had a financial stake in Scanlon's companies. He said no.

Scanlon was even more reticent than Abramoff. He simply faxed
a statement to Schmidt, saying the new tribal governments had
bad-mouthed Capitol Campaign Strategies because they "want to
send business to their own guys." "The bottom line is that," the
statement continued, "my firm delivers. We provide expensive services, in an expensive industry, and we get the job done."

On February 22, 2004, Schmidt's finished piece appeared on
the front page of the *Washington Post*. The headline read: "A Jackpot from Indian Gaming Tribes." The article's lead paragraphs are
worth rereading, if only because they constitute one of the clearest
examples of newspaper journalism acting as the "first rough draft
of history":

> A powerful Washington lobbyist and a former aide to House
> Majority Leader Tom DeLay (R.-Tex.) persuaded four newly
> wealthy Indian gaming tribes to pay their firms more than $45
> million over the past three years for lobbying and public affairs
> work, a sum that rivals spending to influence public policy by
> some of the nation's biggest corporate interests.
>
> Touting his ties to conservatives in Congress and the White
> House, lobbyist Jack Abramoff persuaded the tribes to hire him
> and public relations executive Michael Scanlon to block powerful
> forces both at home and in Washington who have designs on their
> money, according to tribe members.

Schmidt went on to relate how Michael Scanlon had paid $4.7
million, in cash, for the beachside Rehoboth Beach mansion that
housed, in its basement, the American International Center; how
he "or his companies," since 2001, had spent $16 million purchas-
ing real estate, "including a $6.3 million Delaware office park";
how in 2002 he started renting a $17,000-per-month apartment in
the Ritz-Carlton on Washingon's M Street, a few blocks from
Georgetown. Schmidt was yet to discover that when Scanlon trav-

eled between the apartment at the Ritz in Washington and the mansion on the beach in Delaware, he took a helicopter.[8]

And there it was: the profits, the influence, the connections to powerful congressmen, the trading on a career in the conservative movement, the unstoppable attraction to gambling dollars, all distilled into two crystalline sentences. Through contingency—a nonroutine audit and a strategically placed phone call—and curiosity—Robb's and Schmidt's intrepid reporting—a window had been opened onto the world of the K Street Conservatives. Things would never be the same.

On February 21, the night before it was published in the paper's print edition, the *Washington Post* posted Schmidt's story on its Web site. At 10:45 P.M., shortly after the story appeared, Greenberg Traurig lobbyist Neil Volz forwarded it to the "DCCasino" e-mail list.

Duane Gibson, a member of Abramoff's team who had formerly worked for Alaska representative Don Young, was the first to reply to all. "Not that bad," he wrote.

His was the minority reaction. After reading Gibson's response, another lobbyist, Michael Williams, sent an e-mail just to Michael Smith, Kevin Ring, and Neil Volz. "Is he tone deaf, or is it me?" Williams asked, referring to Gibson. "Shouldn't the mention of the FBI alarm a legal eagle like him?"

"This is a total embarrassment," Smith replied. "My friends all have it on their bberry's and are asking a ton of questions. This goes from here to roll call to the hill and on."

"Same here!" Williams wrote. "But they are R's!!" And "What about this statement from the article," Williams asked, including Abramoff's quote that he had no financial ties to Scanlon's firm. The Greenberg Traurig lawyers knew that quote was a lie.

Volz chimed in. "I second that," he wrote, referring to Smith's e-mail a few minutes before. "Just got a call from a friend who read the article—his quote, 'bad news.'"

Shortly after midnight, Ring went online to read Schmidt's piece. "I just woke up and read it," he wrote Volz, Williams, and Smith. "Lots of damning facts in there. To be very honest, the Scanlon stuff makes me sick to my stomach—buying property in cash. I am glad she did not no [*sic*] about AIC [the American International Center], but the firm does."[9]

Then Ring forwarded the article to another friend. "Now what do you think of my partner Jack?" he wrote sarcastically. "Not too shady, eh?"

The friend, Matt DeMazza, replied, "That's a lotta cake."

"Awful," Ring said.

Then the two entered into a revealing exchange.

"So are these Redskins just blindly paying these exorbitant fees based largely on Jack's PAST successes, and not what's going on now?" DeMazza asked.

"They are paying our fees because our firm does good work," Ring replied, "but they are paying the bulk to this outside vendor on our reputation and Jack's recommendation. The firm doesn't see the money, but it seems the others are dipping. Not legit."

"And what of the Michigan Chippewas that have canceled contracts? How much does that hurt your firm and/or Abramoff and Scanlon?"

"Hurts Jack and the firm," Ring wrote. "Firm is losing clients because of Scanlon. Firm doesn't appreciate that. I expect corrective action by the firm or something will have to give."

"So is it 100% Scanlon's fault, or is Jack partially to blame?"

"Jack," Ring wrote, "is equally to blame. He talks tribes into hiring Scanlon."

"That's what I gathered from the story, but I wasn't sure if you knew something that the reporter didn't know. So is your future with G.T. in question?"

"I don't think mine is. But impact will be felt by everyone. Unsettling after buying new house. I know more than article," Ring wrote, "and the truth is worse."[10]

The morning after Schmidt's story appeared, at about 8:30 A.M., Abramoff forwarded an electronic version of it to his clients and associates, typically appending a short personal message. "Not sure if [redacted] had sent this to you yet," he wrote to one unidentified recipient, "but this hit piece was in yesterday's Post. Let me know if you want to chat about it. The reporter was a real racist and bigot, but that seems pretty obvious with the implication that Native peoples don't have the same rights that companies do to defend themselves. Oh well."[11]

This note was only the first. Stung by what Schmidt had revealed, Abramoff entered an e-mail frenzy. "I hope you are well," he wrote another undisclosed recipient, most likely a representative of one of his tribal clients. "I wanted you to see this piece which was in yesterday's Washington Post. As you can tell, the reporter was quite biased, and frankly fairly bigoted. Anyway, I am sure this will come up and I am happy to discuss it with you, though it was pretty obviously a slanted piece. Regards."[12]

At 11:05 A.M., Marc Schwartz sent Abramoff an e-mail with the subject line "ARTICLE." "Well, it wasn't pretty," he wrote. "It sure looks like Scanlon was living a little large, huh! Call me when you get a chance."

"Don't you love Washington?" Abramoff replied. "I'll try to call later today."[13] It appears he never called, instead following up with another e-mail later that night. The *Post* story was the "usual bullshit," he wrote. "Funny part (for me, not Mike) was that 60 [percent] of the over 300 e-mails I got thought it was a puff piece. Thank G-D for ADD!"

He was putting a happy face on a sad story. Internal e-mails show that there was a flurry of activity in Abramoff's corner of the Greenberg Traurig office the day Schmidt's article appeared, which never quite subsided. Abramoff knew he had to respond. He became his own lobbyist, employing the tricks of K Street Conservatism in a counterattack. His methods were dishonorable. His strategy was to ghostwrite letters from his clients to the *Post* in which he accused Schmidt of racism. Unsurprisingly, he subcontracted the actual writing duties.

"Here are the first three letters," Greenberg Traurig lawyer Christine Thomas wrote Abramoff and colleague Todd Boulanger on Tuesday morning, February 24. "They are all a bit different, as you asked for, but we can definitely switch around the three authors as you see fit. I just put in the names randomly, but you may want to change this. Let me know if/how you would like me to edit these pieces, or if there are any arguments you would like me to leave out or build upon."[14]

This is how Washington works. The ghostwritten letters, devoid of personality or verve, exhibited a tenuous internal logic. The argument went something like this: First, by equating the amounts the tribes had spent on lobbying with that of large American corporations, and then pointing out that this money was spent at a time when the tribes had no pressing matters before Congress, Schmidt implied that the tribal governments had made irresponsible decisions. Second, such an implication was an attack on tribal sovereignty. Third, any attack on tribal sovereignty was racist. Q.E.D.

Here's the letter prepared for Milanovich of the Agua Caliente: Schmidt's "racist notions completely undermine the concept of tribal self-determination." Poncho of the Louisiana Coushatta: "It seems that the *Washington Post* has a record of ridiculing groups or ideas that it does not agree with. The current article is reminiscent of the controversial 1993 story in which reporter Michael Weisskopf described the Christian right as 'poor, uneducated and easy to command.'" Martin of the Choctaw: "Susan Schmidt's Sunday attack on Jack Abramoff and his D.C.-based lobbying group constitutes a vicious and baseless assault on the liberty and independence that Native Americans across the country have fought so hard to obtain." Martin went on, "I am deeply offended by Schmidt's total disregard for the decision-making capabilities of my Tribe in choosing our own representation in the nation's capital." Martin called Schmidt's reporting "highly racist." How was it racist?

> Schmidt reports that certain Native American tribes have spent a considerable sum over the past three years for lobbying and public affairs work—one that "rivals spending to influence public policy by some of the nation's biggest corporate interests." With her racially prejudiced disapproval of these dollar amounts, Schmidt

calls into question the ability of tribes to make sound financial decisions, thereby undermining tribal sovereignty and self-deter-mination.[15]

There were other elements to the push-back strategy. A ghost-written op-ed on behalf of the Saginaw Chippewa's chairman arrived on the same day as the protest letters. Abramoff forwarded it to his colleague Todd Boulanger. "Are you going to get this in the washing times?" Boulanger asked. "Should we send this to our friends?"

"Do you think it's positive enough?" Abramoff replied. "We can-not have anything in DC which is not 100 percent with us."

"Probably not," Boulanger wrote. "This is helping Maynard back here and we are getting better press in LA now too . . . I'm going to give Brody all the dirt when the recall goes through and he can pounce on it with full access."

"I take it they are not trying to get something in RollCall this Thursday."

"Not that I'm aware of. I'm sure it's a good idea anyway. The opeds are good because it is our clients. Once the door is slammed in MI, that's a good story too."

"Agree," Abramoff replied.

"You are taking years off my life with this crap," Boulanger wrote. "It's going to be a pricey year for you come xmas . . . . . :)"[16]

The next morning, Wednesday, February 25, Abramoff sent an e-mail to another unidentified recipient. "I just chatted with Chris," Abramoff wrote, referring to his contact in the Saginaw Chippewa tribe, "and he agrees that we must have a letter from Maynard as the chairman of the tribe while we represented them outlining what a great job we did for them and attacking the racism. Can you get a draft moving from someone? The ones [redacted] did were all the same, basically. This needs to be different. Can you get this going?"[17]

The hint of urgency in these e-mails was well-founded. That same morning, Susan Schmidt had another article in the *Washington Post* on Abramoff, reporting that in previous days Representative Frank Wolf, a Virginia Republican, citing Schmidt's February 22 piece, had asked the FBI and Justice Department to open an investigation into tribal gambling. Wolf must have missed the fact that the investigation had already begun.

And others were about to start. Not only did most of the tribes launch internal investigations into whom, and how much, they had paid at Abramoff's request, but Greenberg Traurig also opened an investigation of its own. And among those who unfolded their copies of the *Washington Post* on the Sunday that the paper printed "A Jackpot from Indian Gaming Tribes" was Arizona Republican senator John McCain. McCain reads the paper every day, usually while he eats his regular breakfast of jelly doughnuts. One of the senator's aides told me that when McCain read Schmidt's article, he grew animated, pointing at the paper, saying, "I want hearings on this." McCain sat on the Senate Committee on Indian Affairs and planned to become chairman, for the second time, when a new Congress convened in 2005. On Thursday, February 26, he announced that Indian Affairs Committee investigators, working in tandem with investigators from the Senate Commerce Committee, had launched a probe into Abramoff and Scanlon.[18] McCain's investigation staff was expert. His lead investigator, a lawyer named Pablo Carillo, had directed the inquiry into the government's corrupt leasing of Boeing fuel tankers that led to jail sentences for several of the people involved.

Greenberg Traurig finished its investigation in days. By the end of the week, Friday, February 26, Abramoff admitted to his bosses that he had failed to disclose his business relationship with Scanlon. They asked for his resignation. The firm made a public announcement the next Wednesday, March 3. Abramoff was out of a job.[19]

He entered into talks with two firms, Cassidy & Associates, one of the capital's lobbying giants, and PodestaMattoon, the shop founded by Democrat Tony Podesta. If that didn't work, Abramoff told friends, he would write a diet book.[20] He went with Cassidy & Associates, on March 23 signing a consulting contract that would allow him to focus his energies on the legal battle ahead.[21]

Meanwhile, McCain's team was beginning to subpoena e-mails, correspondence, accounting records, contracts, receipts, promotional material, PowerPoint presentations, anything they could get their hands on. And the press continued its own inquiry, often in tandem with, or ahead of, the various legal proceedings. Correspondence between McCain and Abramoff was quick to find its way to reporters. On March 30, less than a week after Abramoff signed his new contract, the *Washington Post* reported, based on a letter McCain had sent Abramoff the prior afternoon, that the Indian Affairs Committee had found evidence of at least $10 million in payments from Scanlon to Abramoff, which contradicted his earlier claims.

"Predictably, I saw the Post story this morning," Amy Ridenour, Abramoff's College Republicans friend, wrote to him that day. "It still seems to me as though they are making a mountain out of a molehill. One can't go long listening to WMAL or WTOP"— Washington, D.C.'s twenty-four-hour news radio stations—"without hearing lobbying-type ads. That stuff isn't cheap, but we all seem to take it for granted."

Ridenour may have been sympathetic, but she had another reason to write Abramoff, whom she had helped funnel money to various causes, and fund congressional travel, through her nonprofit. "Do you expect that we will hear from the Senate?" Ridenour asked. "From where I sit, it is hard to know what is covered by confidentiality rules and also how much of this matter is reflective of internal fights among the Saginaw group. As most of what we received was from the Choctaws, does that leave us mostly out of it, or am I being unrealistically optimistic?"[22] Abramoff said he would help make sure the National Center for Public Policy Research had its finances in order. He didn't know it at the time, but he would have to be quick. The investigation was about to receive a boost from an unexpected source.

In May, Secretary of State Colin Powell made a memorable appearance on the NBC public affairs show *Meet the Press*. What made the interview noteworthy was the manner in which it concluded. Host Tim Russert interviewed Powell, who was traveling in Jordan, via satellite. Toward the end of the interview, Russert said, "Finally, Mr. Secretary, in February of 2003, you placed your enormous personal credibility before the United Nations and laid out a case against Saddam Hussein citing . . ."

There was commotion over the satellite. At one point the camera panned away, leaving the audience with an empty view.

"Not off," Powell said.

A woman's voice could be heard off camera. "No," she said. "They can't use it. They're editing it. They . . ."

"He's still asking me questions," Powell said, perturbed. "Tim . . ."

"He was not . . ." the woman said.

"Tim, I'm sorry, I lost you," Powell said.

"I'm right here, Mr. Secretary," Russert said. "I would hope they would put you back on camera. I don't know who did that."

"We really . . ."

"I think that was one of your staff, Mr. Secretary," Russert said, "I don't think that's appropriate." Russert was steamed.

Powell barked: "Emily, get out of the way." Emily followed orders. Russert asked his final question, and that was that.

"Emily" was Emily Miller, Powell's press secretary and a former press secretary to Tom DeLay. She had tried to cut off the interview because Russert had gone over his allotted time and Powell needed to use his satellite facilities in Jordan for another interview with Fox News. The episode was an embarrassment for Powell and for Miller, who as a DeLay aide had acquired a reputation for aggressively defending the interests of her boss. She later called NBC to apologize. The dustup was a minor story the next day. Russert fumed to the *Washington Post*, "A taxpayer-paid employee interrupted an interview. Not in the United States of America, that's not supposed to go on."[23]

But something more may have been going on. According to the investigative journalist Jason Leopold, writing on www.rawstory. com, around the time of the Powell interview, Miller's fiancé had called off her engagement. The fiancé reportedly was Michael

Scanlon. Divorced before, Scanlon had become involved with Miller during their time in DeLay's office. But as the wedding loomed in the distance, several anonymous sources told Leopold, Scanlon had fallen in love with someone else and broke Miller's heart. Big mistake. Not long after the infamous Powell interview, according to Leopold, Miller went to the FBI and began telling them everything Scanlon had told her about Abramoff, about his company, about Gimme Five, and so on. Everything.[24] (Those involved decline to comment on Leopold's reporting.)

The summer brought additional trouble. In early June, Wells Fargo Foothill and Citadel Equity Fund asked a federal judge to force Abramoff to pay the $60 million in loans for which he had signed a personal guarantee to buy SunCruz Casinos in 2000. Four years had passed since Foothill and Citadel first sued Abramoff and Adam Kidan. In May 2004, Abramoff had filed countersuit, then sued Kidan for misrepresentation.[25]

Back in Washington, the Senate Indian Affairs Committee issued its first subpoenas, including one to a firm owned by the wife of California Republican congressman James Doolittle, and another to an aide of Maryland Republican governor Robert Ehrlich.[26] In Georgia, Ralph Reed was forced to admit that he had received money, through a convoluted laundering process, from Abramoff's tribal clients. Reporters looking at Abramoff's charity, the Capital Athletic Foundation, discovered the nonprofit had been used as the lobbyist's money bin, funding the Eshkol Academy, trips abroad for friendly lawmakers, and much else. Then, on August 9, Choctaw chief Martin sent a letter to Senators Ben Nighthorse Campbell and John McCain. Months back, Martin had attacked Susan Schmidt and the *Washington Post*. But a little research had changed his mind. "In light of information we have recently obtained from various sources," Martin wrote, "it now appears that our tribe may in fact have been the victim of serious wrongdoing by Abramoff and Scanlon. Without your efforts it is unlikely that this misconduct would ever have come to light."[27] Martin pledged his full cooperation.

The scandal machinery had begun its relentless grind. Abramoff had already hired an attorney, the former Clinton defender Abbe Lowell. "It's inappropriate for me or anyone else to discuss financial affairs," he told the *Post* when the investigators announced their potentially illegal finding.[28] Lowell, it should be mentioned, is a busy man. He was also involved in another high-profile Washington scandal, defending Steven Rosen, the former director of public affairs of AIPAC, the Israeli lobby, against charges that he had conspired with Defense Department analyst Larry Franklin to pass American intelligence to an Israeli diplomat. Scanlon, too, hired a lawyer. Soon one lawyer wasn't enough for either Abramoff or Scanlon.

Those who lived and worked in and around the capital were becoming all too familiar with Abramoff and his friends. They marveled at his main accomplishment, the construction of an elaborate machine of self-dealing meant to line his pockets and those of his associates. They shook their heads when they realized that the individuals who made up Abramoff's coterie were prominent figures in D.C.'s Republican establishment. And they learned that that establishment was all too similar to those that had come before it.

Already known as a powerful insider, Abramoff was slowly turning into something else: a symbol of ideals laid to waste, of criminal hubris, of insatiable greed. His friends were fading away, and he was left alone. A July e-mail from Amy Ridenour captures the mood: "Hope you have a great weekend," she wrote Abramoff, "and that things are going as well as possible."[29]

The Senate Indian Affairs Committee held its first hearing on September 29. Senator Ben Nighthorse Campbell, chairman, called the meeting to order. "While our investigation is continuing," he told the crowded hearing room, "we have come to some very disturbing conclusions, and that is that the accusations in the newspapers were not accurate. In fact, the truth is it's much worse." He paused. "The articles vastly understated both the amounts the tribes paid to Mr. Scanlon and the amounts he gave to Mr. Abramoff. In fact, all told, six tribes paid more than $66 million to Mr. Scanlon, and Mr. Abramoff received more than $21 million from Mr. Scanlon for his share of the scheme."[30]

Abramoff appeared alongside Abbe Lowell. Scanlon was missing. "Last I had heard," Senator McCain said during his opening statement, "Mr. Scanlon was dodging the U.S. marshals attempting to serve him." A moment later, McCain said, "The time for games is over." When he finished his statement, the room burst into applause. Abramoff looked straight ahead, his face inscrutable except for a frown.

The senators were unanimous in their disgust. "Do you refer to all your clients as 'morons'?" Nighthorse Campbell asked Abramoff, who said nothing. "What sets this tale apart," McCain said, "what makes it truly extraordinary, is the extent and degree of the apparent exploitation and deceit." And those were the committee Republicans. "This is the most extraordinary pattern of abuse to come before this committee in the eighteen years I've served here," Sen. Kent Conrad of North Dakota, a Democrat, told the committee. "A pathetic, disgusting example of greed run amok," Sen. Byron Dorgan, Democrat of North Dakota, agreed. (The two Democrats left out that they had both received Abramoff-related campaign contributions, which they have since returned.)

Once the senators were finished with their opening statements, Nighthorse Campbell, who was due to retire from Congress in four months, said a few more words. "I'm going to pursue this matter with some further hearings," he said. "As you know, as my member friends know, I'll be leaving, but it is highly likely Senator McCain will be the new incoming chair as he was before of this committee, and if there is anybody—anybody—within hearing distance or sight of this hearing today that thinks this is going to go away, you're in for a surprise. It's going to be for a long time."

With that, Nighthorse Campbell called his first witness: Jack Abramoff. "Mr. Abramoff," he said, "I'm sure you're aware of this, but by appearing before this committee, you are under oath, but I've been advised to swear you in. If you will stand . . ."

Abramoff stood.

". . . raise your right hand . . ."

He raised his right hand.

". . . and state after me, 'I solemnly affirm that the testimony I give today will be the truth, the whole truth, and nothing but the truth, so help me God.'"

Abramoff's voice was barely audible.

"A little louder, please," Senator Nighthorse Campbell said.

"I do," Abramoff said quietly.

Abbe Lowell spoke up, asking Nighthorse Campbell to invoke a Senate rule that says in cases in which a hearing deals with potential criminal misconduct, the hearing must be held behind closed doors.

"The committee did hear your objections," the chairman replied. "I overruled those objections, and I do so now."

It was time for questioning. But this was an unusual hearing. Various senators asked questions of Abramoff, who then refused to answer, invoking his Fifth Amendment rights against self-incrimination. And yet the senators, eager to vent their outrage before the assembled cameras, kept asking questions anyway. The results were exchanges such as this, with Sen. Daniel Inouye, the Hawaii Democrat, playing Abramoff's interlocutor:

"After listening to all of the statements and after having read the articles, am I to assume that you did make a few dollars?" Inouye asked.

"Senator, I respectfully invoke the privileges stated," Abramoff said.

"As a good citizen of the United States, did you file an income tax return?"

"I must respectfully assert the privileges stated, sir."

"And in your income tax return, how did you describe this income?"

"Senator, I must respectfully invoke the privileges stated."

And so on.

There was a second hearing on November 17. Abramoff was

absent, but this time Scanlon, with his lawyer Plato Cacheris (another standby from the Monica Lewinsky scandal) in tow, testified before the committee, in a manner of speaking. Like his former business partner, Scanlon invoked his Fifth Amendment rights. And like his partner's, his silences only made the senators' rhetorical questions more damning.

"Did you receive $4.2 million from the Tigua tribe?" asked Sen. Kent Conrad, the North Dakota Democrat.

"Upon the advice of counsel, I must decline to answer that question based upon my rights under the Fifth Amendment," Scanlon said. (Scanlon had received $4.2 million.)

"Did you suggest to the Tigua tribe or their representatives that you had special influence with Congressman DeLay here in Washington?"

"Upon advice of counsel, I must decline to answer that question based upon my rights under the Fifth Amendment." (Scanlon had made such suggestions.)

At the conclusion of the hearing, Senator Nighthorse Campbell launched into a ferocious scolding of Scanlon. "Just speaking as an enrolled member of an Indian tribe," he said, "not the chairman of this committee, I have to tell you that for 400 years people have been cheating Indians in this country, so you're not the first one, Mr. Scanlon. It's just a shame that in this enlightened day that you've added a new dimension to a shameful legacy of what's happened to American Indians. You are the problem, buddy, of what's happened to American Indians."

Scanlon sat in silence.

"This committee," Senator Nighthorse Campbell said, "is adjourned."

McCain took over the Indian Affairs Committee in January 2005. He told reporters that his investigation of Abramoff was ongoing, and that he was planning additional hearings. Meanwhile, other politicians wanted in on the action. Sen. Charles Grassley of Iowa, the chairman of the Commerce Committee, said his investigators would look into how Abramoff manipulated tax-exempt organizations. In the spring of 2005, Democratic representative George Miller of California sent a letter to Attorney General Alberto Gonzales urging the Justice Department to look into Abramoff's involvement with the Commonwealth of the Northern Mariana Islands. "While two committees in the Senate are engaged in thorough reviews of allegations concerning Mr. Abramoff and his associates and their involvement with Native American tribes," Miller wrote, "the Committee on Resources has neither begun such a review nor an investigation into allegations of possible improprieties involving the CNMI and Mr. Abramoff and his associates." (By the beginning of 2006, the FBI had begun to examine Abramoff's Marianas account.)[31]

Abramoff's network ran so deep that it would take time to unravel the manifold schemes. Time and money. And manpower. In addition to McCain's staff, and Grassley's staff, and the first few FBI agents who had grown into a federal task force composed of more than thirty from the Justice, Treasury, and Interior Departments, there was now a small army of bleary-eyed journalists devoting thousands of column inches and magazine pages and blog posts to tracing the arc of Abramoff's career, its peaks and valleys, from foot soldier of the Reagan Revolution to action-movie producer to high-powered Washington attorney to disgraced symbol of avarice and greed.

As 2005 went on, though, Abramoff drifted into the background. McCain held three additional hearings, one in June, two in November. But when Abramoff was mentioned at all in the national media, for the most part it was in connection with Tom DeLay, whom a coalition of "good government" groups, working in tandem with the Democratic National Committee, had targeted shortly after the 2004 presidential election. DeLay's fund-raising, always questionable, was subject to the greatest scrutiny of his political career. And his ties to Abramoff, including his 1997 visit to Russia, led even some Republicans to call for his replacement as majority leader. ("Some Republicans" usually consisted of moderate Republicans who had long been opposed to DeLay and would seize any excuse to attack him.) The heat was close to unbearable. It sometimes seemed as though DeLay went through a new press secretary each week.

Once again, the liberals' fixation on DeLay led them to neglect the far seedier Abramoff. And the attacks on DeLay had an unintended consequence. Conservatives quickly rallied to the embattled majority leader's side. A polarizing figure, DeLay angered liberals to such an extent that conservatives reflexively assumed a defensive crouch when he came under attack. In March 2005, a host of conservative groups held a benefit dinner in support of DeLay at the Capitol Hilton, the site of the annual White House Correspondents Dinner. Norquist attended the predinner cocktail hour.[32] The show of strength, and the absence of any hard evidence of corruption (so far), was enough to make the issue slip out of the headlines. For a while.

But law enforcement officials are more serious than political partisans. They were investigating DeLay along with other lawmakers. And they knew all along that Abramoff was the key to the puzzle.

Then it happened. On August 11, 2005, Abramoff was arrested in Los Angeles. A Florida grand jury had indicted him and Kidan on wire fraud and conspiracy charges relating to SunCruz Casinos. Kidan turned himself in the next morning. Abramoff's end was beginning.

Once Abramoff was under arrest, events progressed rapidly. Within a week, police sent Abramoff's attorney a letter requesting his cooperation in the Gus Boulis murder case. The attorney, Neal Sonnett, who handled Abramoff's Florida-based legal troubles, told the *Miami Herald* that his client had "always been willing to cooperate." The problem was that the police "never followed through." The story reporting Abramoff's cooperation appeared in the *Miami Herald* on August 17.[33]

A little over a month later, at about 8 P.M. on the night of September 26, a homicide detective with the Fort Lauderdale police department entered the home of Anthony Moscatiello in the Howard Beach section of Queens, New York. Once inside, he placed the sixty-seven-year-old "caterer" under arrest. Around 11 P.M., a thousand miles away in North Miami Beach, police stormed the condominium where Anthony Ferrari lived with his wife and two children and took the forty-eight-year-old "security consultant," aka "Little Tony," into custody. And the next morning, in Palm Coast, Florida, police arrested twenty-eight-year-old James Fiorillo. Fiorillo, aka "Pudgy," worked at the Builder's First hardware store in Bunnell. "Everybody loves him," Fiorillo's supervisor, Kurt Wright, told the South Florida *Sun-Sentinel*.[34]

Not everybody. A few days earlier, a Broward County grand jury had indicted all three men on charges of first-degree murder and conspiracy to commit first-degree murder. In addition, the grand jury had indicted Moscatiello and Ferrari on charges of solicitation of first-degree murder. All have pleaded not guilty and (as of February 2006) are currently in prison awaiting trial. Several weeks after Abramoff and Kidan's arrest, Florida law enforcement was able to close a case that had been open for years. Someone had squawked.

The pincers were closing in. On September 19, David Safavian was arrested. (He pleaded not guilty.) On September 28, a Texas grand jury indicted Tom DeLay on conspiracy charges unrelated to Abramoff. (DeLay also pleaded not guilty.) The DeLay indictment was questionable. A partisan district attorney, Ronnie Earle, had doggedly pursued DeLay for years over accusations that he had improperly funded state legislative campaigns in 2002 in order to force through a controversial congressional redistricting plan the following year. Earle's initial indictment was flimsy—so flimsy, in fact, that within days he had to empanel another grand jury (his third), leading to another indictment, this one on money-laundering charges. The second indictment stuck. DeLay's future would be decided in the courts.

Each week brought fresh reports of Abramoff's double-dealing—how he had manipulated the system, sent cash back and forth between entities, cross-pollinated his political donations with his personal needs and desires, groomed contacts in the Department of the Interior while calling his tribal clients "troglodytes" and "monkeys" behind their backs. As the investigation dragged on, Abramoff's money started to run out. He closed his kosher deli, Stack's, and sold his treasure, Signatures, where he had treated so many lawmakers to free meals. He divested himself of his businesses. He gained weight, stopped shaving. He began to resemble a petty thug.

On Monday, November 21, Michael Scanlon agreed to a plea deal with federal investigators. It may be difficult to believe, but Scanlon's rise and fall was even more exaggerated than Abramoff's. The former beachbum had graduated from DeLay's office to Abramoff's empire, and found that his new lifestyle allowed him to live in the Ritz-Carlton, in the mansion on the beach, on his estate on St. Barts.

All gone. As part of his agreement with the Justice Department, Scanlon said he would cooperate with investigators and pay back some $19 million that he had been paid by the Indian tribes. He said he would also cooperate with the investigation into the SunCruz Casinos deal—he had, after all, been the company's spokesman. Most important, he said he would plead guilty to conspiracy and bribery charges. In the "charge of information" filed against him, outlining the bribery scheme to which he pled guilty, only Scanlon was mentioned by name. The other characters were "Lobbyist A"—Abramoff—and "Representative A"—Bob Ney.

On December 15, a few weeks after Scanlon's deal, Adam Kidan also agreed to testify against Abramoff in the SunCruz trial and cooperate with investigators looking into the murder of Gus Boulis. One possible reason he decided to cooperate is that shortly before the deal was announced, Anthony "Big Tony" Moscatiello told a Florida paper that Kidan had been involved in the plot to kill Boulis. According to a December 4, 2005, article in the South Florida *Sun-Sentinel*, shortly after his arrest, Moscatiello

> told detectives that [James] Fiorillo traveled to his Queens home
> two weeks after the murder [of Gus Boulis] and confided that

[Adam] Kidan reportedly told Ferrari to kill Boulis, according to court records. Moscatiello said Fiorillo also indicated that he and Ferrari carried out the hit, the documents show. Moscatiello told detectives, "I told Adam what had happened, what I was told and he told me he never made no phone call and after Tony Ferrari told me it was a lie, I never discussed it with Adam."

Kidan denies any involvement in Gus Boulis's murder—and has done so for years.

And yet there was a sense that, even with all the plea agreements, the Abramoff scandal was nowhere near over. In her *New York Times* article announcing the Kidan deal, Abby Goodnough reported that "a half-dozen lawmakers, many former Congressional aides and several of their wives are under scrutiny" in the Abramoff probe, including Tom DeLay.[35]

One by one, however, the pieces fell into place. The last months of 2005 were a season of scandal. It was long in the making. After the September 11, 2001, attacks on the World Trade Center and Pentagon, terrorism became the FBI's top priority. To devote more resources to fighting terrorists, the Bureau handed most of its narcotics responsibilities to the DEA. But that left an opening. Criminal Division lawyers needed work. They found it investigating public corruption. As a *Time* magazine reporter pointed out in that magazine's January 23, 2006, issue, "Since 2002, the FBI has engineered a surge of more than 40 percent in public corruption indictments, with 2,233 cases pending nationwide, compared with 1,575 four years ago."

The results were in the news. California Republican representative Duke Cunningham resigned from Congress after he was arrested on bribery charges. The Securities and Exchange Commission launched an investigation into accusations that Senate Majority Leader Bill Frist of Tennessee had engaged in insider trading. A Democratic congressman, William Jefferson of Louisiana, was implicated in a bribery scandal involving investment opportunities in African businesses.[36] (As of early 2006, Jefferson has declined to comment on the investigation.)

But Abramoff remained the jewel in the crown. He was now a synecdoche, the part representing the whole. Politicians who had received donations from Abramoff or his clients began to return the money. Ralph Reed, running for lieutenant governor of Georgia, began to distance himself from his friend of more than twenty-five years. The Justice Department informed Representative Ney that an indictment was being prepared against him. Abramoff neared his own plea agreement with investigators. Rumors began to circulate in the capital that up to twenty different lawmakers would be implicated in the affair. "This could be the Enron of lobbying," is how Kevin Ring reportedly put it long ago.[37]

This was a fitting analogy. Enron of course implied a spectacular meltdown, a success exposed as a fraud, an illusion that had had the appearance of reality. Based in Tom DeLay's native Houston, the energy trading company had surfed a wave of hubris and fear to stratospheric heights, only to see the wave crash and fortunes and careers get wiped out. In 1995, on the day when DeLay had invited all his lobbyist friends inside the majority whip's suite, a deal had been struck, however tacit, between the Republican Party and the corporate interests that swam in Washington's waters like leathery eels. The result was a machine, and the machine had some considerable successes. But those working the levers turned greedy, and soon they were out of control, overheating the pipes, wearing out the gears. Torpor followed. And then it all broke down.

The Republicans let the lobbyists go wild, and before you knew it, the lobbyists became a problem for Republicans. Tom DeLay created Jack Abramoff, and like Frankenstein's monster, Abramoff in turn destroyed DeLay. The only question was who—and what—they might bring down with them.

On January 3, 2006, wearing a black fedora and trench coat that made him look like a twenty-first century Al Capone, Jack Abramoff traveled to the U.S. District Courthouse in Washington,

D.C., and pleaded guilty to charges of conspiracy, mail fraud, and tax evasion in his dealings with four Indian tribes. The next day, he traveled to Florida, where he pleaded guilty to charges of wire fraud and conspiracy. The star lobbyist was now a star witness. Leaving both courtrooms, Abramoff, his eyes cloudy, wore the expression of a haunted man.

The Saturday after Abramoff entered his pleas and turned state's evidence, Tom DeLay, in his Texas district, announced that he would resign from the post of majority leader. Game over.

THE CURE

SPECTATORS TO AN ORGY OF "REFORM"

Money is like water down the side of the mountain.
It will find a way to get around the trees.
—RALPH REED

T HE MORNING OF January 3, 2006, less than a mile from where Jack Abramoff was pleading guilty inside a D.C. courthouse, Newt Gingrich sat in a television studio on Capitol Hill, a guest on C-SPAN's *Washington Journal*. The show's host asked the former Speaker of the House for his reaction.

"This story is going to go on all year," Gingrich said. "But I think people should look at it not just as a story of an individual gone bad, but [one that] asks a serious question about the nature of power in modern America."

Gingrich was alluding to the question of whether it is possible for a party or political movement to maintain power without compromising its principles. And Gingrich's question contained within it an implied answer: No, it is impossible. That is the correct answer.

Gingrich reiterated his point several days later, on January 6, in a speech before the downtown Washington, D.C., Rotary Club. There is no doubt, Gingrich said, that Abramoff's actions, and what those actions represent, "is a scandal." But there is also no doubt, he went on, that "this is not one person doing one bad thing. And it isn't Abramoff by himself. Remember, it's not about lobbyists' corruption. You can't have a corrupt lobbyist unless you have a corrupt member, or a corrupt staff." Abramoff, Gingrich said in a radio commentary on the January 9 NPR *Morning Edition,* "is only a symptom." The disease is big government. Paraphrasing Lord Acton, and returning to political ground he occupied in the 1980s and early 1990s, the former speaker said, "Big government tends to corrupt, but big government with no party willing to limit its growth is absolutely corrupted."

For many who heard them, Gingrich's words were tangible evidence of Friedrich Nietzsche's theory of the eternal return. One wonders what Nietzsche would have thought of the American capital, which continually experiences cycles of scandal and reform. One party runs to clean up the other party's mess, staying in power only to make a mess of things themselves. In 1974, Democrats enjoyed a spate of congressional victories as voters reacted to President Nixon's Watergate scandal. Twenty years later, Republicans enjoyed a landslide as voters reacted to the Democratic Congress's and President Clinton's own scandals and disagreeable policies. The ground shifts quickly beneath our feet. These cycles go far back into the past, beginning with the reform movements led by Jefferson and Jackson in the early days of the republic, and they will undoubtedly continue far into the future.

The paradox, of course, is that each epoch of reform plants new seeds that sprout during the next season of scandal.

A common reaction to the exposure of Abramoff's crimes is to ask, Why did this happen? For some Democratic partisans, the answer lies in what they see as the natural and self-evident malevolence of conservative Republicans. But this is an explanation that fails to explain. The truth is that the Abramoff case, and the other major bribery scandal in Washington—involving convicted former

representative Randy "Duke" Cunningham—are the outgrowt
a system of politics constructed in the aftermath of the last great
political scandal.

The liberal majorities elected to Congress in 1974 drew several
incorrect lessons from Nixon's wrongdoing. First, they focused most
closely on how the president and his staff manipulated campaign
finances to criminal ends, placing blame not on the activities themselves, which were already illegal, but on the very idea of money in
politics. Second, they saw Watergate not as an isolated criminal incident but rather as an example of an "imperial presidency," which
required them to place constraints on its power. And third, their
fury was so great that they also wanted to reform Congress and, as
it's said, "change the way business is done in Washington."

Our politics is still conditioned by the laws those reformers
enacted. There was Title VI of the Ethics in Government Act, otherwise known as the independent counsel statute, enacted in 1978
and allowed to die a quiet death in 1999. There were the Church
Committee reforms of the U.S. intelligence services, which gutted
the CIA's human-intelligence capabilities. In 1974, Congress passed
comprehensive campaign finance reform, regulating donations to
candidates and candidate expenditures. A Supreme Court decision
two years later rescinded the regulations governing expenditures,
but the strict limits on giving remained. An individual could donate
only $1,000 to a political candidate. Political Action Committees,
or PACs, could donate only $5,000. Those amounts changed over
time. But the idea that the means of politics were subject to regulation by politicians did not.

These reforms did nothing to stop the flow of money in politics.
Remember that political campaigns are expensive. Congressional
campaigns can cost $1 million or more—much more if you are run-
ning for the Senate, a governorship, or the presidency. Raising that
much money in $1,000 increments is difficult and time-consuming.
You need help. And so you turn to lobbyists, who have the resources
and connections to provide maximum individual contributions,
and can also "bundle" money from many different individuals.

This has led to some unintended consequences. The Watergate reforms increased the demand for lobbyists, and in the late 1970s the numbers of them in Washington began to rise. The reforms also gave an advantage to incumbents—who, since they were already in Washington, knew more lobbyists, and could spend more time at fund-raisers held in sports arenas and chic restaurants—and also to the wealthy, who could finance their own campaigns without restriction. "Reform" further changed the nature of the relationship between the electorate and the elected. When campaigns were financed in a variety of ways, and lawmakers had more time for politics as opposed to fund-raising, there was more of an opportunity for them to consider the interests of those they represented. The constant money-grubbing of today acts as an isolation chamber, closing off the avenues through which lawmakers are able to see beyond their donors. Finally, the reforms increased the importance of unregulated "soft money," which often came from shady places, including foreign agents and even foreign governments. (Soft-money was banned in 2002, which led to the use of unregulated 527 groups. Nothing changed.)

Also in 1974, Congress passed, and the president signed, the Budget Control and Impoundment Act. Simply put, this legislation eviscerated the system of checks and balances through which the two elected branches of government are supposed to argue over how to spend your money. Prior to 1974, the president had the authority to "impound"—refuse to spend—money Congress appropriated in its budget. But Congress, frustrated at Nixon's devotion to curtailing wasteful spending, took away the president's power to impound. After this law was passed, the president would have to veto an entire appropriations bill if he wanted to keep costs down—a power that President George W. Bush, for example, did not use in the first five years of his presidency.

The importance of the Budget Control and Impoundment Act becomes obvious when considered in light of another Watergate-era budgetary reform. In February 1973, Wilbur Mills, the Democratic chairman of the House Ways and Means Committee, agreed to let a tax bill out of his committee without invoking the "closed" rule—meaning that any congressman, from whichever party, could propose amendments and riders to the legislation. David Frum summarizes the consequences:

> Before 1973, a corporation seeking a tax favor need worry only about convincing a single man or, at most, a few party leaders. After 1973, any one of the 435 members of the House or the one hundred members of the Senate could write an amendment containing the favor and have a fair chance of negotiating it into law.[1]

With so many new members offering potential favors in exchange for campaign contributions, is it any wonder that the long boom of the lobbying industry began in the post-Watergate era?

The Founders built Washington, D.C., on a swamp for a reason. They could have chosen to have the capital remain in New York or Philadelphia, centers of trade and commerce, capitals of culture and society. They refused. A republican capital, they thought, should be devoted to the people's work and little else. Washington was intended to be a backwater, unattractive to all except the people's representatives, and then only for the limited time that Congress was in session. Everyone has heard the old saw that prior to the invention of air-conditioning, when the humid summers stifled the pretensions of potential yearlong residents, the federal government was small and Washington, D.C., a village. The explosion of lobbyists following Watergate caused a flood of money to inundate the village. Fund-raisers were held in expensive restaurants, hotels were constructed to house itinerant lobbyists, movie theaters and shopping malls sprouted like weeds to entertain and satiate the growing establishment. And that establishment (though largely Democratic during the years of that party's dominance) was essentially bipartisan. Republican or Democrat, its members shared a single overriding interest: Keep the gravy flowing. Keep the restaurants and shops open, the donors rich, the businesses booming. Keep the spigot open, and we will give you what you want. Because in exchange for the money flowing to the incumbents' campaigns, Washington politicians were able to provide their friends with an invaluable commodity: access to the enhanced powers of a larger, more complex government.

The Washington Establishment resisted any impulse to change. It fought against insurgent tides. It bent those who came to do good to its will. And its siren song was hypnotic: *Stay. Be Happy. It's nice here. You'll learn to like it.*

Consider the fate of the contemporary Republican Party.

Under a party claiming to represent those Americans who believe in limited government, government continues to grow. In 2001, when President Bush came into office, the federal government spent $1.8 trillion. In fiscal year 2004, the last year for which we have data, the federal government—all three branches dominated by Republicans and Republican appointees—spent $2.2 trillion. According to conservative economist Steven Moore, government has grown three times faster under President Bush than under President Clinton.[2] And government revenues have not kept pace with outlays. In fiscal year 2004, the federal government ran a deficit of more than $500 billion.[3] That works out to just about 5 percent of that year's U.S. gross domestic product. This may seem small, but it also bears comparison to the worst deficits in the history of the United States. (The Reagan deficits ran more than 5 percent of gross domestic product.) The deficit is at "its highest level in absolute terms since World War II," Moore writes.[4] According to the *New York Times*, "of the 30 [Republicans elected in 1994] who are still in the House of Representatives, 28 sponsored bills in the last Congress that would have increased government spending overall."[5]

Discussions about federal spending typically focus on "pork-barrel" projects. These are line items in appropriations bills that send money to a member's state for what usually turn out to be trivial, laughable, and sometimes insidious purposes. Examples are easy to find. In his book *Rome Wasn't Burnt in a Day,* former Republican representative Joe Scarborough attacks the "$90,000 for the National Cowgirl Hall of Fame in Fort Worth, Texas," the "$350,000 to the

Rock and Roll Hall of Fame and Museum in Cleveland, Ohio," the "$400,000 for the Pennsylvania Trolley Museum, which is located, of course, in Washington, DC," and the "$725,000 to the Please Touch Me Museum in Philadelphia, Pennsylvania"—all appropriations that the Republican Congress passed, and President Clinton authorized, in the late 1990s.[6] In his book, Scarborough reserves particular opprobrium for House Transportation Committee chairman Republican Bud Shuster's 1998 transportation bill, the total cost of which was $217 billion. "By the time the highway bill reached Bill Clinton's desk," Scarborough writes, "it was the most expensive public works bill in U.S. history."[7]

He spoke too soon. The transportation bill that was signed into law by President George W. Bush—known by its official name, the "Safe, Accountable, Flexible, Efficient Transportation Equity Act: A Legacy for Users"—on August 10, 2005, cost $286.4 billion.

Critics of government spending seize on pork-barrel projects because they give us tangible evidence of congressional waste and mischief. It is difficult to criticize government when its size is so staggering as to be almost incomprehensible. But it is easy to criticize the "Please Touch Me Museum in Philadelphia, Pennsylvania." The projects involved are often silly. Sometimes they are worse.

In 2003, during a House-Senate conference, Republican senator Ted Stevens of Alaska inserted a provision into that year's defense appropriations bill leasing a fleet of 100 refueling tankers from Boeing. The cost was stratospheric. It would have been far cheaper for the government simply to buy the planes outright. The Congressional Budget Office estimated that leasing cost taxpayers $5.6 billion more than buying. Later, John Warner, the chairman of the Senate Armed Forces Committee, modified the deal so that the government would lease only twenty planes and buy the other eighty. But this still cost a huge amount of money. Why would the Republican Congress back such a boondoggle, a colossal waste of taxpayer dollars? The *Washington Post* has reported that a month before he inserted the provision into the defense appropriations bill, Stevens received huge fund-raising checks from thirty-one different Boeing executives.[8]

Another example. Contained in the Transportation Equity Act of 2005 was a $223 million appropriation for a bridge connecting the Alaskan city of Ketchikan (population 8,000) to Gravina Island (population 50). Republican representative Don Young and Republican senator Ted Stevens, both from Alaska, and both legendary for their ability to funnel federal tax dollars to their already rich state, entered the item into the bill. The project quickly became known as the "bridge to nowhere." It was a joke.

Alaska congressional staffers point out that the Gravina bridge did actually go somewhere; there is an airport on the island that has only been possible to reach via ferry. What Alaska congressional staffers ignore, however, is that the wife of Frank Murkowski—the former Republican senator from Alaska, current governor of Alaska, and father of current Republican senator from Alaska Lisa Murkowski—owns a chunk of land on Gravina Island and stands to gain much from the bridge. Suddenly, things are less funny.[9] (The Murkowskis reject any hint of impropriety. Senator [Lisa] Murkowski has gone so far as to call the property "worthless." It won't be once the bridge is built.)

The appropriation for the bridge to nowhere was later removed, although a similar amount of money will still be sent to the Alaskan state transportation authorities, to be used at their discretion. The bridge should be considered not as an isolated incident but as merely one earmark in a federal budget that contains tens of thousands of such earmarks. A Republican Congress has allowed these often-wasteful appropriations to spread out of control. In the decade since the Republican Revolution, the number of earmarks has increased by a staggering 873 percent.[10]

All told, however, the dollar amounts Congress directly appropriates every year, known as discretionary spending, make up a relatively small portion of the federal budget. In 2004, the federal government spent $28 billion on pork-barrel projects, a fraction of the total $2.2 trillion spent.[11] The bulk of the money the government disburses goes to entitlements. In Fiscal Year 2004, Social Security, Medicare, and Medicaid combined totaled more than $1 trillion.

Interest payments on the national debt—a wealth transfer from middle-class taxpayers to superrich bond buyers around the world—accounted for another $160.2 billion, leaving about $900 billion in annual discretionary spending for Fiscal Year 2004. Remove defense spending from that amount and one is left with $400 billion in discretionary spending. The United States economy is $12 trillion strong and growing at an annualized rate of a little more than 3 percent. Seen in this light, $400 billion is a drop in the bucket.

America's outdated entitlement programs risk making that bucket much smaller. The trillions spent in Social Security benefits and Medicare and Medicaid disbursements show no signs of slowing down. The aging population of Baby Boomers will only make the problem worse. Here, too, however, Republicans have abandoned whatever principles they held in the past. In 2005, President Bush proposed a Social Security reform that would have introduced personal accounts into the system and indexed benefits for the well-off. The reform went nowhere, for two reasons. The first is Democratic leaders Nancy Pelosi and Harry Reid's success at ensuring that no member of their caucus compromised with Bush. The second is that Republicans were captives of political dogmatism and opportunism. They dogmatically refused to consider raising the cap on payroll taxes, which would make America's most regressive tax (it hurts the poor the worst) more progressive, which is to say equitable—a small price to pay for Social Security personal accounts. And they opportunistically ignored the long-term issue of entitlements, worried that voters would turn on them if they were seen cutting benefits or raising the retirement age.

On Medicare, the Republican record is worse. Democrats, who think government should satiate the electorate's every need and are constantly inventing new needs to satiate, had pushed for years for a prescription-drug entitlement to be added to Medicare. Conservatives, viewing the entitlement as an unnecessary and expensive appendage to a program desperately in need of alteration, happily remembered that Congress was in Republican hands. That changed, however, in 2003, when the Bush White House, eyeing the upcoming presidential election, sought to preempt Democratic attacks by passing an entitlement that Republicans could claim as their own. Once again, conservative principle became the victim of political expediency.

The plan itself was a confusing and complicated morass of misdirection, with plenty of subsidies and handouts to the pharmaceutical industry. The congressional budget resolution that the House voted on, based on numbers from the Congressional Budget Office, stated that the cost of the prescription-drug bill would be $400 billion between 2004 and 2013. But when the Centers for Medicare & Medicaid's chief actuary, Richard Foster, crunched the numbers, he came up with a much different figure: $534 billion over ten years. What accounted for the difference? Since the entitlement would not start before 2006, the Congressional Budget Office's number included two years in which spending would be zero. Here's how economist Bruce Bartlett put it in his recent book, *Impostor:* "CBO had spending going from virtually nothing in 2004 and 2005 to $27.6 billion in 2006, $40.2 billion in 2007, and rising to $65.1 billion in 2013, the last year estimated. In other words, spending would be twice as great in the second five years of the program as in the first five years: $122.1 billion versus $272.2 billion."[12]

It was, in short, an actuarial sleight of hand: By beginning in 2004, the CBO could avoid counting two additional years—2014 and 2015, say—when the government would be forced to spend more than a hundred billion dollars. Moreover, the inspector general of the Department of Health and Human Services eventually concluded that Bush officials had withheld information about the cost of the drug bill from Congress prior to the vote.[13] In 2005, the cost of the bill was revised upward again, this time to $800 billion over ten years. But by then, of course, the vote that betrayed the principles of the Republican Revolution was a distant memory.

The Medicare entitlement was the largest expansion of federal power since the days of Lyndon Johnson's Great Society. Two years later, in the aftermath of Hurricane Katrina, President Bush would propose some $200 billion in spending to rebuild New Orleans, another echo of the federal overreach that characterized the Johnson years. Government expands and becomes more servile, yet the voters government serves continue to view it with suspicion and mistrust. The Medicare plan is unpopular. Congressional approval levels have plummeted. And yet the busybodies soldier on and find new problems to solve, new industries to subsidize, new regulations to issue, new products to tax. The Republicans have "increased the federal role in education, imposed tariffs on steel and lumber, increased farm subsidies, okayed new federal restrictions on campaign finance and corporate accounting, and expanded the national-service program President Clinton began," writes conservative author Ramesh Ponnuru. "No federal programs have been eliminated, nor has Bush sought any such thing. More people are working for the federal government than at any point since the end of the Cold War. Spending has been growing faster than it did under Clinton."[14]

The abandonment of principle has led to a new governing ideology, known as "big government conservatism." The phrase is oxymoronic. For half a century, one of the key tenets of American conservatism has been a belief in limited government. Limited government is not lazy government; it can be active, too—in fact, better equipped to handle crises than a bloated and overcommitted state. To some conservatives, limited government is not necessarily little government. The key to understanding the conservative advocacy of limited government as opposed to "little" government is an understanding that the character of a regime matters more than the size of a regime. There are moral reasons to oppose "Big Government" and to favor responsibility, risk, and individual initiative. By making peace with big government conservatism, however, Republicans have abandoned such moral claims. It is time the Republican Party faced reality. The era of "big government is over" . . . is over. And they, more than anyone else, are to blame.

A consequence of the conservatives' abandonment of principle is the degradation of their movement. This degradation reveals itself in subtle ways. Every four years since 1980, for example, the conservative Heritage Foundation has released a book called *Mandate for*

Leadership. The book is a guide for conservative activists and legislators, laying out the ways in which conservatives can shrink the size of government. However, since it was first published, *Mandate for Leadership* has been shrinking, not government. The first edition (credited with inspiring much of the Reagan agenda) was 3,000 pages long; the 1996 edition was 760 pages; the 2004 edition, 156 pages.[15]

There are two ways to look at this. An optimist says that the cuts in *Mandate for Leadership* are signs of conservative success; as Republicans spend more time in power and enact conservative policies, there is simply less for them to do. A pessimist says that the cuts in *Mandate for Leadership* are signs of conservative capitulation. Most conservatives, of course, are natural pessimists.

Tempted by power and money, some conservative intellectuals have become mouthpieces for the federal government. In January 2005, *USA Today* reported that the Department of Education had paid Armstrong Williams $240,000 to promote the No Child Left Behind Act. Williams has a public relations business and his own radio show, and appears on television. The next week, the *Washington Post* revealed that syndicated columnist Maggie Gallagher had been paid some $20,000 by the Department of Health and Human Services to write policy on the area of her expertise. The Bush administration, Jonathan Alter writes, "has doled out $250 million in taxpayer money to private public-relations firms, twice what had been spent" in prior White Houses.[16] This is all too similar to the column-writing habits of Doug Bandow and Peter Ferrara, who were paid money to write articles favorable to Jack Abramoff's clients, or to Michael Fumento, who wrote columns favorable to the corporate giant Monsanto after receiving a small portion of that firm's profits.

In short, conservatism has been professionalized. It has become a cosmetic affectation, like wearing an American flag lapel pin. It has become a résumé item, a prerequisite set of ideological commitments for the ambitious young. "It's all about forging one-to-one relationships," Katherine Rogers, an intern at the Heritage Foundation, told *New York Times* reporter Jason DeParle in the summer of 2005. "That's where business starts." Rogers, a student at Georgetown University, spent the summer living at Heritage in preparation for her intended career as a pharmaceutical lobbyist. Each summer, Heritage hires sixty-four interns just like her.[17]

In the summer of 2005, Pennsylvania senator Rick Santorum told a group of reporters asking him about the potential consequences of the K Street Project, "For 40 years Democrats have been doing what Republicans have done in the last few years. Maybe I'll find these stories in the archives and show them to you. I think corruption is trying to get people into places where they don't fit in. Helping good people get job interviews—I don't see any harm in that."

Santorum, elected to the Senate in 1994, was saying that the GOP's transformation into the party of K Street was a nonissue because the Democrats had done the same thing "for 40 years." He was admitting, in so many words, that the Republicans were behaving exactly like the people they had overthrown. That it was just business as usual.

No wonder, then, that Republicans and Democrats had the same reactions to the fall of Jack Abramoff.

The first reaction was fear—fear that increased scrutiny would shine a light on the interactions between lobbyists and legislators, revealing the Establishment for the money-laden mutual-advantage club that it is. The lobbyists in particular played down the scandal's impact. "The whole Abramoff matter is atypical," one lobbyist, Ed Rogers, told *Washington Post* writer Jeffrey Birnbaum in that paper's January 4, 2006, issue. Another, John Jonas, told Birnbaum that Abramoff "hurts the legitimate practice of the profession," because the scandal "confirmed everybody's worst fears about lobbyists—that they double-deal, that they're not aboveboard." The Democrats, seeking to gain partisan advantage in the 2006 midterm elections, distanced themselves from Abramoff. "This is a Republican scandal," the Senate Democratic leader, Harry Reid, told Fox News Channel's Chris Wallace in December 2005. "Don't lump me in with Jack Abramoff." Democratic politicians were quick to point out that not a single member of their ranks had received personal contributions from the disgraced lobbyist. But they neglected to mention that they had received plenty of contributions from Abramoff's tribal clients—contributions that some Democrats refused to return.

The Establishment's second reaction was a flurry of reformist posturing, reflecting the assumption that Abramoff's crimes necessitated further regulation of politics by politicians. Both parties forgot that the crimes to which Abramoff and Scanlon had pleaded guilty were already illegal. They forgot that the United States's byzantine system of campaign finance, in combination with our rapidly expanding government and ever-busy regulatory apparatus, had brought us the scandal to begin with. They forgot that Abramoff fed off big government. He looked for clients—the Mariana Islands, the El Paso Tigua—who depended on government's good graces. He forged his career in the interstices between government dependents and government agents. The leaders of both parties forgot all of this. Instead, they gave in to the politician's central imperative: *Do something.* Do anything. Look busy.

The proposed reforms were as cosmetic as they were numerous. In all, *National Journal* magazine counted six different plans. The House Republican leadership plan, proposed by California Republican David Dreier, was typical. It would have banned privately funded travel for lawmakers, lowered the gift amount to $20 a gift and $50 a year, extended the ban on lobbying one's former bosses from one to two years, banned access to the House floor and gym for former lawmakers registered as lobbyists, increased disclosure requirements, required "ethics training" for lawmakers and staff members, eliminated the government pensions of former lawmakers who are also convicted felons, and "curbed" earmark spending.[18] The Democratic plan was much of the same, but would have also "eliminated" the K Street Project, allowed time for lawmakers to read the content of spending and tax bills before a vote, ended the practice of "no-bid" government contracts, and "ensured" that the president's appointees have "proven" credentials. A skeptic would ask whether, had these regulations been in place years ago,

Abramoff would not still be headed for jail. The answer is that he probably would.

But the plastic surgery continued. On January 25, 2006, Republicans ended the routine meetings they had held for a decade with lobbyists to discuss job openings and opportunities for Republican influence peddlers. The "vacancies memo," a several-pages-long list filled with vacancies at lobbying firms, would no longer be passed around at Senate conference meetings. Both decisions were made to draw attention away from the K Street Project. But the idea that failing to distribute sheets of paper would end the relationship between the Republican Party and corporate interests remained farcical. The proposed curbs on privately funded travel, for example, would only mean that there would be more junkets paid for by taxpayers. Meddling with the gift amount would create a whole new set of potential crimes while ignoring the nature of the crimes that had spawned the reform. When the House approved the ban on allowing former lawmakers registered as lobbyists access to the House floor and gym, Harry Reid quipped, "I've never been lobbied in the gym," but, "of course, I'm pretty ugly naked."[19]

Sen. John McCain called for improved disclosure. Since lobbyists need only report their income every six months, it is difficult to track what the industry is up to. Improved disclosure would have allowed the FBI and others to uncover Abramoff's conspiracy quickly. A second sensible reform would have expanded the "cooling-off" period in which former lawmakers and congressional staffers are forbidden to lobby their former colleagues from one to two years. This reform echoed, but did not go as far as, a 2005 proposal by Bruce Reed of the Democratic Leadership Council. "We need a real cooling-off period of at least four years for members of Congress, their senior staff, and senior administration officials," Reed writes in his organization's magazine, *Blueprint*. "Private interests would still be able to hire former officials for their political and policy expertise. But for four years—two congressional cycles, one presidential term—those who've served couldn't lean on those they hired or others with whom they served."[20]

With DeLay gone, the Republicans held elections for a new leader. Two of the three candidates had close ties to the lobbying industry. One, Rep. Roy Blunt, for years DeLay's chief deputy, was, as we've learned, married to a lobbyist—which only demonstrated the impossibility of fully regulating such interactions. Blunt lost to Ohio Republican John Boehner, who boasted during his campaign that he had never approved an earmark. Boehner, elected in 1990, was a soldier of the Gingrich years who promised a return to the ideals of that era.

But Boehner was as much a part of the Republican machine as Blunt. (Arizona congressman John Shadegg ran on a reform platform as well, but was eliminated from the race after the first round of balloting.) Back in the 1990s, he had spent part of his summer vacation cruising the Caribbean with lobbyist friends; he was close to the lobbyists and political action committees tied to Sallie Mae, the quasi-governmental agency that handles student loans; in 1995, he was seen distributing campaign checks from the tobacco industry to congressmen on the House floor.[21] (Boehner says he regrets this.) Blunt remained in the leadership as whip. Still, there was a new boss. The only question was how long it would take him to shed the language of reform and behave like the old.

All of the proposed reforms were based on the assumption that it is the lobbyists who are the problem. There is no question that the proliferation of lobbyists poses a danger to American democracy. But altering the price of a meal those lobbyists can buy a representative will do nothing to lessen that danger. The wrongdoing in the Abramoff case may have been initiated by a crooked lobbyist—but it was facilitated by members of Congress. Congress needs to be reformed. Unsurprisingly, few members have risen to the challenge.

If one is so inclined, here is where he might begin. He would recognize that the explosive growth of the lobbying industry corresponded to three political developments: the growth of government, the expansion of campaign finance regulation, and the proliferation of the regulatory state. And it followed two acts of Congress: the Budget Control and Impoundment Act of 1974 and the changes that year to the Federal Election Campaign Act of 1971. Together, as we have learned, these developments created the world of K Street Conservatism. It is past time that that world is dismantled.

Limited government might seem an impossibility, but if so it is an impossibility worth pursuing. Controlling earmarks and pork-barrel spending is a matter of discipline and restraint, two conservative values. As the sphere of public decision-making expands, so does the pool of potential graft. Solution: shrink the sphere of public decision-making.

The regulatory state issues rules and regulations at a dizzying pace, regulations that corporations, through their lobbyists, attempt to influence to their advantage. Solution: cut regulation. But not in the manner in which Tom DeLay handled Project Relief—by doing the bidding of whichever corporation will fork over the most money. Cut regulation on the one hand, but also end corporate welfare—the myriad loopholes and subsidies that fill appropriations bills to the bursting point. Lessen the demand for lobbyists and soon enough there will be a diminished supply.

As Newt Gingrich put it in his speech to the D.C. Rotary Club: "The election process has turned into an incumbency protection process in which lobbyists attend PAC fund-raisers to raise money for incumbents so they can drown potential opponents, thus creating war chests which convince potential candidates not to run and freeing up the incumbents to spend more time at Washington PAC fund-raisers." The solution: rescind campaign finance law and return to the system in place for most of American history, a system of unlimited individual contributions coupled with full and immediate disclosure. To some, this may sound fantastic. But Democrats, who were hurt by the McCain-Feingold campaign "reform" of 2002, would embrace the issue. Two of that party's chief strategists, Paul Begala and James Carville, make a similar proposal in their book *Take It Back*.

To cut the number of special loopholes and appropriations placed into bills at the behest of lobbyists requires a return to the republican idea of checks and balances. As *Wall Street Journal* deputy editorial page editor Daniel Henninger pointed out in his paper's January 27, 2006, issue, Congress did grant the president "recision" authority as part of the 1974 budget law. Using his power of recision, the president can ask Congress to revoke specific appropriations without vetoing an entire bill. However, for recision to work, two things are required: Congress must honor the president's request, and the president must be willing to back his words with action. Under unified Republican government, both requirements are sorely lacking.

Reform of Congress is unlikely to happen. That is because politics is a profession and lawmakers do everything in their power to secure lifetime employment. Incumbents secure their future careers by regulating campaign finance law and gerrymandering congressional districts to their own advantage. In most districts, competitive elections are a sad and bitter joke. As Ed Kilgore of the Democratic Leadership Council observes:

> According to congressional elections expert Gary Jacobson of the University of California, San Diego, the number of "safe" House seats—defined as those where the winning party's presidential candidate exceeded his national vote by more than 2 percentage points—rose from 281 in 1992 to 356 in 2002. That left 79 theoretically competitive seats in 2002, out of 435. But it turned out to be even worse than that. In the run-up to the 2002 election, only 45 seats were ultimately rated as competitive by the authoritative *Cook Political Report*, and just 15 seats were considered true tossups.[22]

Since legislators will not restrain themselves, it is incumbent on the people to restrain them. More states should reconsider California governor Arnold Schwarzenegger's failed proposal to hand redistricting over to a bipartisan panel of appointed judges. California voters rejected the proposal in 2005 as part of an upsurge in anti-Schwarzenegger sentiment. But the governor should resurrect it as a reform that would increase competition and promote political dynamism. And other governors should urge their state legislatures to fix Congress by fixing the system through which congressional seats become heirlooms. They can start by reminding those legislatures that Tom DeLay's indictment in Texas involved such a gerrymander. They can also remind them that that alleged scheme was part of his undoing.

The term-limits movement rose to prominence in the 1980s and early 1990s, during a time when the American public was frustrated at congressional irresponsibility. And Republican lawmakers, frustrated at the House Democratic leadership, championed the cause. Voters expressed this discontent at the ballot box in 1994. Suddenly, Republicans were in power. All talk of term limits ended. Then the movement suffered another, and perhaps fatal, blow in 1995, when the Supreme Court issued a 5-4 ruling that overturned an attempt by the Arkansas state legislature to set term limits for members of its congressional delegation. Unless the Court overturns the razor-thin decision, and it has shown no interest in doing so, it would require either an act of Congress or a constitutional amendment to limit representatives and senators to a particular number of terms. Neither is likely to happen. It would be better for the republic if the fancy restaurants and luxurious hotels and golf courses and expensive boutiques dotting the Washington, D.C., area would simply disappear, along with the money and culture of insiderism that supports them. But that would mean the Establishment would have to disappear as well. And no Establishment has ever voted itself out of existence.

No one should have any illusions. The prospect for meaningful reform is bleak. Without either a reassertion of conservative principles or a Democratic landslide, government will continue to grow, and with it the number of lobbyists. As Republicans grow more comfortable in power, their standards will drop, whatever restraint they still possess will vanish, and their ranks will swell with more opportunists and con artists. Sclerosis will follow, and then more scandal, followed by yet more "reform." Ambitious young men and women will come to Washington in pursuit of the public good, and find themselves tempted to stay by the gourmet cuisine, the sumptuous homes, the allure of celebrity. Far from being an artifact of the past, Jack Abramoff may well represent the Republican Party's future. And this future will last until the public's last ounce of tolerance is depleted, and the Republican Establishment is overthrown, and a new one emerges in its place.

The faces of this next Establishment will be new, their ideology different. But they will have the same ambition, they will face the same temptations, and they will fall victim to the same hubris, as they sniff out new opportunities in the Capitol and along K Street, returning again and again to the scene of the crime.

NOTES

PROLOGUE: THE DECEMBER REVOLUTION

1. *Washington Post,* October 10, 1993.
2. *Dallas Morning News,* November 27, 1994.
3. Major Garrett, *The Enduring Revolution,* 48.
4. Dubose, *Hammer,* 88.
5. Drew, *Showdown,* 57.
6. Hannah Rosin, *The New Republic,* February 19, 1996.
7. Dubose, *Hammer,* 88.
8. Dubose, *Hammer,* 88.
9. Major Garrett, *Washington Times,* December 5, 1994.
10. Dubose, *Hammer,* 88.
11. Drew, *Showdown,* 57.

CHAPTER ONE: THE GANG

1. Nina Easton, *Gang of Five,* 75.
2. Easton, *Gang of Five,* 70.
3. Easton, *Gang of Five,* 70.
4. Susanna McBee, "Nov. 7 Shaping Up as Series of Prop. 13 Look-Alike Contests," *Washington Post,* September 10, 1978.
5. Susanna McBee, "Nov. 7 Shaping Up as Series of Prop. 13 Look-Alike Contests," *Washington Post,* September 10, 1978.
6. John Cassidy, "The Ringleader," *The New Yorker,* August 1, 2005.
7. John Cassidy, "The Ringleader," *The New Yorker,* August 1, 2005.
8. Easton, 139.

9. Easton, 135.

10. Easton, 138.

11. Easton, 141.

12. Sandra G. Boodman, "The Right Stuff," *Washington Post,* July 18, 1982.

13. Donna St. George, "Students Bone Up on Art of Politics Aiming to Make Better Grades as Voters," *National Journal,* April 7, 1984.

14. Elizabeth Wharton, "Washington News," United Press International, July 19, 1982.

15. Mona Megalli, "Washington News," United Press International, August 11, 1983.

16. "College GOP Pushing Free Emigration from Communist Countries," Associated Press, October 6, 1983.

17. Joseph B. Treaster, "College Republicans Open a Drive Against Student Activist Groups," *New York Times,* March 13, 1983.

18. Bill Prochnau, "Ripon Society Decries New Right's 'Alliance' with Moon Church," *Washington Post,* January 6, 1983.

19. James Conaway, "Young and Restless on the Right," *Washington Post,* January 25, 1985.

20. Easton, 279.

21. John Cassidy, "The Ringleader," *The New Yorker,* August 2005.

22. John Cassidy, "The Ringleader," *The New Yorker,* August 2005.

23. Barbara Slavin, "Ralph Reed: Onward Christian Soldier," *Los Angeles Times,* May 1, 1995.

24. Quoted in the November 9, 1991, *Norfolk Virginian-Pilot,* and Barry M. Horstman, "Regional Report: Christian Activist Using 'Stealth' Campaign Tactics," *Los Angeles Times,* April 5, 1992.

25. Ralph Reed Jr., "Casting a Wider Net," *Policy Review,* Summer 1993.

26. Ralph E. Reed, *Politically Incorrect* (Dallas: Word Publishing, 1994), 222–23.

27. David Von Drehle, "Life of the Grand Old Party," *Washington Post,* August 14, 1994.

28. Marc Peterson, "The Gospel According to Ralph Reed," *Time,* May 15, 1995.

29. Andrew Ferguson, "A Lobbyist's Progress," *The Weekly Standard,* December 20, 2004.

30. Sidney Blumenthal, "Staff Shakeup Hits Conservative Group," *Washington Post,* July 27, 1985. Lehrman quoted in James Verini, "The Tale of 'Red Scorpion,'" Salon.com, August 17, 2005.

31. James Verini, "The Tale of 'Red Scorpion,'" *Salon,* August 17, 2005.

32. Dan Balz and Ronald Brownstein, "God's Fixer," *Washington Post Magazine,* January 28, 1996.

CHAPTER TWO: THE K STREET PROJECT

1. Drew, *Showdown*, 117.
2. Confessore, "Welcome to the Machine," *Washington Monthly*, June 2003.
3. Franklin Foer, "What it Takes," *The New Republic*, October 2003.
4. Drew, *Showdown*, 114.
5. Jim VandeHei and Juliet Eilperin, "Targeting Lobbyists Pays Off for GOP," *Washington Post*, June 26, 2003.
6. *National Journal*, January 22, 2005.
7. All the above statistics were drawn from Thomas B. Edsall, "Big Business's Funding Shift Boosts GOP," *Washington Post*, November 27, 2002.
8. http://www.opensecrets.org/industries/indus.asp?Ind=K02
9. http://www.tray.com/cgi-win/lb_directory.exe?DoFn=
10. Jeffrey Birnbaum, *Washington Post*, June 26, 2003.
11. http://www.thehill.com/thehill/export/TheHill/News/Frontpage/081705/k.html
12. http://www.publici.org/lobby/profile.aspx?act=industries&in=18
13. http://www.publici.org/lobby/profile.aspx?act=industries&in=34
14. http://www.publici.org/lobby/profile.aspx?act=industries&in=3
15. John B. Judis, "Tammany Fall," *The New Republic*, June 21, 2005.
16. Confessore, "Welcome to the Machine."
17. All figures: http://www.publicintegrity.org/lobby/profile.aspx?act=firms&year=2003&lo=L000155
18. http://www.publicintegrity.org/lobby/profile.aspx?act=firms&year=2003&lo=L001666
19. Jim Barlow, "Intellectual Capital Still a Resource," *Houston Chronicle*, January 20, 2002.
20. Jeffrey Birnbaum, *Washington Post*, June 22, 2005.
21. http://www.publicintegrity.org/lobby/profile.aspx?act=firms&year=2003&lo=L003198
22. Grover Norquist, *Rock the House*, p.1.
23. Norquist, 10.
24. Norquist, 10.
25. See: http://www.heritage.org/about/community/insider/2000/may00/welcome.html.
26. Drew, "Selling Washington," June 2005.
27. Dubose and Reid, 164.

CHAPTER THREE: THE PETRI DISH

1. Greg McDonald, "Mexican Guest-Worker Plan in U.S. Is Pushed by DeLay," *Houston Chronicle,* January 6, 1998.

2. Franklin Foer, "Isle of Blight," *The New Republic,* June 18, 2001.

3. Dubose and Reid, 181.

4. http://www.epa.gov/region09/cross_pr/islands/northern.html

5. http://www.doi.gov/oia/StateIsland/ch3a.html

6. http://www.spc.int/prism/country/mp/stats/Social/Popn/pop_Census.htm

7. "Economic Miracle or Economic Mirage? The Human Cost of Development in the Commonwealth of the North Mariana Islands." Report by the Democratic Staff Committee on Resources, U.S. House of Representatives, April 24, 1997.

8. Dubose and Reid, 187.

9. "Economic Miracle or Economic Mirage?"

10. William Branigin, "Amid Criticism, U.S. Commonwealth Trying to Win Congressional Favor," *Washington Post*, February 22, 1997.

11. Abramoff memo, January 4, 2001.

12. Ken Silverstein, January 12, 1998.

13. W. John Moore, "American Dream or Pacific Nightmare?" *National Journal,* December 13, 1997.

14. Ken Silverstein, "Congress's Beach Boys," *The Nation,* January 12, 1998.

15. Jock Friedly, "Memo Raises Questions about Marianas Lobbying," *The Hill,* March 25, 1998.

16. Silverstein, January 12, 1998.

17. Dubose and Reid, 187.

18. Friedly, March 25, 1998.

19. Silverstein, January 12, 1998.

20. Silverstein, January 12, 1998.

21. http://www.spc.int/prism/country/mp/stats/Social/Popn/pop_Census.htm

22. Mark Krikorian, "Slave Trade," *National Review,* September 14, 1998.

23. George Miller, "Beneath the American Flag: Labor and Human Rights Abuses in the CNMI." March 26, 1998. Written with the assistance of the Democratic staff of the House Committee on Resources. The quote is found on page eight.

24. Peter Stone, and Paul Singer, "From the K Street Corridor," *National Journal,* May 14, 2005.

25. Stone, *National Journal*, May 14, 2005.

26. "GOP Platform on U.S. Territories." *The Associated Press*. August 3, 2000.

27. AP, May 6, 2005.

28. Peter Stone, "Grover and Jack's Long Adventure," *National Journal*, October 1, 2005.

29. Kate Zernike, "Associate of Lobbyist Tied to DeLay is Questioned on Island Contacts," *New York Times,* April 29, 2005. The CNMI's further comments were reported in Ellen Gamerman, "How Lobbyist's Troubles Felled Columbia School," *Baltimore Sun,* May 18, 2005.

30. Walter F. Roche, Jr., "Enron Doused Island Electric Plant," *Baltimore Sun,* April 3, 2000.

CHAPTER FOUR: ROGUES' GALLERY

1. Lisa Myers, *NBC Nightly News,* April 28, 2005.

2. R. Jeffrey Smith, "The DeLay-Abramoff Money Trail," *Washington Post,* December 21, 2005.

3. Ledger of the Capital Athletic Foundation, December 31, 2002. Government ID: MB-001952.

4. Easton, 162.

5. Alan Cowell, "Four Rebel Units Sign Anti-Soviet Pact," *New York Times,* June 6, 1985.

6. Peter Worthington, "Can We Trust Savimbi?" *National Review,* May 9, 1986.

7. Christopher Hitchens, "Minority Report," *The Nation,* May 22, 1989.

8. Foer, "Founding Fakers."

9. Easton, 172.

10. Radek Sikorski, "The Mystique of Savimbi," *National Review,* August 18, 1989.

11. Verini, "The Tale of 'Red Scorpion.'"

12. Fred Bridgland, "Angola's Secret Bloodbath," *Washington Post,* March 29, 1992.

13. Easton, 170.

14. "Police Manipulated Student Group," *The Guardian,* July 26, 1991; Easton 165.

15. Phillip Van Niekerk and David Beresford, "SA Student Body Admits State Aid and Disbands," *The Guardian,* August 2, 1991.

16. Dele Olojede and Timothy Phelps, "Front for Apartheid," *Newsday,* July 16, 1995.

17. Verini, "The Tale of 'Red Scorpion.'"

18. Richard Grenier, "Weaning Mozambique," *National Review,* February 5, 1988.

19. Robert Pear, with James Brooke, "Rightists in U.S. Aid Mozambique Rebels," *New York Times,* May 22, 1988.

20. Robin Birley, "Brave New Order," *National Review,* October 19, 1992.

21. Grover Norquist, "Reality in Mozambique Punctures a State Department Myth," Heritage Foundation Reports, September 22, 1987.

22. Neil A. Lewis, "A 6-Pointed Star and Mozambique," *New York Times,* November 30, 1987.

23. David B. Ottaway, "Reagan Affirms Support for Mozambican Leader," *Washington Post,* October 6, 1987.

24. David B. Ottaway, "Carlucci and the Mozambicans," *Washington Post,* November 10, 1987.

25. Tucker Carlson, "What I Sold at the Revolution," *The New Republic,* June 9, 1997.

26. Ibid.

27. Jack Friedly, "Burton Aided Mobutu After Contributions," *The Hill,* May 14, 1997. Information about André Soussan in Sam Skolnik, with contributions by T. R. Goldman. "Zairian Dictator Knocks Hard on U.S. Door," *Legal Times,* July 3, 1995. Also: Thomas W. Lippman, "GOP Activists Push for Mobutu Visa," *Washington Post,* August 6, 1995.

28. Sam Skolnik, "Zairian Dictator Knocks Hard on U.S. Door," *Legal Times,* July 3, 1995.

29. Letter from Jack Abramoff to Omar Bongo, July 28, 2003. Released by the Indian Affairs Committee, November 2, 2005.

30. The case of Abdurahman Alamoudi is detailed in the criminal complaint filed in *United States of America* v. *Abdurahman Alamoudi aka Abulrahman Alamoudi/Abdul Rahman Al-Amoudi/Abdulrahman Mohamed Omar Alamoudi.* United States District Court, Eastern District of Virginia. Filed September 30, 2003.

31. Paul Starobin, "Crescent Conflict," *National Journal,* November 19, 2005.

32. Byron York, "Fight on the Right," *National Review,* April 7, 2003.

33. Mary Jacoby, "Friends in High Places," *St. Petersburg Times,* March 11, 2003.

34. Janus-Merritt lobbying disclosure forms can be found in *Hearing Before the Committee on Governmental Affairs, United States Senate, One Hundred Eighth Congress, Second Session, on the Nomination of David H. Safavian, to be Administrator, Office of Federal Procurement*

Policy, April 29, 2004. U.S. Government Printing Office, 94-485 PDF. Washington: 2004.

35. In addition to the FBI affidavit, information about the SAAR Foundation, the SAFA Trust, et al., can be found in Edward Aiden, "The Money Trail," *Financial Times* of London. October 18, 2002. Also see Judith Miller, "A Nation Challenged," *New York Times,* March 21, 2002.

36. Susan Schmidt and Jeffrey R. Smith. "Aide was Reticent on Lobbying for Foreign Clients," *Washington Post,* September 21, 2005.

37. Margot Dudkevitch, "Parents of Victim of Hanawi Terror Waited Ten Years for Justice." *Jerusalem Post,* November 15, 2005. See also: Gretchen Ruethling, "Judge Awards $156 Million in Terror Death," *New York Times,* December 9, 2004.

38. David Tell, "Is the President a 'Dictator'?" *The Weekly Standard,* December 3, 2001.

39. Richard Willing and Deborah Sharp, "Indictment: Smiling Face Hid Hatred," *USA Today,* February 26, 2003. Norquist's award was reported in Kristin Szremski, "National Coalition to Protect Political Freedom Holds Fourth Annual Convention," *Washington Report on Middle East Affairs,* October 31, 2001.

40. Eric Boehlert, "'Betrayed' by Bush," *Salon,* April 3, 2002.

41. Byron York, "Fight on the Right: 'Muslim Outreach' and a Feud Between Activists," *National Review,* April 7, 2003.

42. "Transaction Detail by Account" of the American International Center, Inc. Dated July 15, 2004. Released by the Senate Indian Affairs Committee, November 2, 2005.

43. Josephine Hearn, "Abramoff's Mysterious Lobbying Firm," *The Hill,* April 14, 2005.

CHAPTER FIVE: THE HIT

1. Andy Friedberg, "Suspects plentiful in Boulis murder," *Sun-Sentinel,* February 8, 2001. Susan Schmidt and James V. Grimaldi. "Untangling a Lobbyist's Stake in a Casino Fleet," *Washington Post,* May 1, 2005.

2. Schmidt and Grimaldi, *Washington Post,* May 1, 2005.

3. The details of Boulis's biography can be found in: Terry Spencer, "Florida businessman built empire, made enemies, died violently." Associated Press, March 28, 2001.

4. Ibid.

5. Details of a raid on Boulis's ships can be found in: "Suspended Hialeah

official indicted," *Miami Herald,* December 4, 1998. Boulis's 1998 indictment is mentioned in the indictment for *United States of America* v. *Adam R. Kidan and Jack A. Abramoff* (05-60204).

6. Jay Weaver and Wanda J. DeMarzo. "Pair accused of SunCruz deal fraud," *Miami Herald,* August 12, 2005.

7. Schmidt and Grimaldi. May 1, 2005.

8. Ibid.

9. Ibid.

10. Ibid.

11. Ibid.

12. *United States of America* v. *Adam R. Kidan and Jack A. Abramoff* (05-60204), p. 6.

13. Ibid.

14. Jeff Shields, "Casino Cruise Partner Kept at Bay by Restraining Order," *Sun-Sentinel,* January 31, 2001.

15. A summary of the various litigation in re SunCruz is found in Jeff Shield, "Boulis Estate Sues to Evict Hollywood Restaurant," *Sun-Sentinel,* June 14, 2001.

16. Wanda J. DeMarzo, "Kidan's Tale 'Stranger Than Fiction,'" *Miami Herald,* October 2, 2005.

17. Selwyn Raab, "John Gotti Running the Mob," *New York Times,* April 2, 1989.

18. Pete Bowles, "Feds Want to Bar 3 Gotti Lawyers," *Newsday,* February 23, 1991.

19. Elaine De Valle, "Sobe Sex," *Miami Herald,* December 10, 1995.

20. Michele McPhee, "Rise and Fall of a Playboy Molester," *Daily News,* April 14, 2002.

21. Michele McPhee, *Mob Over Miami* (New York: Onyx Books, 2002).

22. Brian Fannin, "A blast for bartenders," *Washington Times,* February 7, 1995.

23. John McCaslin, "Inside the Beltway," *Washington Times,* February 17, 1995.

24. Schmidt and Grimaldi, May 1, 2005.

25. Unless otherwise noted, e-mails in this chapter are from Schmidt and Grimaldi, May 1, 2005.

26. Jeff Shields, "Payments Revealed After Boulis Slaying," *Sun-Sentinel,* August 10, 2001.

27. Ibid.

28. Jeff Shields, "SunCruz DeLays Suits with Bankruptcy Filing," *Sun-Sentinel,* June 23, 2001, Also see John Holland, "Deal Gives SunCruz to Boulis Estate," *Sun-Sentinel,* July 11, 2001.

29. Jeff Shields and Ardy Friedberg, "Boulis Slaying Investigation Loses Impetus," *Sun-Sentinel,* February 3, 2002.

CHAPTER SIX: THE TRIBES

1. Testimony of Nell Rogers, Public Hearing of the Senate Committee on Indian Affairs, June 22, 2005.
2. Abramoff quote from Susan Schmidt, "A Jackpot From Indian Gaming Tribes," *Washington Post,* February 22, 2004. Norquist can be seen defending the Choctaw as early as Kirk Victor, "Rolling the Dice with the Republicans," *National Journal,* December 16, 1995.
3. Contributions to ATR from Choctaw are reported in Robert Dreyfuss, "Grover Norquist: 'Field Marshal' of the Bush Tax Plan," *The Nation,* May 14, 2001.
4. Peter Ferrara, *The Choctaw Revolution* (Washington, DC: Americans for Tax Reform Foundation, 1998).
5. Doug Bandow, "Taxing a Native American Success Story," *Washington Times,* June 26, 1997.
6. Pundit payola was first reported in Eamon Javers, "Op-eds for Sale," *BusinessWeek Online,* December 16, 2005.
7. Peter H. Stone, "Grover and Jack's Long Adventure," *National Journal,* October 1, 2005.
8. All e-mails, unless otherwise noted, were released by the Senate Committee on Indian Affairs on September 29, 2004; November 17, 2004; June 22, 2005; November 2, 2005; and November 17, 2005. All are available at http://indian.senate.gov.
9. Reed's Enron contracts reported in Richard A. Oppel Jr., "No Violations Found in Hiring of GOP Consultant by Enron," *New York Times,* March 11, 2003.
10. The memo was first reported in Joe Stephens, "Bush 2000 Adviser Offered to Use Clout to Help Enron," *Washington Post,* February 17, 2002.
11. Reed quoted in the *San Juan Star,* February 8, 1998.
12. David Briscoe, "House Approves Plan that Would Add 51st Star to U.S. Flag," Associated Press, March 5, 1998.
13. The $2.3 million figure is found in Juliet Eilperin and Amy Keller, "Puerto Rico Battle Costs Money, Seat?" *Roll Call,* March 5, 1998. The Abramoff lobbying registry is found in Senate disclosure reports.
14. Phyllis Schlafly, "What Money Can and Can't Buy," *Copley News Service,* January 5, 1999.

15. Russ Baker, "Stealth TV," *The American Prospect,* February 12, 2001. See also Ruth Coniff, "Left-Right Romance," *The Progressive,* May 1, 2000.
16. Ibid.
17. Jim Suydam, "Board Delays Vote on Channel One," *Austin-American Statesman,* September 14, 2002.
18. Jodi Enda and Josh Goldstein, "With Big Stake in China, U.S. Firms Are Beijing Ally," *Philadelphia Inquirer,* May 19, 1997.
19. Peter Stone, "Ralph Reed's Other Cheek," *Mother Jones,* November/December 2004.
20. Document released by the Senate Committee on Indian Affairs. Available at http://indian.senate.gov.
21. Ibid.
22. David Firestone, "Bush Loyalists Compete for Spots on President's A-Team," *New York Times,* July 21, 2003.
23. Susan Schmidt, "Ex-Lobbyist Is Focus of Widening Investigations," *Washington Post,* July 15, 2004.
24. Documents released by the Senate Committee on Indian Affairs. Available at http://indian.senate.gov.
25. Dollar amounts from criminal information in the case of *United States of America* v. *Michael P.S. Scanlon.* United States District Court for the District of Columbia. Criminal Number: 05-411.

CHAPTER SEVEN: THE SHAKEDOWN

1. All e-mails, unless otherwise noted, were released by the Senate Committee on Indian Affairs on September 29, 2004; November 17, 2004; June 22, 2005; November 2, 2005; and November 17, 2005. All are available at http://indian.senate.gov.
2. Testimony of Richard Milanovich, Senate Committee on Indian Affairs Hearing into Tribal Lobbying Practices, September 29, 2004.
3. Testimony of Gail Halpern, Senate Committee on Indian Affairs Hearing into Tribal Lobbying Practices, June 22, 2005.
4. Document released by the Senate Committee on Indian Affairs. Available at http://indian.senate.gov.
5. Shawn Zeller, "K Street Cooled Off in 2002," *National Journal,* April 19, 2003.
6. Testimony of David Grosh, Senate Committee on Indian Affairs Hearing into Tribal Lobbying Practices, June 22, 2005.
7. Testimony of John McCain, Senate Committee on Indian Affairs Hearing into Tribal Lobbying Practices, June 22, 2005.

8. Document released by the Senate Committee on Indian Affairs. Available at http://indian.senate.gov.

9. Testimony of Amy Ridenour, Senate Committee on Indian Affairs Hearing into Tribal Lobbying Practices, June 22, 2005.

10. Ibid.

11. Ibid.

12. Document released by the Senate Committee on Indian Affairs, November 17, 2004. Available at http://indian.senate.gov.

13. Ibid.

14. Testimony of Marc Schwartz, Senate Committee on Indian Affairs Hearing into Tribal Lobbying Practices, November 17, 2004.

15. Document released by the Senate Committee on Indian Affairs, November 17, 2004. Available at http://indian.senate.gov.

16. Philip Shenon, "Records of Two Democrats Are Subpoenaed," *New York Times,* May 13, 2005.

17. Dodd statement entered into the record by Senator Byron Dorgan, Senate Committee on Indian Affairs Hearing into Tribal Lobbying Practices, November 17, 2004.

18. James V. Grimaldi and Susan Schmidt, "Lawmaker's Abramoff Ties Investigated," *Washington Post,* October 18, 2005.

CHAPTER EIGHT: THE SORCERER'S APPRENTICE

1. Safavian biographical information contained in *Hearing Before the Committee on Governmental Affairs, United States Senate, One Hundred Eighth Congress, Second Session, on the Nomination of David H. Safavian, to be Administrator, Office of Federal Procurement Policy, April 29, 2004.* U.S. Government Printing Office, 94-485 PDF. Washington: 2004.

2. T. R. Goldman, "How Much Must Pundits Disclose?" *Legal Times,* March 24, 1997.

3. Members of the Internet Consumer Choice Coalition are listed in John W. Moore, "Conservatives at Odds on Casino Gambling," *National Journal,* January 10, 1998.

4. Safavian's note can be found at http://www.fsta.org/advocacy.shtml.

5. Cannon quoted in Robert Gehrke, "Critics Question Cannon's Motives in Opposing Internet Gambling Bill," Associated Press State & Local Wire, June 26, 2003.

6. Robert Gehrke, "Cannon Staffer Had Questionable Lobby Link," *Salt Lake Tribune,* November 23, 2005.

7. http://www.house.gov/cannon/press2002/june19a.htm

8. Ibid.

9. Criminal Complaint in *United States of America* v. *David Hossein Safavian*. United States District Court for the District of Columbia. Case Number: 05-0501M-01.

10. Unless otherwise noted, all e-mails in this chapter come from the criminal complaint in *United States of America* v. *David Hossein Safavian*.

11. Criminal Complaint in *United States of America* v. *David Hossein Safavian*. United States District Court for the District of Columbia. Case Number: 05-0501M-01.

12. *Hearing Before the Committee on Governmental Affairs, United States Senate, One Hundred Eighth Congress, Second Session, on the Nomination of David H. Safavian, to be Administrator, Office of Federal Procurement Policy, April 29, 2004*. U.S. Government Printing Office, 94-485 PDF. Washington: 2004. P. 18.

13. *Hearing Before the Committee on Governmental Affairs* . . . pages 44–45.

14. Stephen Barr, "Teaching Uncle Sam to Be a Better Buyer," *Washington Post*, January 21, 2005.

15. Criminal Complaint in *United States of America* v. *David Hossein Safavian*. United States District Court for the District of Columbia. Case Number: 05-0501M-01.

16. R. Jeffrey Smith and Susan Schmidt, "Bush Official Arrested in Corruption Probe," *Washington Post*, September 20, 2005.

CHAPTER NINE: THE UNRAVELING

1. Testimony of Kevin Sickey, Hearing of the Senate Committee on Indian Affairs, November 2, 2005.

2. Testimony of Senator John McCain, chairman, Hearing of the Senate Committee on Indian Affairs, November 2, 2005.

3. Brian Lamb interview of Susan Schmidt. *Q & A*. C-SPAN. January 15, 2006.

4. Ibid.

5. Deborah Howell, "Getting the Story on Jack Abramoff," *Washington Post*, January 15, 2006.

6. Susan Schmidt, "A Jackpot from Indian Gaming Tribes," *Washington Post*, February 22, 2004.

7. Michael Crowley, "A Lobbyist in Full," *New York Times Magazine*, May 1, 2005.

8. Interview with James Grimaldi, *The Newshour with Jim Lehrer*, PBS, November 21, 2005.

9. E-mails released by Senate Committee on Indian Affairs, November 2, 2005. (Pages 289–91.)

10. E-mail exchange between Kevin Ring and Matt DeMazza, February 22, 2004. Released by the Senate Committee on Indian Affairs, November 2, 2005. (Pages 284–86.)

11. E-mail from Jack Abramoff to undisclosed recipient, February 23, 2004. Released by the Senate Committee on Indian Affairs, September 29, 2004. (Page 75.)

12. E-mail from Jack Abramoff to undisclosed recipient, February 23, 2004. Released by the Senate Committee on Indian Affairs, September 29, 2004. (Page 74.)

13. E-mail from Marc J. Schwartz to Jack Abramoff, February 23, 2004. Released by the Senate Committee on Indian Affairs, November 17, 2004. (Page 102.)

14. E-mail from Christine Thomas to Todd Boulanger and Jack Abramoff, February 24, 2004. Released by the Senate Committee on Indian Affairs, November 2, 2005. (Page 297.)

15. Martin letter to the editor, Released by the Senate Committee on Indian Affairs, November 2, 2005. (Page 302.)

16. E-mail from Jack Abramoff to Todd Boulanger, February 24, 2004. Released by the Senate Committee on Indian Affairs, November 2, 2005. (Pages 304 and 305.)

17. E-mail from Jack Abramoff to undisclosed recipient, February 25, 2004. Released by the Senate Committee on Indian Affairs, September 29, 2004. (Page 76.)

18. Susan Schmidt, "Think Tank's Directors Tied to PR Firm; McCain Plans Investigation," *Washington Post*, February 27, 2004.

19. Susan Schmidt, "Lobbyist Quits as Firm Probes Work with Tribes," *Washington Post*, March 4, 2005.

20. Brody Mullins, "Abramoff Shops Himself on K Street," *Roll Call*, March 23, 2004.

21. Paul Kane, "McCain Makes Progress in Indian Lobby Probe," *Roll Call*, March 24, 2004.

22. E-mail from Amy Ridenour to Jack Abramoff, March 30, 2004. Released by the Senate Committee on Indian Affairs, June 22, 2005. (Documents part II, page 145.)

23. Howard Kurtz, "Colin Powell Interview with Russert Is Cut Off," *Washington Post*, May 17, 2004.

24. Jason Leopold's reporting on Miller can be found at http://www.raw-

story.com/news/2005/How_Jack_Abramoff_and_Michael_Scanlon_0103.
html.

25. Patrick Danner, "Former SunCruz Owner Sues Partner," *Miami Herald,* June 8, 2004.

26. Doolittle's firm's subpoena reported in Susan Schmidt and James V. Grimaldi, "Lawmakers Under Scrutiny in Probe of Abramoff," *Washington Post,* November 26, 2005. Edward Miller's subpoena first reported in John Bresnahan, "Aide to Ehrlich Receives Subpoena," *Roll Call,* August 2, 2004.

27. Letter from Chief Philip Martin of the Mississippi Choctaw to Sens. Ben Nighthorse Campbell and John McCain, August, 9, 2004. Released by the Senate Committee on Indian Affairs, September 29, 2004. (Page 77.)

28. Susan Schmidt, "Probe Finds $10 Million in Payments to Lobbyist," *Washington Post,* March 30, 2004.

29. E-mail from Amy Ridenour to Jack Abramoff, July 30, 2004. Released by the Senate Committee on Indian Affairs, June 22, 2005. (Documents part II, page 151.)

30. Opening statement of Senator Ben Nighthorse Campbell, Hearing of the Senate Committee on Indian Affairs into Tribal Lobbying Practices, September 29, 2004.

31. Zach Coleman, "Mystery Firm Linked to U.S. Lobbyist Scandal," *The Standard* (Hong Kong), January 21, 2006.

32. Cassidy, "The Ringleader."

33. Wanda J. DeMarzo, "Cops to Quiz High-Powered Lobbyist About Boulis Murder," *Miami Herald,* August 17, 2005.

34. John Holland and John Burstein and Brian Hass, "Man Linked to Plot Had Gun Bust," *Sun-Sentinel,* September 30, 2005.

35. Abby Goodnough, "Casino Partner Pleads Guilty in Fraud Case," *New York Times,* December 16, 2005.

36. Allan Lengel, "Ex-Aide Pleads Guilty to Bribing Congressman," *Washington Post,* January 12, 2006.

37. Susan Schmidt and James V. Grimaldi, "The Fast Rise and Steep Fall of Jack Abramoff," *Washington Post,* December 29, 2005.

EPILOGUE: THE CURE

1. David Frum, *How We Got Here: The '70s* (New York: Basic Books, 2000).

2. Stephen Moore, *Bullish on Bush* (New York: Madison Books, 2004), p. 96.

3. Historical budget data comes from http://www.cbo.gov/showdoc.cfm? index=1821&sequence=0.

4. Moore, 96.

5. Sheryl Gay Stolberg, "The Revolution That Wasn't," *New York Times,* February 13, 2005.

6. Joe Scarborough, *Rome Wasn't Burnt in a Day* (New York: Harper-Collins, 2004), pp. 80–81.

7. Scarborough, 110.

8. R. Jeffrey Smith and Renae Merle, "Rules Circumvented on Huge Boeing Defense Contract," *Washington Post,* October 27, 2003.

9. http://www.cagw.org/site/PageServer?pagename=news_porkerofthemonth; see also John Fund, "Don Yang's Way," OpinionJournal.com, February 7, 2006.

10. George F. Will, "Hammering Away," *Washington Post,* January 26, 2006.

11. Michael Crowley, "Learning from Newt," *The New Republic,* January 14, 2005.

12. Bruce Bartlett, *Imposter* (New York: Doubleday, 2006), p. 68.

13. Bartlett, 70.

14. Ramesh Ponnuru, "Swallowed by Leviathan," *National Review,* September 29, 2003.

15. John J. Miller, "The Heritage Mandate," *National Review Online,* January 20, 2005.

16. Jonathan Alter, "The End of 'Pay to Praise,'" *Newsweek,* February 7, 2005.

17. Jason DeParle, "Next Generation of Conservatives (by the Dormful)," *New York Times,* June 14, 2005.

18. "Key Provisions of the Leading Reform Proposals," *National Journal,* January 28, 2006, pp. 34–35.

19. Dana Milbank, "An End to Treadmill Lobbying," *Washington Post,* February 1, 2006.

20. Bruce Reed, "Swamp Thing," *Blueprint,* vol. 2005, no. 2, p. 9.

21. Jonathan Weisman, "Lobbying Colors GOP Leadership Contest," *Washington Post,* January 11, 2006.

22. Ed Kilgore, "The Fix Is In," *Blueprint,* vol. 2005, no. 2, pp. 12–13.

INDEX